Nina Lugovskaya was born in Moscow on 13 December 1918. She survived her long imprisonment, married, and became a painter. But she never wrote again. She died in 1993, just after the end of the Soviet Union.

Acclaim for *I Want to Live*:

'Nina's diary is touching: it will strike both teenage and adult readers with a terrible pang of recognition . . . remarkably mature and intelligent'
Charlotte Hobson, *Daily Telegraph*

'Astonishingly well-written and perceptive'
The Times

'Carries poignant echoes of Anne Frank's diary. Both offer an innocent young girl's perspective on horrifying world events . . . but the essential difference is that Nina's diary was the reason for her arrest'
Mail on Sunday

'Extraordinarily frank and eloquent diary [which] proved to be her undoing . . . Modern readers will be struck not only by Nina's perceptiveness and intelligence, the elegance with which she could write when her adolescent gloom lifted, her confused feelings for her father, her interest in current events and the well-informed hostility she nurtured for the Bolsheviks – but also by the sheer recklessness of her act of self-expression'
Times Literary Supplement

'Could do for the Russian experience of Stalin's terror what Anne Frank's *The Diary of a Young Girl* did for worldwide understanding of the Holocaust'
Financial Times

www.rbooks.co.uk

'Remarkably well informed and perspicacious ... a monument to a girl's reckless defiance of indoctrination and intimidation'
Literary Review

'Riveting, if painful, reading ... singularly moving ... Her diary has inspired comparisons with Anne Frank – and rightfully so'
Daily Mail

'Nina's is an account of a stifled teenage life in a time of terror, a tale of fear and self-loathing ... it is extraordinary that such an account should have reached us at all ... There is some excellent reportage about food shortages ... some unfathomably well-informed commentary on the famine in Ukraine; dangerous personal delight in the murder of a Politburo member ... Nina's depression and angst were seen as signs of criminal degeneracy and the idea that her most intimate, self-sabotaging thoughts were also there to be policed now seems almost heartbreaking'
Observer

'A poignant and ultimately tragic diary that recounts what it was like to grow up in Stalin's Soviet Union has been hailed as Russia's answer to Anne Frank'
Sunday Herald

'Will capture the imagination of teenagers and help them understand the 1930s in the same way as Anne Frank's diaries have helped students to understand the Holocaust. If you read a book like this you're touching the past. It brings the period to life in a way that nothing else does'
Sunday Tribune

I WANT TO LIVE

The diary of a young girl in Stalin's Russia

Nina Lugovskaya

Translated by Andrew Bromfield

BLACK SWAN

TRANSWORLD PUBLISHERS
61-63 Uxbridge Road, London W5 5SA
A Random House Group Company
www.rbooks.co.uk

I WANT TO LIVE
A BLACK SWAN BOOK: 9780552772907

First published in Great Britain
in 2006 by Doubleday
a division of Transworld Publishers
Black Swan edition published 2008

Addresses for Random House Group Ltd companies outside the UK
can be found at: www.randomhouse.co.uk
The Random House Group Ltd Reg. No. 954009

The Random House Group Limited supports The Forest Stewardship
Council (FSC), the leading international forest-certification organization. All
our titles that are printed on Greenpeace-approved FSC-certified paper carry
the FSC logo. Our paper procurement policy can be found at:
www.rbooks.co.uk/environment

Typeset in 11/14pt Giovanni Book by
Falcon Oast Graphic Art Ltd.

Printed in the UK by CPI Cox & Wyman, Reading, RG1 8EX.

2 4 6 8 10 9 7 5 3

CONTENTS

Foreword by Anne Fine   7
Introduction   9
Nina's Friends and Relations   17

The First Notebook   21
The Second Notebook   133
The Third Notebook   253

Excerpts from the Letters of Nina's Father   355
Bibliography and Further Reading   375
Picture Acknowledgements   379

FOREWORD

WHAT IS SO SPECIAL about Nina Lugovskaya's diary? Here they all are, the usual complaints about dreary lessons and even more tiresome exams, the crushes on schoolmates and celebrities, parties and daydreams and longings, arguments with sisters and parents, fretting in front of mirrors, fears for the future – the whole teenage gamut of black moods and unruly feelings.

The difference is that Nina was a born writer. And it was our good luck – if not her own – that she was keeping her diary through one of the most extraordinary periods of Russian history, just as the Bolsheviks she so despised were tightening their grip on Russian society in advance of the Great Terror that would send her family, like her father, into punishment exile.

The virtue of history books is that they offer a sober overview. But a diary as raw and honest as Nina's can tell us with vivid immediacy just what it's like to cheek a policeman searching your home for evidence against your family; to be horsing about in class one moment and ripping propaganda posters off the door the next; to be called away from doodling on your workbook to face interrogation from the state police.

We read Nina's diaries with knowledge of the future. We see the full danger of the streak of rebellion in this irrepressible teenager, bored in school then bored out of school, so cripplingly embarrassed on the outside, filled with such soaring feelings within.

Meanwhile the power of the state, ever stronger, creeps closer. Nina is, like her committed father, just the sort of clear-sighted, free-thinking citizen a system like Stalin's will have to crush if it's to triumph.

So, as with *The Diary of Anne Frank*, and *Zlata's Diary* from the Bosnian conflict, we read on, appalled and aghast. Nina is lively, clever, sensitive, and so alive to the nuances of the politics around her – the sort of teenager we'd all be proud to have been, or to have raised, thrilled by literature, exhilarated by high winds and snowstorms. 'I want to be great and extraordinary.'

Be careful what you wish for, warns the old saying. In its way, this is both a great and extraordinary diary. Nina herself finally died in 1993. The words she wrote will live as long as people still ask the question, 'What was it like to be there in those times?'

Anne Fine
Children's Laureate, 2001–2003

INTRODUCTION

Nina Lugovskaya began writing this diary in 1932, when she was thirteen years old. She lived with her family in a flat in Moscow during the time of Stalin's Great Terror. The last entry in Nina's diary is dated 3 January 1937, the day before the NKVD (Stalin's secret police, later called the KGB) raided the flat and confiscated all the family's papers, including schoolgirl Nina's diaries. Her father, Sergei Rybin, was already serving a prison sentence at the time as a counter-revolutionary, and this caused his whole family to fall under suspicion.

Nina's diary was recently discovered in the newly opened KGB archives. It had evidently been studied very carefully by the NKVD – passages felt to contain incriminating evidence were underlined with a red pencil (darker type has been used instead here). Ironically, her diary is a typical adolescent fug of obsessions about her looks, boys, homework, the meaning of life and parties. Yet, because her father, an activist in the Socialist Revolutionary Party, which opposed the Bolsheviks, was persecuted for his political views and usually away in prison or in exile from Moscow, Nina occasionally raged against Stalin and his regime as well. Passages like 'I felt such rage and frustration against him, who took away my father from me' and 'I dreamt for hours about how I would kill him. His promises, the promises of a dictator, a villain and bastard, the vile Georgian who is crippling

Russia' were taken as evidence of 'terrorist intent against Stalin', and were enough to convict her as an enemy of the people.

Apart from her father, Nina seemed to be the only one in the family who was interested in politics and read newspapers. Nina's sisters were preoccupied with their art and music classes and their boyfriends, and her exhausted mother, a teacher, was kept busy struggling to feed the family. After relative prosperity in the 1920s, when Sergei had run a bakery under Lenin's New Economic Policy, his arrest in 1929 plunged the family into poverty. Nina mentions in passing, as if she takes it for granted, the constant hunger (their diet consisted of tea, potatoes and bread), the freezing cold and the lack of clothes – she had only one dress to wear to school and to parties alike.

By the early 1930s, the idealism of the Communist revolution had given way to suspicion and fear. By December 1929, Stalin had largely liquidated or silenced all of his opponents in the ruling elite of the Communist Party and had started to consolidate his despotic reign of terror. Thinking people had to keep their opinions to themselves – informers were everywhere. In this sense, Nina Lugovskaya, like Anne Frank, had to live underground in a hostile world, where speaking out meant certain death. After a warning from her mother, Nina went back and deleted some passages in her diary that might have been construed as counter-revolutionary. Yet, like Anne Frank, in her diary, Nina was mostly preoccupied with the usual self-centred adolescent problems: unrequited crushes on boys in her class, insecurity about her friendships with girls, fights with her mother and sisters, despair about her grades at school, agony about her looks (especially about an unfortunate squint which made her very self-conscious).

But she was also very interested in what was going on in the world around her, and her clear and sober vision of Soviet reality is impressive, given the climate of repression and propaganda at the time. Her diary was important to her because, again like Anne Frank, she harboured ambitions to become a writer. Nina had a good eye for detail and a surprisingly clear understanding of current events. As early as 1932, she calls Stalin 'a scoundrel' who is stifling freedom in Russia. She also describes the famine in the Ukraine and gives a vivid first-hand account of public events, like the ceremony to celebrate the rescue of the crew of the *Cheliuskin* by Soviet pilots. She was outraged by the arrests that followed the murder, in 1934, of Sergei Kirov, First Secretary of the Leningrad Communists as well as Stalin's main rival for popular appeal. Her comments on this episode are quite extraordinary for a girl of fourteen: she is indignant that, for one Bolshevik life, dozens of people were summarily shot without trial while, after the assassination of the Tsar at the beginning of the Revolution, only one person was executed.

Stalin's stranglehold on the whole of Russian society was tightening. During 1935, most of the old-guard revolutionaries were arrested and forced to sign testimonies of their alleged involvement in a vast conspiracy to assassinate Stalin and other leaders and re-establish the capitalism from which Stalin had supposedly rescued the country. The purges began, starting with members of the Party: half a million were expelled, and many of these were arrested and forced to sign public confessions. Enemies of the people were avoided like the plague; their spouses divorced them or were arrested themselves. Children were encouraged to denounce their parents. After harsh round-the-clock interrogations and torture, show trials were conducted at which the accused confessed publicly to all sorts of fantastic and obviously fabricated crimes. The purges affected all walks of life. People disappeared without trace. No one was immune from a sudden knocking on the door in the small hours of the night, being dragged out of bed and led away, usually for ever. A few weeks after Nina's flat was searched, it was the turn of her friend Ira:

> And now they had taken away Ira's dad, destroyed her happiness and peace of mind, shattered her whole way of life and her routine, everything that was important to her. We had a good life too, before Dad was arrested, but . . . afterwards, it was as if we'd tumbled down from heaven into an abyss of deprivation and uncertainty. And these people, who ate butter in the morning and drank coffee – they would lose everything too if he was sent off to somewhere in Ust-Sysolsk, to a little town in the north . . . Ira would do her lessons and store up her hatred for them in her heart. Oh, you bastards! You villains! How dare you do this!

A total of over two million people were arrested in this period, and at least forty thousand were executed. Over one million civilians were sentenced to hard labour in camps in Siberia, in Stalin's notorious gulag archipelago, and many died there of hunger, cold, disease and exhaustion.

Nevertheless, Nina's diary is not all about the horrors of Stalin's Terror. Even under this brutal regime, Nina's preoccupations were those of any normal teenager, her mood typically changing from excitement to frustrated hope and tormented despair. Her diary is often witness to a lonely introspection: she feels ignored by her popular older twin sisters, insecure about her own popularity. Yet, at other times, she is full of giggles at silly pranks and fooling around at school, or shows herself to be a ringleader of rebellion against her teachers. Now she is elated, now miserable. Love courses through the pages, always unrequited. Anyone who has been a teenager can identify with Nina's emotional turmoil and self-doubt: 'This diary gives a good insight into my character – the pettiness of my soul stands out; nothing can disguise it. To understand me, you only have to look at what I usually think about. Today, I read some of the entries and, I must confess, I felt ashamed: pessimism and boys, boys and pessimism.'

Pessimism, indeed: among the passages underlined by the NKVD there are moments of intense depression and thoughts of suicide. At one point, she even makes a real suicide attempt, using opium found in her grandmother's medicine cupboard. But the dose wasn't strong enough, and nobody even noticed the attempt. The NKVD considered these suicidal thoughts unpatriotic and treasonous. And yet, poignantly, the emotion that repeatedly wins out over despair in the diary is hope, as she proclaims time and again, 'I'm a human being. I want to live!'

But Nina's wish to go out into the world and live was doomed. When she was eighteen, two months after the family's papers were confiscated, the NKVD came back. Nina, her mother and sisters were arrested, brutally interrogated and sentenced to five years' hard labour in the notorious Kolmya prison camp in the gold-mining region of north-eastern Siberia, one of the harshest in the gulag archipelago, and one which contained a high proportion of political prisoners. Miraculously, all the family survived, but their imprisonment was followed by seven further years of exile in Siberia. Nina married a fellow prisoner and became a painter. But, as far as we know, she never wrote again.

A note on this edition

Nina wrote in her diary irregularly, sometimes twice a day, sometimes nothing for three months or more. As time went on, she wrote less often, and the diary entries are more sporadic near the end. Contained in three thick notebooks, her diary was discovered in the archives of the KGB by Irina Osipova while researching the opponents of the Bolshevik regime and cases of resistance in the camps. She came across the file of Sergei Rybin, Nina's father, which contained Nina's diary. Irina Osipova was immediately impressed by the clear style and vibrancy of Nina's writing, a living voice from the past. It was a rare find because normally all the diaries and letters confiscated during arrests were later destroyed, except for the few that could be used as incriminating evidence.

After its discovery, the diary was published by the Russian publisher Glas. For this present edition, we went back to the original diary and translated it in full, then edited and abridged it to about half the total length in an effort to make it more accessible to an English-speaking audience, taking out repetitions but retaining passages judged 'too personal' by the Russian editors, as well as all the passages underlined by the NKVD. We have also added short commentaries giving contextual background information, which we hope will highlight the interest and historical relevance of Nina's words and experience. To make for easier reading of names, where possible we have replaced initials used in the original with proper names. The occasional italicized passages within the diaries are those underlined in the original by Nina herself, while the passages in darker print are those underlined by the NKVD.

The diaries have been edited and abridged by Michèle Hutchison, with grateful acknowledgement to the excellent work on previous editions of Irina Osipova, Natalya Perova and Elena Kostioukovich.

A note on dates

During Stalin's regime, the calendar was revised several times and, as a result, dates in the diary were inconsistent. These have been corrected where possible.

Nina's Friends and Relations

The following is a brief list of the people whose names occur most frequently in Nina's diary. Many of Nina's friends are often called by nicknames or diminutives (i.e. an added '-ka'), and the boys are sometimes called by their surnames. Where possible, these individuals are cross-referenced in the alphabetical list below. The names of Nina's sisters are Eugenia and Olga, but Nina calls them Zhenya and Lyalya. To add to the confusion, some names, such as Zhenya, are used for both boys and girls.

Andrei B.: college friend of Nina's sisters

Betka: the family poodle

Crocodile: Valya's nickname

Dima or **Dimka**, see **Linde**: boy in Nina's class

Dusya: girlfriend of Nina's sisters (object of Zhenya G.'s love)

Eugenia (Zhenya): one of Nina's sisters, Olga/Lyalya's twin

Ira (Irina) Sharova: Nina's best girlfriend

Kolya K.: boy at school Nina suspects of being an informer

Kolya (Nikolai): Nina's cousin

Ksyusha (Ksyushka or Ksenya): Nina's girlfriend, sometime best friend

Linde: one of the boys Nina develops a crush on, also known as **Dima**

Liza: girl at school who acts as an informer

Lyalya (Olga): Nina's other sister (Zhenya's twin)

Manya: the family maid

Lyovka (or **Lev**) **Ivanovka**: schoolmate (maths teacher Yulia's son; the first boy Nina develops a crush on)

Margosha: another boy in whom Nina is periodically interested

Maria Fyodorovna: Nina's aunt

Musya Ivyanskaya: Nina's schoolfriend, object of Margosha's affections

Nikolai Keller (Kolya): Nina's cousin

Nina K.: friend of Nina's sisters

Nina P.: in college stage production with Nina's sister Zhenya

Olga (Lyalya): one of Nina's sisters, Eugenia/Zhenya's twin

Schechtman: boy at school who writes Nina poems

Sergei Keller: Nina's uncle (Sonya's husband, lives in Kashira)

Sergei Fyodorovich Rybin: Nina's father (their family name, however, was Lugovskoy/-kaya, after the region they came from)

Shura Kobalenskaya: neighbour whose parents are murdered

Sofia: an aunt who lives in the country

Sonya: Nina's aunt, married to Sergei Keller

Valya Leitin (Crocodile): one of the boys at school

Volodya Zelenin: schoolmate, one of the Zelenin brothers

Yulia Ivanova: Nina's favourite teacher (mother of Lyovka)

Yura T.: friend of Nina's sisters (becomes Zhenya's boyfriend)

Yurka Zelenin: schoolmate, the other Zelenin brother
Zhenya (Eugenia): Nina's older sister (Lyalya's twin)
Zhenya G. (Zhenechka): male college friend of Lyalya and Zhenya (Nina develops a big crush on him)
Zhorka: college friend of Nina's sisters who becomes Lyalya's boyfriend

Other schoolmates
Girls: Mila, Natasha, Raya, Stasha, Tamara, Tanya, Vara, Zina/Zinka
Boys: Alka, Antipa (Antikpa/Antipochka), Boris M., Budulya, Filya Moskal, Girya, Sakharov, Shunya, Tolka, Timosha, Uklon, Zinok, Zyrik

Teachers (apart from Yulia Ivanova, see above)
Evtsikhevich: social studies teacher
Tatyana Sergeevna: German teacher
E.V. (full name not given): literature teacher

THE FIRST NOTEBOOK

7/IV 1995г.

*N*ina's diary opens when she is thirteen, a couple of months before her fourteenth birthday. She is living in an apartment in Moscow with her parents and her older twin sisters, Eugenia (also called Zhenya) and Olga (also Lyalya). Her father had just returned from three years' exile in Siberia and the family were under surveillance. The social climate was one where the government expected complete loyalty from all citizens, as well as discipline and productivity. Housing was an issue, particularly in large cities where the population was rapidly expanding, and each urban dweller had an average of 45 square feet of living space. The Lugovskys' apartment appears to have been relatively spacious.

Nina's best friend at school was a girl called Irina Sharova, sometimes shortened to Ira. Another significant figure was Lyovka (Lev), a fellow pupil on whom she had a crush. He was the son of Yulia Ivanova, her maths teacher, whom Nina adored as well. She was two years behind at school, which often made her feel out of place with her friends, who were all younger. We don't know whether she was held back because of a failure to reach the expected standards, or whether she had been ill as a young child. Later in the diaries she seems to suggest that her parents may have been in some way responsible.

8 October 1932

Yesterday at school, our first lesson was double social studies, and the teacher, Evtsikhevich, arrived even more dressed up than usual, and that set us off laughing and making all sorts of jokes about him. He gave some of the boys reports to write, including Staska, and I promised to write his report for him, which I really regret doing now.

In the fourth lesson, before the German teacher arrived in the classroom, Lyovka was standing by the glass tank of newts and prodding them in the back with his pen. One of them grabbed hold of the tip of his pen, and Lyovka thought that was hilarious. He burst out laughing and made a dash for his seat, almost skipping along.

'Ugh, what horrible faces they have, ugly as sin!'

'Just like yours,' Irina quipped, and Lyovka answered back, slightly embarrassed: 'No, like yours.'

Something's changing, imperceptibly but irresistibly, in the way I feel about the boys, and we are becoming friends (something I've dreamt of for ages). I don't feel anything special for Lyovka now; I kind of like him, that's all. After school I went to Ira's place and stayed there till late. When I got home, Zhenya and Lyalya weren't back yet.

Now it's half past ten. Zhenya is sitting playing the piano and I'm trying to note down as fast as I can the way music makes me feel. You wouldn't believe how much I love it, but it can be weirdly painful and bitter. It's impossible to explain the powerful and complicated emotions it gives me; something fragile and delicate begins to stir somewhere deep inside me, setting me on edge in a good and a bad way, something that wants to be let out.

At moments like this I'd love to be able to join in and sing with my sisters, to let out all my feelings and make beautiful music, but all that comes out is a thin, tremulous wheezing, and I go quiet, letting the confusing tide of feelings ebb away. All the different melodies – playful and mischievous or full of deep, distressing emotions – send me into a dreamworld.

Love! How can you not think about it when everyone goes on and on about how great it is! How can you not dream about it? Take these words:

> *It was on the outskirts of Granada,*
> *Where the Spaniards are known to dwell,*
> *And endless serenades fill the air.*
> *There the beauties all smoke cigars,*
> *And eternal summer reigns,*
> *There guitars thrum and jangle*
> *And castanets clatter night and day.*
> *One night in a remote alley,*
> *Don Rodrigo Jerez del Malaga*
> *Was out walking at his set hour,*
> *Leaning upon his long sword.*
> *The sword glinted bright 'neath the moon,*
> *The streets were flooded with light,*
> *When Don Malaga suddenly beheld*
> *The bright image of Señora Lolita*
> [anonymous; probably a poem set to music]

I really like them, and the tune is really simple and playful.

It makes me feel as if I'm gazing curiously out into the distance, into a wide expanse filled with the obscure phantoms of some different, romantic life.

Almost nothing interesting happened at school today. The first lessons were dull, and in physics we carried on with questions and answers, and I was bored, so I drew a picture of Lyovka in Zina's rough book. He was getting on my nerves, spinning around all the time, but I couldn't tell him to stop because I didn't want him to know I was drawing him.

Ira once said to me: 'It would be a good idea to write all this down, Nina, and read it back at the end of the year.' 'There's no point,' I said in an innocent voice, secretly laughing to myself.

9 October 1932

When I went for the bread it was half past ten. The sun was already quite high in the sky, illuminating the earth with its pale autumnal rays. There was a smell of autumn in the fresh, dry air. The immense vault of the bright-blue sky seemed to cover the entire earth, with only the misty wreaths of the thujas spreading silently along the horizon, like dense smoke. These calm, yellow trees seemed to radiate the tender, warm light from inside themselves, and the sky glimmered through the lacy network of branches and dry leaves. It's a long time since the weather has been so good.

I walked to school alone today, because Irina and Ksyusha were late. When I got close to the school I saw our boys, including Lyovka. They were standing on the brightly lit sports pitch in the schoolyard, and he was conspicuous in the cheerful motley crowd, a slim figure in his baggy black shirt.

During woodwork, Lyovka, who was standing with his back to us, turned round to loosen a screw on his friend's lathe and, noticing that I could see him, laughed and wagged his finger at me. I told on him, of course. We went straight from our lessons to have lunch (Zina and I handed them out), and without even realizing it, I paid too much attention to Lyovka.

In geography there was another question and answer session. The three of us – Zina, Ira and I – sat together. There was an empty desk behind Lyovka and I teased Ira that she should sit there, but she wouldn't. Then, suddenly, Budulya and Lyovka brought all their bits and pieces over and joined the second team, really near to us. I tried drawing him again, but the result wasn't particularly accurate. 'He really is good-looking, though,' I said to Ira, and saying it gave me a nice feeling but not a real thrill.

'Yes, but only from a distance, from close up he's not so handsome, he's got a snub nose,' Ira said.

But I've got used to seeing his face, with those big, deep eyes, as handsome, even from close up.

Just before I reached our house, I suddenly noticed the weather: the air was warm and it was quite light, with a strip of sky still glimmering dull pink in the west and a bright yellow moon slipping through the clouds.

Woodwork was a typical lesson in the new 'polytechnical' syllabus, in which manual and technical skills were valued over academic and intellectual thinking. Since the October Revolution in 1917, education had been a much-argued point amongst the Party leaders and their advisors. While activity-based practical education was considered ideologically sound, it led to a diminution of key skills such as reading, writing and arithmetic, and in knowledge of history and literature.

11 October 1932

Today I have a day off school. In the morning I went for the bread; it was cold and dreary outside. Afterwards, we – that is, me, Zhenya, Lyalya and my cousin Nikolai – played cards. We lost to him. I'm in a foul mood at the moment. I don't want to do anything. I keep remembering yesterday at school and feeling annoyed. In the singing class Lyovka and Staska kept whispering to each other all the time and pointing at us, and Ksyusha was unbearable, as usual. What's happening to me? I promised myself I wouldn't sit close to Lyovka, and I sat next to him; I swore I wouldn't wait for him outside school, but instead I kept a sharp look-out for him and as soon as I saw him I acted just like everybody else and shouted wildly. Nothing I plan to do works out in the real world.

Being alive is just awful. I can feel my black mood coming on again, my brief recovery is over, I don't long to go to school any more, and those blue eyes hardly excite me at all. How could I fall in love so unexpectedly and so seriously and fall out of love again so soon? I used to think badly of people who fell in love and then cooled off quickly, I thought of love as a firm, strong, constant feeling. But now remembering that seems strange and a little bit ridiculous.

What's life all about? What's the point of living? Live until you die, they tell you. Easy to say! Just fall in love while you're young, then get married, have lots of children and spend your old age cooking and moaning all the time – is that all there is to life? Do I really want a life like that? I want to be great and extraordinary. Dreams, dreams! It's dreams that give me a chance to be happy, at least some of the time.

Oh, I love writing! Now I've written this, I feel calmer, as though some invisible hand has tidied up everything in my heart so that there's not a single little thing left to worry me.

13 October 1932

The first lesson was biology. We reached the classroom after the bell had rung, and the teacher was already there. Alka came up and gave me a small scrap of paper. He said with a laugh, 'Read the announcement.' Then he went back to his seat. I unfolded it and read the following: 'Group five has gone crazy because a chimpanzee has fallen for Lugovskaya.' How could I not laugh? I glanced round at the boys. Lyovka stretched his big mouth wide open and shouted: 'What do you think of that, Luga?'

'It sounds about right to me,' I answered. It was a lively, cheerful lesson.

The second lesson was PE, but the teacher didn't come.

The class didn't behave particularly well, and soon the teacher from the next room came in. She looked like a working-class trainee who had just been promoted. She set us a story to write using the words 'imperialists', 'capitalism', 'opportunists', 'enthusiasts', 'shock workers', 'new society', and then went away but came back to check up on us during the lesson.

After lessons, Ira, Ksyusha and I said goodbye to Zina, then walked to the next side-street, turned into it, perched on the low wall and started waiting for Yulia Ivanova, our maths teacher, and her son, Lyovka. It was very dark and the weather was really warm, and there was no one around at all. We had waited for them often before, but we had never dared go so close to the street that they had to walk along.

Nina was a student at a 'seven-year secondary school', a former primary school with an extended intake, the usual age range being between eight and fourteen years. The seven-year schools were not renowned for their high academic standards and pupils in general did not go on to further education. However, at the beginning of the 1932/33 school year, grades 8–10 were reinstated to allow students to reach the level necessary for university entry. Pupils could then leave school at either fourteen or seventeen.

14 October 1932

I walked to school alone, because I was late and the girls had already gone. I didn't mind. The first lesson was Russian, and the teacher called Lyovka out to the front. He walked calmly up to the board, picked up the chalk and paused expectantly. His slim, elegant figure reminded me somehow of Yulia Ivanova's. I could tell from his answers that he hadn't done his homework. The entire class prompted him in chorus, and I asked pointedly: 'Ira, why do you think everybody helps him?'

In German Lyovka got so boisterous that the teacher was forced to move him to a different seat, but even then he didn't settle down. He and the other boys started tossing his cap backwards and forwards, and twice he even threw it on to our desk.

You wouldn't believe what went on in the woodwork lesson. The teacher gathered everybody around one lathe to explain how it was made but then left the room to get something. The boys started trying to trip each other up, and the way they dodged about was really comical. Lyovka leapt up on a desk and roared with laughter watching Staska pulling horrible faces and falling over on the slippery stone floor.

By the way, about Staska – I think I notice something special in the way he acts when he's around me, and almost every time I've glanced at him in lessons, our eyes meet. How rarely I see those blue eyes, but how often I see his brown eyes, looking at me! It gives me a feeling that's pleasant and unpleasant at the same time, as though someone is tickling me gently.

17 October 1932

Mum has just come home and told my sisters to go for the

groceries. As usual, it started a row, with all three of them shouting and yelling at each other, and I sat shivering in my room as though I had a fever, praying to God that they wouldn't remember I was there. Zhenya and Lyalya are still bickering now. Oh, God! It's really so absurd and pitiful to look at them and think that we're really not that close at all. Mum and Dad grumble and grouse quite a lot, but we three are far worse.

21 October 1932

Yesterday we were sent back into the classroom for bad behaviour. Lyovka came running up to my desk, grabbed a pen and exclaimed: 'Ah, Luga, you forgot your pen!'

I grabbed hold of his hand firmly, took back the pen and said, 'Thank you!' in a rather ironical and mocking voice. He went back to his seat without saying a word, but I could feel the touch of his slim, supple hand for a long time afterwards. All I can think about now is whether he notices me, at least a little bit. Of course, it's not easy to tell, but there is still a tiny glimmer of hope in my heart . . .

Life! It's so complicated, but so simple at the same time. **Maybe I should just poison myself? Sometimes I want to, you could say I dream about it, but I know for certain that I won't do it.** Why not? Zhenya and Lyalya are already at college, but I have to carry on at school for ages, for an unbearably long time, it will be so long before I can just casually say that I'm going out 'to see some friends'.

This is the first place in the diary where the NKVD, the Bolshevik secret police, underlined Nina's words as evidence of counter-revolutionary thought. (The underlined words are set here in darker print.) To them, suicidal thoughts were not typical of adolescent depressions but a sign of degenerate 'thought crime' against the state.

22 October 1932

When Mum got home, Aunt Maria Fyodorovna told us that a father, mother and daughter had been killed at six in the morning on one of the side-streets. It didn't make much of an impression on me, and an hour later, sitting in front of my diary, I had forgotten all about it.

At about 10 p.m. there was a loud knock at the door. 'Ask who it is,' I warned Mum when she went to answer it.

'Who is it?' she asked.

'It's us,' the girls answered.

Mum opened up. Zhenya and Lyalya came in, looking very serious. 'Go through to Granny's room, girls, we've left you something to eat there.'

'No,' Lyalya answered in a flat voice, without looking at Mum.

'What's wrong? Why are you looking so sad?'

The girls went through into their room, and Mum and I followed them. 'What's happened?'

'Wait a moment . . . I can't say it,' Zhenya said, wrinkling up her face, and Lyalya leaned her elbows on the table and began to cry.

'Tell me what's happened! Has your dad been murdered?'

33

'No.'

'What, then?'

Perhaps my sisters' friend Vanya's shot himself, I thought.

'Tell me then, see how worried I am,' Mum insisted.

'Shura's mum's been killed!'

'What? My friend Kolebanskaya?' Mum exclaimed in an agonized voice.

'Yes, this morning. They were still in bed. They cut her dad's head off and split her mum's head open down to the brain with an axe, and Shura's alive, but she'll probably . . .'

'But who killed them?'

'Some madman. He lives in their flat. Shura woke up and screamed and dashed to the window, but he hit her in the face with the axe.'

I stood there with a calm expression on my face, filled with a strange, heavy feeling and anger – desperate, hopeless anger – at this disgusting murderer. Oh, what terrible things can happen! I remembered a story I'd read, by Kuprin, 'Temptation'. God, how awful! I had to struggle to understand what had happened, to imagine Shura fighting back as her mother lay there wounded. She was in our flat only yesterday, a cheerful, pretty fifteen-year-old girl with huge brown eyes and such soft, tender skin on her face and hands. Very cheerful and a little bit scatterbrained. I recalled our conversation. How terrible! What was happening to her now, there in the hospital?

I felt offended by the idea that life would just carry on as normal after this tragedy. Zhenya was getting ready to do some drawing, Lyalya went to bed, Mum did something else – as though everything was all right. How appalling, as if nothing had happened. I was overcome by a powerful desire to kill that villain, who would probably escape punishment because he was mad. I just can't believe it! My own joy and all the events of this day seem so petty and insignificant now in comparison with the sheer obvious significance of this terrible thing that has happened.

It is probably true that this attack was an act of criminal insanity as described above, but this was a time of terror, when men, women and children were routinely and brutally tortured and killed on the slightest pretext. The fact that a stranger was living in the Kolebanskys' flat was not unusual – the urban housing shortage meant that the government forcibly allocated tenants to people with larger flats or houses.

A. I. Kuprin (1870–1938) was a well-known Russian writer. The story 'Temptation' (1910) is devoted to musings on the nature of chance. After long wanderings, a husband returns to his beloved wife and at the last moment perishes under the wheels of the same train on which he arrived.

27 October 1932

Nothing special's happening at school. Lyovka? But I think that's all over for me. More than once today, when I caught his glance, I didn't feel a thing apart from a slight amusement, and when I noticed him looking at other girls, I hardly paid any attention at all. All in all, things are pretty dull.

Yesterday I went to the theatre to see *The Cricket on the Hearth*. At first I didn't like the show at all, but the original stage setting brought things to life. During the interval Ira and I went to the foyer, mingling with the crowd in bright-coloured silk dresses. The women had enjoyed dressing up, but their glad rags didn't make much of an impression on me.

Nina saw a play based on the book by Charles Dickens performed by the Moscow Arts Academic Theatre. Theatres had been nationalized after the October Revolution and were relatively inexpensive. Stalin had decreed that the arts should portray the ideal of the worker hero and Soviet society, and Dickens's portrayal of the working classes probably fitted the bill.

31 October 1932

In the workshop, when the teacher was explaining the parts of the lathe, Lyovka and Girya stood a little behind everyone else and mangled the names of the parts so mercilessly that Lyovka was simply choking with laughter. The fourth lesson was singing. As usual, we sat so that we could see Lyovka. He was sitting beside the piano, and in the middle of the lesson he started writing 'Luga' on the lid in chalk. And he went on and on writing like that, looking at me and laughing, showing those long, attractive dimples in his cheeks. When we went upstairs to the fourth floor, Lyovka was in front of us, but he waited for us to go past and followed us.

1 November 1932

I've developed a new desire – to learn to play the piano. It's not a bad idea, of course, only it's impossible. But I really do want to! This evening, when Zhenya and Lyalya came back from the institute, they played the piano and sang, and I joined in. My heart felt strangely light and calm. I love that feeling of overwhelming, undiluted goodness. Often, I'm quite worried by the thought that if I can't play I'll feel awkward at parties in the future. No, I simply can't imagine how I'll cope; it makes me feel a bit frightened and curious.

Does a life of pleasure attract me? Yes, it does, definitely. When I hear the foxtrot and other dance music, I can't help picturing boisterous young people, carefree, but not frivolous. I dream of being the life and soul of the party, but for me it's only a dream. Reason keeps telling me I don't suit the part, that I'm not good enough to join this company of witty people with lively intellects and high-minded motives. And so, firmly believing in one thing, I continue to think of another and imagine my brilliant future.

Dreams, dreams! Oh, does every girl dream the same way at my age? If they do, there's no hope; if they don't, then perhaps I'll still be able to live the way I wish and know the happiness of life and youth.

2 November 1932

I had just started writing when Mum called me to come

and have a cup of tea. Leaving the diary on the table, I joined them in the room. It was half past eleven. I was enjoying myself, telling Mum about school. We were laughing and joking together. Suddenly, there was a sharp, loud knock at the door. Betka the poodle started barking furiously and I quickly leapt to my feet with a nervous start, the way you sometimes do when you hear a sudden noise. 'Who's there?' I asked, going up to the door and holding Betka by the scruff of her neck with one hand.

A coarse male voice shouted: 'The janitor.' I realized what was happening, but there was still a vague hope left somewhere in my heart and, letting go of Betka, I opened the door a little warily. The light wasn't on in the corridor, and it was dark on the stairs, too, so all I could make out was the vague outline of a man's figure in a threadbare jacket, with a peaked cap and a big moustache. Further away, I glimpsed another man's face. Perhaps, just for a second, I hesitated, thinking: Yes or no? – but then I stepped aside to let in the janitor, two military men and two Red Army officers.

Just then, Mum appeared in the doorway.

'Who lives here?' asked the first man, a Russian wearing a brand-new greatcoat.

'The Lugovskys.'

'Does Rybin live here?'

'Yes,' said Mum, pointing to Dad. After going through all the formalities, the same military man pulled two sheets of paper out of his greatcoat and handed one to Dad and one to Mum, saying: 'This is for

'All right, next time we'll warn you.'

'Then we'll sprinkle even more on,' Mum muttered in a low voice.

The time passed slowly. Lyalya was worried about her diary, and I was worried about mine even more – when I remembered what was written in it, I felt terrified. When he went into my room, the tension became absolutely unbearable. The three of us stayed in the room; the door was open. A Red Army man walking along the corridor looked in at us and smiled. Soon, the second investigator came into my room, too. Dad was walking up and down the corridor.

'He's spent all his life like this,' Zhenya remarked.

'Who, Dad?'

'Yes, it makes things interesting.'

When he had finished in the room, the blond man moved into the corridor. He wasn't wearing his cap, and I noticed the crown of thick, wavy hair on his head. He opened the linen cupboard and, without bending down, shoved aside the dirty old shoes with his foot, then he moved on to the chest and opened the lid. The contents of the box weren't particularly clean, so he turned to Mum and said: 'Sort through it, please.'

'That's not my job,' Mum snapped back. And the janitor began taking out the dirty felt boots.

We all gathered in the corridor and followed the investigators' actions with an ironical smile. But then the search was over, and everyone (apart from us three) got together in Mum's room. I walked backwards and forwards past the door and tried to reconstruct the conversation they were having from the fragments of words that I heard. At about three o'clock, just before the end, we were sitting on the bed, wondering tensely whether they would take Dad away. The minutes went by very slowly. It was absolutely quiet in Dad's room. And then there was the sound of steps, and all five visitors came out into the corridor.

'Goodbye!'

'Do come again.'

They laughed and slammed the door.

'Hooray! Everything's all right.'

In the morning I desperately wanted to tell Ira about what had happened, and lessons were almost over before I finally relaxed.

Surveillance and police raids were a normal part of Soviet life in the 1920s and 1930s. A series of arrests, expulsions and executions had begun in the 1920s. The NKVD focused first on kulaks (wealthy land-owning peasants), then nepmen (traders or businessmen), priests and spetsy ('bourgeois specialists') came under attack. Because of Nina's father's status as a counter-revolutionary, he was a prime target. Raids, with the aim of confiscating incriminating material such as diaries, letters or illegal newspapers, became commonplace and often took place at night. Increasingly these raids were followed by arrests. Nina's description of the Jewish soldier would be seen as racist in our time, but it was both typical and acceptable in 1930s Russia.

5 November 1932

Today they herded us out to march round the streets, which made me absolutely furious and aggravated my feeling of helplessness even more. Walking over the cold, grey ground in the damp, dull light of an autumn day, stamping my frozen feet during the halts and cursing Soviet power to myself, with all its lying and bragging to foreigners and all the rest . . . and wincing at the tuneless, discordant singing. I decided definitely not to go to the demonstration, and that calmed my insulted pride a little.

Good Soviet citizens were required publicly to demonstrate their support for the state. On this occasion, as on many others, the school authorities had sent the students out into the streets to join the rally. Public rallies involved marching to brass-band music and popular Soviet songs and carrying posters of Stalin or the Soviet flag, and took place at any opportunity, such as Stalin's birthday, a state funeral, or the workers' May-Day bank holiday. They were public, outdoor celebrations of the communist spirit. This one may have been a rally for the fifteenth anniversary of the revolution. Nina's decision not to take part in the demonstration after school would have been seen as unpatriotic, or worse.

8 November 1932

How incredible. Ira has just come to see me, and she simply couldn't bring herself to ask me to tell her about what happened here on 2 November. She's such a child! I answered her questions until she guessed the truth, and then – would you believe it – I saw a strange expression appear on her face. I realized she was afraid to mention it, even though it had no special significance for her. Yes, she was too young to hear about such things.

Oh, how funny it felt to look at this little girl, who thought it was somehow improper to talk about a raid. When the door slammed behind her, I stood at the window, looking out at the pavement that she had to walk along, and laughed ironically as I whispered: 'She's still too small. She's really only a little girl still.' Oh, my God, how naïve people can be. I was right when I told her before that she was too young. Ha-ha! She wasn't expecting that. **And probably she's quaking now and thinking that they'll arrest her dad because she comes round here. To see me! When I've had a raid. Ha-ha!**

12 November 1932

Just recently, everything has gone back to normal and I have nothing at all to write about. The only noteworthy event yesterday was the funeral of Stalin's wife, Alliluyeva. There were masses of people there, and I had a rather unpleasant feeling looking at the jolly, excited crowd of curious people shoving forward with happy faces to get a look at the coffin. Boys shouted, 'Hoorah!' as they dashed along the roadway, stamping their feet.

I walked backwards and forwards, trying to listen to the passers-by talking. I managed to catch a few words filled with surprise and rather spiteful irony. Somehow

I didn't feel sorry for this woman – after all, Stalin's wife couldn't be even the slightest bit good, especially since she was a Bolshevik.

And then that report, that announcement in the newspaper – that had set me against her. A great queen, just imagine that! It was strange to hear that Stalin had a son and used to have a wife. I had never thought of him as having a personal life and a family. In the evening, when Zhenya and Lyalya came home, for some reason I felt incredibly angry with everyone – that was how their lively chatter and laughter and their unrestrained admiration for Alliluyeva's hearse affected me.

They began telling me about their institute, about their drawing, and I began feeling envious again, or perhaps not quite envious but, anyway, something of the kind. My sisters can draw and sing, play the piano and dance and do all sorts of other things that I can't do and know I'll never be able to. But what makes me any worse than they are?

All that's left is this miserable writing, which is absolutely no good for anything at all except simply wasting time. And you need time so badly for everything; whatever you try to do, you need time.

Stalin had married his second wife, the teenaged Nadezhda Alliluyeva, in 1919. It was rumoured that the marriage was strained. Nadezhda was found shot in the head in her bedroom, a revolver by her side, apparently having committed suicide – although, in the press, the death was reported as being due to peritonitis, and there were also unsubstantiated rumours that Stalin had had her murdered. The couple had a daughter,

Svetlana, who would cause an international furore by defecting to the United States in 1967. Nina is probably referring to a eulogistic obituary with the words 'great queen'.

16 November 1932

Today I told Mum about Natasha's party and, just as I thought, she has nothing against me going and even seems to approve. I told her everything about it. I've just washed the dress that I'll wear. It's the only one I have. I'm drying it over the oil-stove.

I got dressed and went to Granny's room first to have something to eat. Lyalya was there. She squinted at me slyly and remarked: 'What's this, Nina, going to a party?'

'Yes,' I replied casually, with exaggerated coolness. I went to Ira's place at half past five – of course she was home – and I was delighted to see that she hadn't got dressed up at all. The minutes went by and, when Ksyusha still didn't come, I started worrying. But then she arrived, and we all set out together. It was pleasantly cool outside, the streetlamps shone with a dim light, and I tried not to think too much about the party as it was making me nervous. Ksyusha too.

Then, there we were at Natasha's house, and we went up to the fifth floor. I imagined I could hear noise and laughter behind the door. Ira rang the bell and someone opened the door. We went into the hallway and looked around. There was nobody there. 'Surely we're not the first, are we?'

'Oh, no.'

In one room there was a grand piano, and lots of mirrors hanging on the walls. We sat down, not knowing what to do or what to talk about.

Fortunately, everybody else soon turned up, someone played the piano and we began playing lotto. Then Yulia Ivanova and Lyovka arrived. Glancing sideways at them, I saw his face turned towards us, underneath a fashionable cap with a long peak.

'Ah, Lyovka! I'm going to beat you,' Alka shouted.

'He's wearing riding breeches again,' Ira whispered to me.

After a while, Yulia Ivanova came over to us: 'Stop playing this game, let me see you running about and enjoying yourselves.' Then we played charades and forfeits. They made me the oracle and I had to accept it. They brought the boys to me one by one and asked: 'What does the future hold for this one?'

'A tram will cut his legs off.' They laughed. At first I gave quite good answers, then things didn't come to me so easily, I didn't know what to say any more, I felt myself blushing unbearably under the shawl, and Yulia had to prompt me.

Ksyusha had to go up to someone and kiss them, and she chose me. We set out a row of chairs facing her, sat the boys down and blindfolded Ksyusha.

'Luga, let's swap places,' Alka whispered.

'All right.' I sat him in my place, covered him with the shawl and moved to his seat. Ksyusha came up and gave him a warm, strong hug, and was about to kiss him. I pulled her away hard, dragged him away and quickly sat back in my own place. But she noticed. My God! How everybody laughed! Alka blushed and remarked as he sat down: 'What a hugger.'

While we drank tea, we were sitting quite close to Lyovka and Alka, and I wasn't at all bored. As always, I watched everyone else without speaking, feeling perfectly at ease. Lyovka stayed standing beside the piano, his hand propped against the lid in an artistic pose. When we started playing lotto again, he stood beside me and I brushed against his knees. All in all, we had a wonderful time, and even though I'm not mad on those kinds of games, I really enjoyed myself.

5 December 1932

My God! In the last few days I must have cursed school at least ten times. Not a single minute of free time. No matter how upsetting it is, I'm forced to break my own rules. For instance, take biology. OK, you think, fair enough, but then tomorrow there's geography, and after that maths! And I so want to write, read, play the piano, and dream a little too. But I haven't got a single minute of free time.

Today I woke up at eight o'clock. I had to study my biology. It wasn't light yet outside. I lay there in a half-doze, with my head buried in the cool pillow, enjoying that moment of peace that I wanted so desperately to prolong, but which I couldn't possibly. Perhaps I could stay at home? The treacherous thought flashed through my mind. It was growing stronger. I ran through in my head what lessons we had that day and wondered drowsily what to do.

One voice was insisting that I had to get up, that every single day was important now, while another was telling me in a whisper, low and weak but so tempting: 'Stay at home, stay at home.' And my mind conjured up vague images of a whole day spent in peace and idleness or, rather, doing my own work. For a while the second voice was winning, but reason overcame desire. I got up and sat down to study.

30 December 1932

Yesterday, we broke up for the holidays. My wish has come true at last. It's so great not to think about school for a while, not to rummage through exercise books, not to cram on ancient Babylon or the physical properties of soils, not to have to put off writing my diary any longer. I haven't even touched it this last week.

It's terrific to have so much free time: if I want, I can draw; if I want, I can write or read, or else pick up my skates and go to the ice-rink. The ice is so smooth and transparent I can never wait to get on it, and the figures dart along like arrows. On the ninth there's going to be another party at Yulia Ivanova's flat, and although I try not to be nervous, whenever I think about it I get a kind of prickly feeling inside.

I haven't touched my diary since 24 December. I've been putting it off till the holidays. That day was stranger than any other I can remember. In the first place, it was my birthday. I wasn't mad keen on any of my presents, which was a bit embarrassing, especially with Mum, and it was really all because Yulia had decided to have a party.

Earlier I had decided not to go, but when it came to it and I found I'd backed myself into a corner, I began to change my mind. By the time lessons were over I wanted so desperately to go to the party, I could hardly restrain myself and tried to stifle the voice that was trying to persuade me to stay at home.

I made up my mind to go. But Mum didn't want me to, and I had to stay at home after all. I felt upset the whole day long. I didn't do anything, just walked around the flat and almost cried, I was so annoyed. I really wanted to write, but I'm not in the mood any more. I feel like writing some kind of story, but I can't decide what about. Every now and then something flashes through my mind, but it's vague, unclear and formless.

4 January 1933

New Year's Eve was nothing special. As always, I read a book and waited for Mum. At midnight they played the 'Internationale' and a choir sang. Oh, I love that song! So now it's the New Year, I've been to the ice-rink twice, and now my legs are aching quite badly. As usual, I'm busy doing nothing and beating myself up over all the hours I've wasted. But, unfortunately, that's just the way I am, and it's hard to shake it off.

For instance, today I just wanted to keep on day-dreaming, so I did. I only pretended to read Chekhov in Granny's room because there's always someone in there, but while I was reading I still managed to dream about something else. Everybody has their faults. I'd love to be able to just dash off a beautiful drawing and write something good and play the piano well, and read a lot. Just try to pull that off! That'd be something! And then, on top of it, I have to get the potatoes and go to German lessons and the ice-rink.

The party at Yulia Ivanova's flat is coming up. Irina isn't going and I don't want to go either, but my pride forced me to say I would – I felt embarrassed, not feeling able to go without her, so I decided to go on my own, even though I'm nervous about it. I hardly think about Lyovka at all, and when I do, I only picture him very dimly and vaguely, but that still doesn't mean I feel nothing for him. He has such lovely eyes, and so does Yulia Ivanova. I love their eyes, and I can't even tell whose I love the most.

The 'Internationale' was the Russian national anthem until 1941. It was based on a famous French socialist song of 1870 which became the anthem of international revolutionary socialism. The chorus begins: 'So comrades, come rally/And the last fight let us face/The Internationale unites the human race.'

18 January 1933

Towards the end of the holidays, just two days before lessons were due to start again, I was suddenly overcome by a powerful hatred of studying and school. I so badly want not to go back to school and cram lessons when all those hours could be used to finish the interesting books I've got into during the holidays. Now I have to tear myself away from them and swap this life for boring lessons that won't lead to anything any time soon.

But that mood didn't last long. Recently, I've been living by two rules that lift my spirits so much that quite often I actually feel contented. The first rule comes from the proverb that says, 'Study is bitter, but its fruits are sweet.' When things are really getting me down, this phrase instantly pops into my mind from somewhere deep inside and I feel calmer.

The other rule is to live for the future. When I get hungry, I tell myself: Never mind, things will be better in the future. Or if I want a drink so badly it feels like my stomach's on fire, I stop thinking about it and say: There will be lots of sweets soon, and then you can drink as much tea as you like. Sometimes I really long to read, but I have to do my lessons. What can you do?

I went to school in a new dress. At first it felt awkward, but I forced myself not to be superstitious and not to worry about it. Both days I've been to school it has been so unbearably cold there that my pen kept falling out of my blue fingers and I felt a feverish tremor running through my body.

Lyovka has had a haircut, and it's made him look funny and spoilt his looks. When I look at him, I can't help remembering Zhenya and Lyalya laughing and telling me three or four years ago that once a month the boys at their school all looked ghastly because they'd had their hair cut. Lyovka looks completely different – his usual head of wavy hair and the thick hair at the back have been cropped short now, the back of his head looks all pointy and his ears seem to have grown bigger. Despite the cold, I've been feeling very cheerful these last few days, especially since during the second or third lesson we put our coats on and warmed up a bit, snuggling down into our collars and huddling against each other.

19 January 1933

Yesterday or the day before yesterday, in social studies, when Evtsikhevich was saying something about qualified personnel and how there are new colleges opening up, I started thinking it would be a good idea to ask him why the old colleges are being completely disbanded now. While I was thinking about it, I told Irina, still feeling perfectly calm, but when I suddenly decided that I definitely was going to ask, my heart began pounding so hard . . . I sat there waiting for Evtsikhevich to stop speaking, telling my heart over and over again: Shut up, will you. But it didn't shut up; on the contrary, it began pounding even louder . . . **Of course, in response to my question, he blinded me with merciless logic, and I didn't feel like objecting any more**.

Stalin considered the Russian education system outdated. Rabfaks – evening colleges with less demanding entry requirements – were established for the peasant and urban worker population, who had previously received little or no education. Meanwhile, the old university colleges, which were seen as remnants of the privileged bourgeois system, were closed or remodelled, and new polytechnics with a greater emphasis on practical skills were set up. As Nina's pounding heart suggests, challenging her teacher and questioning the Party line were provocative and dangerous things to do, even for a schoolgirl.

21 January 1933

Twenty-seven degrees below freezing [$-27\,^{\circ}C$]. Lacy patterns and fluffy hoarfrost have appeared on the windows. I was on my way to a German lesson with Tatyana Sergeevna. I put my coat on and went out on to the stairs, my head swirling with German phrases from the poems that I'd been cramming all evening and all morning. As I went down the steps, I repeated them to myself, straining my memory to the limit. I was on the last flight before the ground floor when I suddenly stopped. All the German instantly evaporated from my mind.

The sky was a pale, clear, matt pink; whichever way you looked, the pink light washed over everything; the air was densely permeated with it, making objects on every side look vague and ambiguous, enveloping them in a pink membrane. The twenty-seven degrees of frost froze my face and sent a pleasant chill running across my body. The firm snow squeaked loudly under my feet. I hid my hands in my sleeves and strode out cheerfully along the street, muttering poetry again. The frost bit hard at my nose, taking my breath away.

I came to Ira's house (I always called for her). I went into the yard and closed the small gate behind me. On the right, the wall of a big grey building towered up over me; on the left stood a little one-storey house with frosted-over windows. The pink sphere of the rising sun lit up the gleaming snow with a hazy glow. I went into the warm hallway, tugged at the closed door with its leather upholstery and then knocked three times.

For a while no one came, but then I heard steps. Lusha, the maid, unlocked the door.

'Nina?' Irina's mum called from her room.

'Yes,' I answered and I went into the room exclaiming loudly: 'Hello!' Ira was sitting at the table sideways on to me and carefully sorting through something. 'What's that you're doing?'

She didn't answer.

'Listen, Nina,' Ira's mother began, 'Irina won't be coming to school today . . . her dad's been arrested . . .' Her voice broke, and none of us said anything for a while.

'Aa-ah,' I said slowly and just stood there indecisively, not knowing what to do next.

'Don't tell anyone, and don't try to tell your teacher why Ira isn't there.'

'All right, all right,' I said firmly and confidently.

No one would find out anything from me. My thoughts swirled round in my head like a whirlwind. This family, sitting there without saying a word, amazed me: silent Alyonushka, Irina and their weeping mother. Let her suffer, too, as I suffered. And I remembered what had happened to us four years earlier, when they'd taken our dad away, too, and I'd woken up in the morning, not knowing anything.

I remember Granny coming in and asking: 'Will you go to school, now your dad's been arrested?'

'No,' I answered. When she went away, first I burst into

tears. Then I felt my heart swelling with anger and spite for the person who had dared to take my dad away from me.

And now they had taken away Ira's dad, destroyed her happiness and peace of mind, shattered her whole way of life and her routine, everything that was important to her. We had a good life too, before Dad was arrested, but . . . afterwards, it was as if we'd tumbled down from heaven into an abyss of deprivation and uncertainty. And these people, who ate butter in the morning and drank coffee – they would lose everything too if he was sent off to somewhere in Ust-Sysolsk [*one of the main centres of the state prison-camp system*], to a little town in the north . . . Ira would do her lessons and store up her hatred for them in her heart. Oh, you bastards! You villains! How dare you do this!

I walked round the room, grinding my teeth, stopping now and then and saying to myself: But Ira's mother won't go out to work. My mum worked, but she won't. She'll age ten years in about three, but she won't be able to work. And what about Ira? Would she stop loving her father after being separated from him for three years? I stopped loving mine. It took me a long time to get used to him again, I even spoke to him almost as if he was a stranger.

Oh, you Bolsheviks, you Bolsheviks! What have you done, what are you doing? Yesterday Yulia Ivanova gave our group a talk on Lenin and of course she talked about our socialist regime. It hurts me so much to hear those shameless lies from the lips of a woman I idolize. Let Evtsikhevich tell his lies, but not her, with that way she has of getting genuinely carried away, lying like that. And who to? To children who don't believe her,

who smile silently and say to themselves: Liar, liar!

Last night I had a horrible dream. I can't remember it all, but one part has stuck firmly in my memory: even while I was still asleep I thought there was something familiar about it, but I couldn't remember what. A man, naked to the waist, I think he had a handsome face, contorted in pain, struggling with someone, and the other man seized him in his arms and put his rifle across his chest, pressing down so hard I could hear the bones cracking. I was overwhelmed by a strange feeling of revulsion, I started to feel sick . . .

This is ironic, given Nina's condemnation of her friend back in early November for being so cowardly that she couldn't bring up the subject of the raid on Nina's flat, presumably because she was afraid of her own father being arrested because of Nina and Ira's friendship. Nina's anti-Bolshevik views must have been influenced by her father.

6 February 1933

I have just been flicking through my diary. How stupid everything that I used to find absolutely fascinating seems to me now. And why does time fly by so fast? It's just unbelievable.

13 February 1933

Time, time! I'd give anything to make it go more slowly.

Sometimes you lie in bed looking at the black hand of the clock moving remorselessly on and you think: I wish it would stop. But no, time marches on and on without any stoppages or delays . . . A month or two ago, when I was still quite interested in Lyovka, I didn't notice the hand of the clock racing round. I was hurtling along in some kind of vortex without any time or clocks. The days rushed by, and all they left behind them was a vague pleasant memory.

But now that I'm back in the old routine it's so disappointing that I don't feel that thrill in my heart any more when I meet Lyovka or gaze at him lesson after lesson without taking my eyes off him. Although I do still sometimes look in his direction, somehow I just can't look for very long any more, and the moment he turns his head towards me, I immediately turn away. Generally speaking, my inner condition is fairly tolerable right now. I sometimes even feel I'm starting to get enthusiastic about my studies. I'm not exaggerating, but I don't have a single free minute now. I study and study, sometimes I read, and I don't go out at all. And I don't feel at all interested in what's going on around me.

Sometimes I really long to walk off into some boundless snowy expanse, disappear into the white, fluffy snowflakes and just stroll about and revel in nature. But I just don't have the time. Recently, I've stopped hoping for anything in the future. I haven't been hoping for anything and definitely haven't even been thinking about anything. Only 'dreaming' sometimes. This is a quite special feeling: I used to be totally transported to a different world, into the future, of course. Before, when I was younger, I used to call this a 'game', but now I don't think I call it anything at all.

15 February 1933

Right now I'm reading a biography of Lermontov ... Usually, when I read the biography of any writer, the first thing I look for is some definite feature that he and I have in common. When I find something (which happens only very rarely), I always feel glad somehow, as if that gives me greater hope of becoming a writer.

But all the same, I don't know how to write. What kind of talent is it, when I can't even write a single page properly? I have to ponder every phrase. How far can you get like that? Sometimes I think that it will come as the years pass, plus the fact that I started writing when I was still little, but Lermontov only began writing from the age of thirteen, and he wrote very well anyway.

It's strange, as if I write my diary for somebody else, not for myself, and I often feel afraid of writing something I shouldn't. I try to suppress this feeling somehow, but it's useless. Feelings in general are very unruly things: you say one thing, but they say something quite different.

There's no particular news at school. I go on following Lyovka around, nothing special or unusual, of course. Yesterday, during break, I was standing by the radiator on my own. Lyovka came out of the classroom and, as he walked past, he looked at me and asked: 'Feeling warm, Luga?'

'Yes,' I replied. And when he walked away I thought in surprise and delight that I sometimes used to feel warm in exactly the same way when he was around. It's nothing special really, but . . .

And how awful it is that Lyovka's younger than me. Of course, it's just stupid pride, but it really is a shame, isn't it? Putting this boy on my own level when, after all, I'm not a child any longer.

24 February 1933

Since the last time I wrote, I've done a lot of thinking and experienced an awful lot of feelings. Sometimes I was desperate to write it all down, but rotten, lousy time . . . there wasn't a single minute. And what's the point of writing now?

I'm becoming more and more withdrawn and uncommunicative. Is that good or bad? I don't laugh or joke any longer with my family, and I'm gradually separating myself from them. I live as if I were asleep, calmly, quietly, without anything happening to me. Nothing ever does happen, of course, but I have inner experiences, and sometimes quite strong ones. What do they mean by a person's inner world? Perhaps I'm mistaken when I say that I don't have one. And what difference does it make whether it's an inner world or just inner experiences?

The human heart is just bizarre – it's capable of hoping in any situation. When it looks as if everything is lost, in some corner, somewhere, hope starts stirring timidly, gradually expanding until eventually it fills your heart completely. I've experienced this destruction and resurrection of hope for myself several times just recently. How it hurts to feel hope (especially long-cherished hope) suddenly disappear. Your heart feels weirdly empty and tired.

The first time it happened was in school, and to do with Lyovka – I suddenly lost all hope that he loved me (how funny to say that word). It happened during technical drawing, I probably did something the boys thought was funny. They started laughing at me, then they started shouting, 'Fool,' and I even thought I heard Lyovka shout, 'Squinty-eyes.' I blushed from head to toe, and although I carried on calmly drawing, I suddenly felt something in my heart collapse. Moments like that are so painful . . .

Of course, my heart's back to normal now, although, if I think about it sensibly, it's all self-deception. But the greatest disappointment I've suffered since that last time is the end of faith in my literary talent, something that's kept me going for years. I have no talent, there's nothing left now but pain and emptiness beyond words. That's why I whisper bitterly again and again: **'Life, if you glance around with a dispassionate eye, is such an empty and stupid thing.'** [*A modified quote from Lermontov; Nina often repeats this expression in her diary.*]

12 March 1933

Spring is in the air. Its scent is in every gust of wind. There is something new, fresh and young in every current of air. Spring . . . She creeps up imperceptibly and inaudibly, and we seldom really feel her warm breath. Yesterday there was a thaw; there is already quite a lot of heat in the sun, and damp, black stripes are appearing on the road. Spring has percolated into my heart and is luring me irresistibly, 'far and away', into the forest and the open fields.

On our last day of school, when I was sorting out my papers, I came across the piece I'd written about my walk on the Sparrow Hills last year, and others. And I suddenly wanted to write again so badly, it was almost unbearable. Is it really all just self-deception? Do I really have no talent? Can anyone my age really write a heap of manuscripts on various themes if they want to and there's really nothing to it?

18 March 1933

What's happened to my motto: 'Live and hope'? It's all over, I don't believe in it any more. I don't believe and I don't want to believe.

24 March 1933

The holidays are already half over ... Everything's so boring, stupid and dull. What is life? **I walk around with a strange, unpleasant feeling in my stomach and every five minutes I ask: What is life? There is an answer, an answer that hits it right on the head: Life is an empty and stupid joke. It's easy to say, but somehow I don't want to believe that life really is a joke, and a stupid one at that.**

Yesterday evening, I was walking along the street,

looking around at the blue twilight, listening to the shrill voices of the nannies calling to their children on the boulevard, looking at the big, tall houses and the dark figures of the people flitting by, and thinking: Well, what is life? Going to the shops, shouting at the children. Why were they built, these houses, and this road that is so well surfaced? [*Nina was evidently walking down a street where the well-paid Party officials lived.*]

Zhenya and Lyalya were sitting in their room singing, and I walked up and down the corridor for a long time listening to them, then went into the room and sat by the window. From time to time, a breath of fresh air reached me from the small open top window. The room was lit up by the sun and the flowers cast dark, tremulous shadows on Zhenya's back. I stood there, listening, looked at Zhenya's brown jumper and the delicate shadows, and thought, this time with a strange feeling of annoyance: What is life?

And then they refused to give Dad his passport. God, I was raging. I didn't know what to do. I was filled with fury, helpless fury. I began to cry. I ran around the room, cursing and swearing, decided that the bastards had to be killed. Ridiculous as that sounds, it's no joke. For several days, when I was in bed I dreamt for hours about how I would kill him. His promises, the promises of a dictator, a villain and bastard, the vile Georgian who is crippling Russia. How did it happen? Great Russia and the great Russian people have fallen into the hands of some corrupt monster. How was it possible? For Russia, who fought all those centuries for freedom, who had finally won it – for that Russia suddenly to enslave herself. I clenched my fists tight in my fury. He must be killed ... [*illegible*] ... as soon as possible! I must avenge myself and my father ... [*illegible*] ... kill ... [*illegible*].

That day, when Dad's fate was being decided, I couldn't stay at home waiting, so I put my coat on and went outside. The air was damp, the dark streets were blanketed in cold fog. Occasionally, rips would appear in patches of the living shroud ... and for a moment you could make out the forms of objects quite clearly, and then everything was veiled in fog again. Every now and then, grey, indistinct human figures slipped through it and disappeared into the darkness. I gazed in loathing at the dull, grey fog, and it was then for the first time that the thought came to me: What is life? Fate can be cruel.

Here Nina is referring to the Moscow residence permit in her father's passport. He had only recently returned from his first period of exile in Siberia. Without the passport, he would have to leave the capital within ten days. Urban residents had to have a permit allowing them to live in the cities – an attempt to control urban overcrowding. It was also a way of excluding 'undesirable elements', and her counter-revolutionary father was clearly one of these. The illegible sentences in this entry are those crossed out by Nina when her mother advised her to be careful after she read her diaries in August 1935. Nina's anxiety about her father sent her into a typically over-the-top rant. But as the NKVD's underlining suggests, these empty, angry words were taken as a literal threat to kill Stalin, and this was highly incriminating.

29 March 1933

It's over. Dad's gone. He left this morning. Where to? I'm afraid to write it: the walls will see and report it. But he's not with us any more. What difference does it make where he's gone? Dad has gone away – ill, blind in one eye – and I'm sitting here writing my diary.

There is no other mention of her father's illness or partial blindness in the diary, so it is hard to ascertain what this was caused by.

Evening

At about five o'clock, while I was sitting in Granny's room reading a book, Dad came home again. As I have been doing recently, I just gave him an inquiring look: Well, what now? I don't often go any further than this. What would be the point, anyway? **In the last few days I've started loving Dad very much. Before, I didn't care too much about him, but now that they've refused his application for a passport, in other words, ordered him to get out of Moscow within ten days, things are quite different. I love him as a revolutionary, I love him as a man with an idea, a man with a cause, a man who clings staunchly to his own views and doesn't barter them for an easy, comfortable life. Just recently, he has got very thin and yellow, and the wrinkles have started to stand out more sharply on his stern, worried face.**

30 March 1933

Yesterday, I didn't have enough patience to write down everything I wanted to say. I will only say briefly that Dad went to the militia to find out if they would let him stay in Moscow for an extra two days on a doctor's certificate. We waited impatiently for him to come back. An hour went by. He didn't come. Then another half-hour. We had agreed between ourselves that if he was refused, he would go straight round to see Mum at work. Aunt Sonya kept looking out of the window, walking around nervously, saying something for the sake of it; Granny was lying down and only occasionally glancing at the clock. It no longer made any sense to think that he would come back, but . . . it is in man's nature to hope, and I hoped, just as the others hoped.

At about eight o'clock, someone opened the door. I raised my head from my book and started listening. Was it him or not? This time, my hope had not deceived me. I went back to my reading, listening intently for his footsteps, but when the door opened unhurriedly, my cheeks were burning and I could feel myself slowly blushing with joy. I was happy at this minor reprieve of two days.

Dad sat down, smiling, cheerful. The trivial questions began.

'At last you've come,' said Granny. 'I thought my heart was going to burst. At least before I could get to sleep, but now . . .' Her voice quivered and trembled and faltered on the high notes. She began crying and fell on the bed, sobbing convulsively. Dad began making excuses. Sonya took out some kind of drops.

I glanced at Dad. His face didn't look worried now and something rather like a bewildered smile seemed to have settled on it. He was embarrassed, and I thought I saw something like tears glint in his eyes. I said something reproachful to him and was surprised at the loud sound of my voice, breaking off at every word, as if there was something blocking my throat and I had to force the words out with an effort.

Later, Zhenya and Lyalya came and, soon after them, Andrei Lashok arrived. A very stout, solid man with a pot belly, thick, springy thighs in tight-stretched trousers and a broad, good-natured face. I didn't use to like him. I used to find his entire unwieldy, bulky figure and his overly apathetic and calmly self-satisfied face physically unpleasant. I used to see him exclusively as a man in the full sense of the word, and I couldn't look at him without feeling disgusted. He made me feel slightly nauseous, as if I were looking at some repulsive reptile. **But even my feelings for him have changed since the beginning of this business. I've begun to see him as a person who is first and foremost a revolutionary. Very much the same as Dad.**

I'm reading *Anna Karenina* now, and it's really making a powerful impression on me. Tolstoy was a true artist, to describe people and their experiences with such vitality and skill and, above all, so truthfully. Two or three years ago, I started reading *Anna Karenina* and gave up without finishing it. I still didn't understand then what is so clear and obvious to me now. I even reread certain parts two or three times.

Andrei Grigorievich Lashok was a Left Socialist Revolutionary and member of the Anthill workers' co-operative. He was arrested and exiled in 1929, together with Nina's father. After his release from exile, he returned to Moscow.

The eponymous heroine of the novel Anna Karenina *is unlucky in love and throws herself under the wheels of a train. It is easy to see why it made an impression on Nina.*

31 March 1933

School tomorrow. I can feel how hard it's going to be to study this last term. I want to fall into a trance so that I won't be distracted. To walk around like a machine, to do my lessons and not want anything, at least for a while. And it feels like these two months will fly past so quickly and then afterwards, afterwards! Afterwards, there's the wide-open expanse of a happy life. I'll forget completely about school and studying.

Today, Dad will go to the militia again and they'll give him an answer. Sonya was going to go with him, with Noskova, a very pleasant, unpretentious woman, a good friend of Sonya's and a member of the Moscow Soviet. As Dad says jokingly, they've taken him into their care. They know someone in the militia, and with his help they hope to obtain a very brief reprieve for Dad. Everyone is more or less calm now after the first explosion of outrage and despair.

Almost everything at home has gone back to the way it was before, at least on the outside. Dad has been working in the evenings, reading the newspaper in the morning, walking round the room, going out somewhere or other and coming back. We have stopped attacking him; those trivial quarrels that used to happen between us have completely stopped. Because of that, or for some other reason, I've almost begun to enjoy doing my homework, and I only start scowling every now and then, when I get really fed up.

Now Dad has gone out again. 'Well, goodbye, Nina. Perhaps we won't see each other again!' He gave me some final insignificant instructions about the plants and left, but he said that they might grant him a reprieve of five days. If my father is hoping, that means a lot. I do love him after all, and I like to feel this love, which I once doubted. Those doubts really tore me up inside.

Nina's father would end up living and working in Marfin Brod in the Mozhaisk District, a small provincial town not far from Moscow and just outside the 10km exclusion zone. It was an area where many exiles lived.

30 April 1933

They're broadcasting different kinds of dances on the radio. And I imagine brightly lit halls, gleaming mirrors, parquet flooring and furiously swirling couples . . .

1 May 1933

I didn't go to the demonstration today. There hasn't been a single year when I stayed home for the first of May. But . . . nothing lasts for ever, and I've left behind my old habits. I always used to go with Mum, but she has gone to spend these holidays with Dad in Mozhaisk, and I've been left alone. It's been so unbelievably boring! Everything seems pointless when Mum isn't here. I feel totally miserable.

When I went outside today, I was quite startled to see that the city was absolutely deserted, as if all life had died out. There were the odd few young men dressed in their holiday best strutting slowly by. My shoes made a lonely clatter, and the echo of their tapping sounded loud in the empty street. On a warm, sunny day filled with invisible life, it was strange to see the dead, brightly lit street.

I called in to see Ira for a minute. All across her yard, the trees had begun to unfold their buds, and the young, bright-green leaves, so delicate and tender, were timidly emerging. When I got home, they were broadcasting from Red Square on the radio. I could hear an orchestra playing a march; somewhere in the distance someone shouted, 'Hoorah!' and those sounds were like a homecoming to me.

The May-Day holiday was known as International Workers' Solidarity Day and was massively celebrated with military parades and aviation demonstrations. Even though Nina hated the Communist ideals that were being celebrated, she was still enough of a child to hanker after the excitement of the occasion.

2 May 1933

School tomorrow. I even feel quite glad about it – everything is far too nauseating and disgusting at home. If it wasn't for the homework, I wouldn't have wanted to go to school, I would have found something to amuse myself and keep me happy, but now ... now I want to run away and hide from this free time, which has to be taken up with studying. In school I won't notice the time passing so much. Oh, if only Mum would come back soon!

Mum! Nothing makes sense, everything seems pointless, without you here. I'm missing you so much, I just want to die. What's to stop me? Why shouldn't I poison myself right now? Why? 'Life! Why do you seduce me with yourself, if only God would give me strength, I would destroy you.' [*A quotation from a poem by A. V. Koltsov (1809–42), 'A Reckoning with Life', dedicated to V. G. Belinsky.*]

But somehow I can't put an end to my life. Either living is still not disgusting enough, or God really isn't giving me the strength. I want to shake off this hypochondria, and I will shake it off, but not completely, it's not in my power to free myself from it completely.

Evening

How I hate the idea of studying. My God! **I want to drop everything, abandon everything and live. I do want to live, after all. Live! I'm not a machine that can work without a break or a rest, I'm a human being. I want to**

71

live! Forget my problems! I'm glad there's school tomorrow. It'll give me a little break from myself, but then again, I won't know my social studies. But to hell with the new society, anyway! Genka's the only one who can get enthusiastic about it and spend hours reading what Lenin and Stalin said and what advances our Soviet Union has made. Ah, life, life! I wish the dogs would tear you to pieces.

And again I ask myself: What does Lyovka mean to me now?

> *Passion has passed, and now its ardent thrill*
> *No longer wrings this heart of mine,*
> *And yet I find that I must love you still!*
> *Where you are not, all is vain falsity,*
> *Where you are not lies drab frigidity.*

But I have to say that it's you that is vain and false.

> *But . . . I cannot join in this life's banality,*
> *My love, dear friend, free of all jealousy,*
> *Remains the same love as it ever was.*
> ['The Passion Has Passed', by A. K. Tolstoy]

5 May 1933

Today I spent the whole evening reading Turgenev's *Smoke*. I haven't read his works for a long time. I'm finding so many brilliant things in a book I found boring and disgusting a year ago. The more I got into his language – sonorous and always subtly changing – and the beauty and fluency of his style, the more I became convinced that I possess absolutely no talent at all. But what I had read left me with a strange impression overall. I felt the memory of it weighed me down like some dark, solid, heavy lump. I just don't understand why the two sweethearts don't have more get-up-and-go. Either I've never been in love or they are just made differently. I don't know, but I just can't sit back and accept that despicable resignation the hero displays after he's fallen in love with Irina. But look how poorly developed my language is – I can't even express the most basic impressions and feelings.

13 May 1933

It feels as if only recently it was still January and I was thinking in horror that I had to study for so much longer, but now? Now there are only two weeks left! And then I'll be free. Sometimes my doubts get on top of me: will I be happy when I leave school? Will there be an end to all this hard work that has exhausted me? Will everything still be the same as before? But that would be the worst!

For the last few days I've been feeling really awful. I torment myself more than ever for being so ugly. It's at least two years since I was amazed that Zhenya, Lyalya, Mum and Dad, everybody we know, including my girlfriends, could look at me, talk and laugh with me the same way as with other people: how they could bear how hideous my eyes look; after all, I can't even bear to look at cross-eyed people myself. Any kind of ugliness is bad, but I think this is one of the worst kinds.

When I was a bit younger, about eleven or twelve, the way the boys mocked me used to really upset me; I'd be hurt by the things they shouted. A time came when this started to feel less painful and, now, I pay even less attention to them, but in myself I feel terrible. Sometimes I just want not to think about it, to forget and take no notice, but I can almost never forget about it. And it's impossible to be happy with that . . .

Yesterday, I spent the whole day wondering what it is that keeps me from poisoning myself. There is a simple and easy way out. And all my torments would be over. What holds me back? What makes me walk round these streets, stealing glances at the passers-by, what makes me learn those stupid, boring subjects, what makes me listen with bitterness in my heart as Lyovka, who I really like after all, sometimes goes walking past and chuckles in a low voice: 'Luga's boss-eyed'?

There is a means to free myself from all of this, there is a way to put an end to all this suffering. What hold has this hideous life of torment got over me anyway? How could I be attracted to this 'empty and stupid joke'? And yet I still dream of a wonderful childhood, when that door is closed to me for ever. And I still dream of being a pretty girl – with my cross-eyes! How stupid is that?

It seems the short-sighted Nina suffered from a pronounced form of strabismus (cross-eyes) due to an imbalance in the eye muscles. It is also possible that she suffered from amblyopia (lazy eye): the

two conditions are linked, with the second deriving from the first
– the crossed eye effectively stops focusing in order to prevent
double vision.

18 May 1933

And life . . . is an empty and stupid joke! But not only that, it's a malicious joke. My last hope has just been ruined. Only just recently I was enjoying planning the summer, thinking that I was happy. But I'm not looking forward to it now. How can I relax when I know that in three months' time the same old stupid, boring life will start all over again? And, just like now, I'll be shaking with fear before the biology oral and spend hours swotting up things that are absolutely no use . . .

I'd be so happy if they'd just leave me completely alone, give me books and let me withdraw completely into myself and forget everything that's happening in the world – then, perhaps, I'd be totally calm and happy. And now these 'First Year of the Second Five-Year Plan' loan bonds have come out. It makes me absolutely furious. Yesterday, I couldn't stand it any more and I tore the poster with the slogans off the door. At school yesterday, the biology teacher gave us work to do for the summer and told all of us to do it, because the Party had ordered it. The Party! How dare it give us orders like that! Some band of villains has got together and is bossing everyone around as if we're obliged to obey them, as if we had to listen to what every scumbag says and revere Stalin.

Today, Zhenya announced that she was going to a demonstration to support the issue of the loan bonds. 'You're going?' I exclaimed in amazement.

'They ordered us to go. I didn't bother arguing, because it's pointless.'

'You go and demand the loan then. I wouldn't go for anything.'

'We were just like you when we were at school,' Zhenya retorted calmly, even pretending to be slightly ironic. Oh, the villains! And they say it so calmly and indifferently: 'They ordered us.' How small-minded can you get!

Ah, Russian people, what can you expect from ignorant peasants and the working masses when perfectly well-educated people, students, act so low without the slightest embarrassment? They'd probably call anybody who dared to oppose the Party a fool. 'I'm going so I won't get on anybody's wrong side,' Zhenya remarked in passing. Ha-ha! Afraid of getting on the wrong side of the bosses. And if that's what students say, what can you expect from the masses?

No, the Russians cannot win their freedom and they cannot live free lives. Ever since the Slavs invited the Varangians to rule over them, they have been under someone else's power. *And they always will be.* You have to agree with Turgenev when he says that 'what the Russian people needs least of all is freedom', and they don't need it, because they can't hold on to it.

The population of Soviet Russia was forced to buy state bonds issued for specific purposes, such as financing the Five-Year Plans.

This was in effect a form of taxation, because the state loan bonds were never redeemed. It was not until the 1980s that any payments were made against these bonds, and then the amount returned to investors was effectively only a hundredth part of what they had invested forty years before. By that time most families had simply thrown the bonds away as useless pieces of paper.

The first Five-Year Plan was introduced in 1928. It was Stalin's economic manifesto and imposed high agricultural production quotas for the collective farms and accelerated industrialization with an emphasis on heavy industry at the expense of the production of consumer goods. The second Five-Year Plan began in 1933.

It's clear that Nina's sisters did not share her political views – they were both happy to go along with whatever they were told for an easy life, which is ironic in the light of their ultimate fate of being condemned with Nina.

21 May 1933

Just recently, absolutely everything gets on my nerves and makes me angry: Zhenya and Lyalya's animated discussions and their arguments too, and my family's attitude to politics, and just the whole intolerable regime we have now. I'm in such a state that I can't even answer politely when my family ask about school and how I'm doing in the exams. I just want to be left alone. I'm finding even the slightest attempt by other people to penetrate into my inner world painful and hard to bear. I can tell that I'm hurting the feelings of everyone who cares about me, but I can't change the way I'm behaving. Well, it's not exactly that I can't. It's not all that difficult to say something, but a little bit later you get that confused, dislocated feeling inside ... I'm afraid that the walls of my world are going to fall in.

24 May 1933

Yesterday, I only got 'good' in the first exam (and so did Ira). I don't think it's my fault – the teacher is partly to blame because she didn't give us enough time or the books to work through the subject material, and because she didn't explain anything to us at all. So I'm not very upset but, even so, it's left a nasty taste in my mouth, and this is the only exam that I can't think back on and feel happy with.

Yesterday evening, Mum and I sat in Granny's room for a long time, waiting for Dad to arrive. I realized, to my own surprise, that in my heart of hearts I didn't want him to come home. It was a shock. How terrible, how awful! Now, I have no idea how such a feeling could have sneaked up on me. I was sitting calmly in an armchair at the table reading, and knowing that, if Dad came, my peace would be interrupted. I'd have to tear myself away from the book, force myself to smile and, probably, even worse than that, tell him about myself.

Dad came home at about midnight, when we had almost given up waiting for him. Trying to stifle my annoyance, I got up and went into the hallway. The chat and the questions began. He told us how good it was out there in Mozhaisk and invited me to join him as soon as

I finished school. I agreed, of course, but . . . my plans for the summer – will I really never realize my dreams? From what Dad told us, it sounds great where he is. Bird cherry and lilac, the river nearby and little groves of trees everywhere: birches, hazelnuts, bushes – and hundreds of nightingales in them.

The NKVD underlined Nina's comments suggesting that her father returned from exile to visit his family illegally, under cover of darkness. They also suggest that getting 'good' (a B rather than an A) in an exam was not something a loyal citizen should feel unhappy about.

25 May 1933

Yesterday, the moment I got out of bed, before my feet even touched the floor, my eye was caught by the bottom drawer of my desk, where I keep my diary under the spare bedding. The drawer was not completely closed, and there were white scraps of material sticking out of it, as if they had been stuffed back inside in a hurry. I rushed across and opened it. The diary was lying right at the edge and was barely even covered with bedding. Very suspicious. Had someone actually taken it? The idea that someone else had found out about my inner life, my desires and aspirations, discovered my most secret thoughts and feelings, stirred up a storm of indignation in my soul. Surely no one would have taken it! A bit later, Zhenya brought me a small red silk pillowcase with a knitted one slipped over it. 'Here, Nina, this is yours, isn't it?'

'Yes,' I said, and took it calmly. But as soon as she left, I threw the pillowcase on the desk in a frenzy, clutched my head in my hands and exclaimed: 'Oh, the bastards! The pigs!' The pillowcase had been in that bottom drawer, so now there was no doubt in my mind: everything was quite clear. I squatted down on the floor, not sure what to do, but then I remembered a rusty old key that had been lying on the windowsill for years. Maybe it would fit. I grabbed it and, after several attempts, I managed to turn it and the drawer was locked.

I wasn't even very angry with whoever it was who had taken the diary: I knew they wouldn't take it again, that I was perfectly safe now. But then, when I returned to my room in the evening, I noticed signs of another attempt; it was obvious that someone had tried to open the drawer, but the key had saved me. I decided to find out who it had been and what they were after, so I asked Lyalya: 'Have you been going into my drawer? Everything's been turned upside-down.'

'I don't know what's upside-down or what isn't, but I tried to open it. Do you lock it, then?'

'Yes.'

'What for? I needed to get the herbarium.'

There was nothing I could say to that.

Zhenya and Lyalya are still at it, playing and singing and chattering away merrily. My heart aches, I can feel a heavy lump in my throat. This is a terrible life! Sometimes I want to tell someone about everything, everything that's stifling me. I feel like snuggling up against Mum or the girls and bursting into violent sobs and bitter tears like a child. And making myself feel a little bit better. But what, what am I going to do? I can't live like this. **If only I could get hold of some poison.**

2 June 1933

Here I am back in Moscow. I arrived early yesterday evening, and I left on the morning of the thirtieth. Did you think I'd be disappointed by the countryside I saw while I was with Dad? Oh, no! I couldn't get enough of it.

Mum and I left Moscow on the nine o'clock train. There weren't many people in the carriage, and the train was exasperatingly slow, clanking its wheels loudly and painfully. There was a cool, gusty wind blowing in at the window, and the sky was grey and overcast, covered with unbroken low clouds. The fields, forests and small villages rushed by. An endless line of low fir trees planted close together stretched out right beside the bed of the track. Their dark greenery mingled strangely with small bushes of delicate, light-green acacia.

I looked through the open window at the flickering birches, firs and the occasional slim, reddish-brown aspen. Is it really possible to represent nature in words, to describe it so that you can picture it in bright and natural colours? It can't be, that unattainable, indefinable 'something' can't be expressed in words, you'd have to be an artist of genius to catch it. Ever since I began to write, my goal has been to depict nature. I've struggled with it a lot but . . . I haven't got anywhere. I've decided to try describing it with a brush instead of a pen, or with a pencil – after all, I used to be able to draw once. And after school I could go to the art department in the textile institute. Of course, I'd have to work really hard, but so what? Having a goal makes it easier to live, and this is quite definitely what I've decided to aim for.

3 June 1933

After walking a few steps along the multiple railway tracks, we saw Dad. He was moving slowly towards us, leaning on a thick white stick. The slightly stooped, haggard figure and the bearded, suntanned face both expressed extreme weariness. Time was taking its toll.

The three of us went into one of the rooms at the station, which had a plaque saying 'hall' and 'buffet'. On the right-hand side, just by the entrance, newspapers and magazines were on sale. A short queue had formed, and Dad joined the end of it. Mum and I went across to one of the tables, put our things on the chairs and waited. A few minutes later, Dad came across with a newspaper, and we set off. After walking all the way through the town, we started along a wet clay road between endless vistas of green fields and reddish-brown plough land.

We walked across a small bridge and started climbing up the slippery road. Standing in front of us, we saw two little single-storey stone houses connected by a semi-circular arch, its plaster crumbled away in places, through which the road passed. We went into the yard, climbed up some rickety, rotten steps and into a corridor. Dad opened the last door and we went inside. I saw a small, low room, its walls covered with light-blue wallpaper. Despite the rather musty air, the first impression was very welcoming. The room was filled with a pleasant half-light from the small window, and there were fluffy branches of bird cherry with white dangling flowers standing in bottles.

Beside the window there was a table covered with white paper and, set against the wall, there was a simple iron bed covered with a dark-blue quilt. On the wall behind it, in the corner, was a broad shelf with small items standing on it, and there was another shelf exactly the same on the wall opposite the window. Underneath it there was a little locker covered with white paper. There was a whole heap of hazel-switch fishing rods lying in the corner. To the right of the door there was a small brick stove. This wretched little room with its poor furnishings was really quite dirty and would have seemed very unattractive if it hadn't been for the white sheets of paper on the table and the little locker, the fragrant bunches of bird cherry and the bluish half-light, the soft glow of which made all the objects look somehow more beautiful and elegant.

4 June 1933

I've never enjoyed myself so much as during this visit to see Dad. I caught a breath of something special, something out of the ordinary and poetic, from that remote spot. It was so much fun to come back from the river chilled through, soaking wet and hungry, to light the stove, get warm, collapse on the bed and relax, physically *and* morally.

I felt so untroubled and happy, my heart beat so steadily, as I sat there at the table beside Mum, barely able to keep my eyes open, waiting for Dad. It was superb to be reading Turgenev's stories and listening at the same time to the monotonous thrumming of a guitar on the other side of the wall, the light, regular banging of the factory machinery and the abrupt, hollow sound of falling drops of water. It was heaven to lie down on the hard, straw-filled mattress, cover myself with the warm quilt and fall into a deep, healthy sleep with no dreams.

The next morning, Mum and I began getting ready to leave: the wind had died down a little, the rain had stopped and, instead of dark stormclouds, the sky was covered with a dense, motionless, yellow-grey film suspended way up high. A thick white mist was rising from the river. We left the house at about nine o'clock, and I gave my father an especially warm kiss when we said goodbye, because I felt slightly ashamed that I wasn't staying there with him.

The yellow dirt road stretched out in front of us in an endless ribbon. A few hours later we saw Mozhaisk. We made our way through the back lanes and allotments out on to the road leading into the suburbs of the town, where little tumbledown houses stood along the sides of the street. We walked up a steep hill along a very muddy road full of potholes to the central part of the town. Then we walked across the square and set off along a small boulevard towards the railway station.

It was made beautiful by low, scraggy trees sticking up here and there among the grass and a solitary flowerbed close to a statue of Lenin. **This monument was probably one of the sights of the town of Mozhaisk. The person who made it must have been trying to create a caricature and cannot possibly have expected that his work would end up in a position of such great honour. The pedestal was painted to look like marble and standing on it was a little dwarf of a man with inordinately short legs and a big, bald head. It was this head, with its small, jutting beard and the orator's pose, that made it possible to identify the dwarf, who looked from behind like a badly trimmed block of stone, as none other than Lenin.** It was still not twelve o'clock when we arrived at the station, quite worn out, and got into the train for Moscow.

After his death Vladimir Ilyich Lenin achieved iconic status. Every town in the Soviet Union had not one but several statues of Lenin, many of which were torn down in 1991 when the union collapsed. On Lenin's death, his body was embalmed and placed in a granite and marble mausoleum in Red Square, where it remains today. His brain was removed to assist research into genius at a specially created Brain Institute in Moscow.

10 June 1933

The days go by, monotonous, dull, but incredibly fast, so fast I feel that these three summer months will pass without a trace, that I won't have time to come to terms with my new situation and adjust to a different routine. I almost feel impatient for classes to begin, so that I can get away from myself and my troubles and not think about anything.

4 July 1933
Mozhaisk – Marfin Brod

The weather is disgusting today, and I must admit that I'm thoroughly bored. There's absolutely nothing to do. Zhenya and Lyalya are drawing, and I'd be only too happy to read for a while, but there aren't any books: everything was left behind in that ill-fated bundle. It's a good thing that we've now moved into a different room, a big room that seems about three times the size of the last one and has a beautiful view. The walls and the ceiling are whitewashed, there are two big Venetian windows that look out on to the open meadow and the park, and in the evenings the setting sun casts its warm rays through the panes of glass on to the floor and the white walls.

Several times we (Zhenya, Lyalya and me) have started arguing about the way things are these days, about how the workers are being treated, about culture and lots of other things of the same kind. They tried as hard as they could to defend the system we have now, but I, on the other hand, denounced it; even when I had to stop arguing because I had run out of arguments, I always stuck to my own opinion. I can never agree with their acceptance of the present order as socialism, with them regarding the current batch of horrors as being just the way things are.

8 July 1933

On the evening of the fifth, Mum and Dad went to Moscow. It just makes me so miserable. It's strange to look at Mum's empty bed and, listening to an owl's crazy hooting or its long, drawn-out call, to think that my lovely Mum is far, far away. For the last two days the rain has been falling almost continuously, taking only short little breaks. Yesterday and today we went prowling through the wet woods, looking for mushrooms. Soaking wet and chilled to the bone, with our skirts black from the rain, we forced our way between the birch trees under the bright-green branches, from which thousands of cold drops came showering down at the slightest breeze. When the sun suddenly peeped out and scattered the bright beams of its light through the forest, all the raindrops hanging on the leaves and the lush green grass began glinting like millions of tiny lights. Everything around us was lit up, and there were dozens of bright little suns staring out at me from the depths of the forest, from the shaggy, moss-covered tree trunks.

I once called all young people of today, in particular Zhenya and Lyalya, limp rags. And it's only too true. How can the students of the old days be compared with the modern ones? Is there really any similarity at all between these coarse people, for the most part entirely undeveloped intellectually, who are capable of doing anything mean and nasty for the sake of even the slightest gain to themselves, and the young people of the last century, so full of life, so intelligent and serious

(with a few exceptions), ready at a moment's notice to suffer for an idea?

12 July 1933

For two days now I've been tormented by indecision: should I go to Moscow on the fifteenth with Mum or stay here with Dad until the seventeenth? Both choices are so appealing that I really don't know which to go for. Yesterday evening, my sister Zhenya, who was in a desperately grouchy mood – as she so often is – was being rude to everyone and getting angry with everyone, and she was especially unbearable with me. The abuse and the caustic remarks just kept on coming. Oh, was I angry! All the indignation, offended pride and wounded feelings that have built up while we've been living here boiled up inside me and begged to be let out.

But I didn't say anything – I concealed my resentment and will just wait patiently for the time to come when I won't have to exchange a single word with Zhenya and will almost never have to see her. I'll try to be as cold and reserved with her as possible, I thought, not argue about anything, do as few things together as possible. But these are only thoughts – how can you put them into practice, living in the same room, spending the nights in the same bed, with all those domestic chores bringing you into close contact all the time?

We've quarrelled the whole summer. We've descended to such pettiness that we won't even hand each other a cup and tend to answer the simplest request with: 'Do it yourself.' I'm particularly good at this, but my sisters are driving me absolutely crazy with their constant demands: 'Give me this,' 'Bring me that,' 'Close that whatever,' etc., etc., etc. We're daggers drawn, and things got especially bad when we were all living together without Mum. Those days it was just incredible – we called each other names morning till night, and the air rang with: 'Bitch', 'Fool', 'Idiot'.

Even now, with the bickering still going on, I feel terrible when I remember what we were like when Mum wasn't here. What can I blame for our unforgivable behaviour, the total inability to hold back and the constant, ridiculous pettiness? God, how life can make you behave! Was Mum like this at our age? And surely we never used to be like it either! Of course not. But it's no easy thing not to be petty when you have to barter and trade between yourselves over every piece of bread, not to abuse each other or get angry, when that unbearable hunger is sucking and gnawing away inside your belly.

After I thought all this over yesterday, I decided to go to Moscow on the fifteenth. It's time for a rest, I've suffered enough this summer, I told myself. And I felt a longing to go to Moscow, to the familiar, old setting, to my own room, to the old, cosy way of passing the time.

21 August 1933

Sixty kopecks for a kilo of white bread! Fifty kopecks for a litre of kerosene! Moscow's grumbling. The angry,

hungry, tired people in the queues abuse the authorities and curse life. Nowhere can you hear a single word in defence of the detested Bolsheviks. Prices at the market are shooting up because of the increased prices for bread and other everyday stuff. And you can't help asking yourself what's coming after this, when the price of bread has already doubled, and potatoes cost five roubles for an eighth of a pound at the market and there aren't any at all in the state shop. What are the workers going to eat in winter, when there aren't any vegetables or anything else now?

All the shops in Moscow are divided into several categories. There are commercial shops, where there is loads of all sorts of food which is sold to anyone who wants it. In these shops the atmosphere is lively: crowding around the counters are painted and powdered, elegantly dressed women, the ones referred to (only in secret, of course) as the Soviet aristocracy. They're mostly Jewish women, the wives of communists and administrators. There are no ordinary people here at all, and the large shopfloor is saturated with the smell of various kinds of perfume.

The commercial shops are located on the bustling central streets of Moscow. The displays in their big windows are magnificent, and at first glance no one would ever suspect that everything is exorbitantly expensive. It's for that very simple reason there are no workers to be seen in the shops. The state has been engaging in this kind of business for about two years now, ruthless in its extermination of the private nepmen and creation of the state nepman.

Looking very inconspicuous beside these swanky shops, there are modest little shops with small windows also full of all sorts of foodstuffs, and more than one passer-by has been tempted to go inside, but they are always halted at the door, after reading the sign that says 'Restricted distributor'. Not everyone can get their groceries there.

Along Tverskaya Street and especially Petrovka Street, among the various bright-coloured signs, you come across the word 'torgsin' [*trade with foreigners*] in large letters over an entrance door. These shops are something like museums or exhibitions of the pre-war days. Here you can find absolutely anything – compared with them, the commercial shops seem quite primitive. The trade with foreigners is very lively and, actually, they are also quite happy to sell to Soviet citizens: just bring along your gold and silver. These *torgsins* provide a graphic demonstration of how far the value of our money has fallen and show that our rouble is only equal to one kopeck in gold.

And finally, the fourth and most numerous category of shops is the state co-operative, kiosks, etc. These are scattered throughout the broad suburbs of Moscow, far away from the chic city streets. Most of the time there is no one to be seen in them at all, except for those days when the factory and office workers are issued with their pitiful rations. Then, there are immense, jostling queues here, and the air is blue with swearing and shouting.

As industrialization shifted the population from the countryside to the city, one of the main problems was a shortage of food and consumer goods. The collectivization of farms was a disaster, leading the peasants to revolt and destroy what would become state-owned property and animals. Coupled with bad weather, crops inevitably failed and famine followed. Shops and markets disappeared, to be replaced with government stores. This led to the infamous system of queuing and the introduction of food rations. Rations were allocated by class, with industrial workers receiving the largest share, followed by ordinary workers and then white-collar workers. The Lugovsky family, being middle-class, were in the lowest category and therefore received a very low ration. Nina knew what it meant to feel hungry.

Evening

What a terrible mood I was in for the first two or three days. I kept asking myself in horror: What's going to happen next, if I'm in this state already? For entire, long evenings of idleness and boredom, I slouched from corner to corner, from room to room, and at times I thought I was going mad. What despair and hopeless, agonizing yearning filled my heart! The room was filled with the sounds of a piano and mournful songs. **My God! What is it with us? I asked dejectedly. Is it really going to be like this every day? (And the thought of opium kept coming into my mind over and over again.) My indignation and fury were choking me, it felt as if my nerves were about to snap at any moment.**

I was suffocating. The atmosphere was appalling, so oppressive. I gnawed at my fingers, clutched at my head, I felt like sobbing and wailing . . . But I put up with it, spoke to Mum with a calm expression on my face, and then, when I turned away, I bit my lips until it was agony, scarcely able to hold back the tears. I felt a half-formed desire to throw myself on someone's neck, to press myself against someone's loving, all-understanding breast and burst into tears without holding myself back, like a child. Oh, how lonely I felt during those moments, how abandoned and unwanted.

Suicide was taken very seriously by the NKVD, and any suspicious deaths were closely investigated. It was assumed that the act of suicide was a subversive message to the state, a rebellious act undertaken as a criticism of the Soviet regime and a betrayal of the Communist Party. It was often interpreted as evidence of guilt, particularly of illegal political involvements.

28 August 1933

Life is just one long string of disillusionments. What is it that's been there waiting for me ever since the day I was born? Disillusionment after disillusionment after disillusionment. It's dogged my footsteps all my life, for as long as I can remember. First, disillusionment with people, and then bitter and painful disillusionment with life. I remember the time when I thought the world and everything in it was beautiful. In those days I never used to brood over all the strange injustices of life, I didn't know how vile people were, I only saw the beautiful façade of life and I didn't glance behind the scenes. And that was such a happy time! It was childhood, with all its ups and downs, happy and carefree. But it passed . . .

And now my disillusionment with absolutely everything carries on. Disillusionment with Mum, with Dad, with my sisters . . . I see everything now in the cold light of reality, and I am bitterly convinced that there is nothing beautiful in this world. The only thing I have not become disillusioned with yet is myself. Ha-ha! That's strange, isn't it? But I do still believe in myself, I believe that I can be happy. But the time will come when this faith too will dwindle away, and the days of even more excruciating disillusionment, disillusionment with myself, will begin.

31 August 1933

There are strange things going on in Russia. Famine, cannibalism . . . People arriving from the provinces tell all sorts of stories. They say they can't clear all the dead bodies off the streets fast enough, that the provincial towns are full of starving peasants dressed in tattered rags. That the thieving and banditry everywhere is appalling.

And what about Ukraine, with its vast, rich fields of grain? Ukraine . . . What has happened to it? It's unrecognizable now. Nothing but the lifeless, silent steppe. No sign of the tall, golden rye or the bearded wheat; their swelling heads of grain no longer sway in the wind. The steppes are overgrown with high weeds.

Not a trace left of the cheerful, bustling villages with their little white Ukrainian houses, not a single note left of those resounding Ukrainian songs. Here and there you can see lifeless, empty villages. The people of Ukraine have fled and scattered.

Stubbornly, without end, the refugees flow into the large towns. They have been driven back time and again, whole trainloads of them despatched to certain death. But the struggle for life has proved stronger, and people dying in the railway stations and on the trains have kept on trying to reach Moscow. But what about Ukraine? Oh, the Bolsheviks were prepared for this disaster too. The insignificant little plots of land sown in the spring are harvested by the Red Army, sent there especially for the purpose.

Nina is describing the famine that resulted from the campaign of 'dekulakization' and collectivization in the countryside, the confiscation of virtually all the food harvested by the peasantry to meet the needs of industrialization, immense communist construction projects and the production of military arms. How could Nina have known about conditions in the Ukraine? It is likely that she copied or paraphrased an article from the Menshevik Socialist Herald or another émigré publication. It was illegal to possess such newspapers, but her father may have brought them home and this may have been amongst the other family material confiscated in the 1937 raid on their house.

5 September 1933

The first attack of pessimism since school began. Not very strong and over quickly, but that's not the point: it's proof that I won't be able to stand even a month. I want to finish school as soon as possible. How do Zhenya and Lyalya manage to do everything so well? Get excellent results at school, and play the piano, and sing, and dance and draw? There's no doubt they were born under a luckier star than I was, they can do everything, everybody loves them – quite often people really admire them. And me? What am I good for? Recently, I've begun feeling convinced that I have no talent for anything, and even if sometimes I have managed to come first in some things, it is only because I try so hard.

Ah, Zhenya and Lyalya! In just one month they went right through the ninth class programme and got 'excellent' in the entrance exams for college. And at school they didn't do a thing, but even then they were always top of the class. And me? Who would believe that just for the biology exam I studied so hard it made me feel dizzy and sick, that I swotted up all the biographies by heart?

Soviet schools used a five-grade marking system: 5) Excellent, 4) Good, 3) Satisfactory, 2) Unsatisfactory and 1) Fail.

22 September 1933

Oh, my God, it's torture! . . . I curse the day that I was born, when I first saw the light of this world. I understand now why adults are so fond of reminiscing about their childhood, why they regret so much that it is over; but two years ago I didn't understand that, did I? What's good about it? I thought. I used to think that everything was so bad but, now, what wouldn't I give to bring it all back! But there's no way that's going to happen! You can't bring it back, and in a another few years I'll finish secondary school and go to college . . . Oh, then I'll regret my childhood even more, then I'll really miss school, the fun and the freedom. Yes, the freedom, because, after all, it is freedom compared with what will come afterwards.

At school I forget about myself, about my painful, hopeless thoughts, I start living and doing things. The lessons are not so boring and unbearable as being at home. I'm surrounded by people I am close to, whose lives are filled with the same interests and thoughts as mine, it makes me feel big and strong, I feel that 'they' are all living inside me, and I am in them – all for one and one for all.

Yesterday, at the Young Pioneers meeting, Liza spread vile, slanderous lies about our girls who have left the Pioneers, and about me. No one liked her before anyway, and now she's made herself even more unpopular. We talked about it a lot during break and decided to boycott her. Today, almost everyone agreed and supported us. Oh, we'll get our own back on her! We won't let her laugh at us, we'll make her sorry for that sharp little tongue of hers. A general boycott is no joking matter!

It was compulsory for school children to join the Young Pioneers –

a kind of Communist youth club based on Baden-Powell's scouting movement. When founded in 1922 by the 5th Komsomol Congress, its original purpose was to teach children between the ages of ten and fourteen the principles of discipline, hard work, morality and collective thinking. They had similar rituals to the boy scouts, including a variation of the 'Be prepared' motto. Activities included marching and singing songs, as well as summer holiday camps. To leave the Pioneers or decline to be a member was an overt declaration of opposition.

A boycott (when everybody refuses to speak with a certain member of a group, class, etc.) was a form of social ostracism widely practised in Soviet schools.

28 September 1933

Homework – my God, so many assignments. Those lousy Bolsheviks! They don't think about us young people at all, they don't think about the fact that we are human beings too. Some Bubnov or other [*a reference to Andrei Sergeevich Bubnov (1884–1938), the People's Commissar of Education, who was responsible for the school reforms of the 1930s*], some kind of poor excuse for a human being, just spews out any old nonsense that comes into his head. He writes articles for the newspapers about the need to improve the level of study and discipline, but none of them understands the very simplest thing – that all they actually do is slow us down. I'm far worse at studying than I used to be, I've lost all interest in it now, it's all become so pointless and annoying. I thought to myself this morning, The sooner I can grow up and leave this land of barbarians and savages, the better.

17 October 1933

Today, Ksyusha and I went for a walk to the Novodevichy Convent. Just as we got near, we had to stop at a turn in the road and wait quite a while to let a vehicle turning the corner go past. It was a strange-looking kind of vehicle. From a distance it looked a bit like an ambulance or as if it was used for transporting patients – big windows and a brightly lit interior . . . It went past us slowly, very close, so I got a clear look at the people sitting on the benches along the sides. There were five or six of them, two in civilian clothes and the others in uniform.

They were sitting there without speaking or moving, looking at the people on the street in an odd sort of way, very tensely and intently. [*one line crossed out*] The soldier by the window closest to us gave us a long look as he went by and even turned his head. Was it really him? It couldn't be, we had to be mistaken, surely! I didn't believe it; even now I don't completely believe it. We started walking faster. Quick, quick! We had to get to the convent in time to catch up with him there.

We were almost running. There were a lot of people at the last stop. The wide-spaced street lamps gave off a dull glow, shrouding the streets in gloom. Ksyushka and I walked across to the gates of the cemetery. [*line crossed out*] Through the narrow wicket gate in the big cast-iron one, we could see the asphalt track of the entrance, the occasional figure walking along it and, on the right, we could vaguely make out the workers' wooden barracks. Ahead of us was the gaping black void of the descent to the pond, with the thick convent wall running alongside it. Black, crooked willows leaned down over the water, and in the distance we could see a wide line of bright lights – that was the embankment.

Looking into the empty blackness was frightening. We stood on the roadway by the big gates, speaking in low voices, almost in a whisper. 'The vehicle could be over there, behind the wall, by the pond, there's no one there.' But the darkness over there was so scary, we didn't dare go any further and just carried on standing there, talking quietly and waiting for someone to come along the path. Eventually, some man or other walked past us in the direction of the pond.

We set off after him, making our way down the steep slope. The dark, peeling wall looked terrifying, the water was calm and still, with street lamps reflected in it here and there, and there were houses in the distance on the opposite bank. Behind us, we could clearly hear the voices of either women or children, and that encouraged us, so we walked on rather quickly until we came to a turn. The light of the city did not reach this far, and at this point everything was drowned in total darkness. Ahead of us, I heard shouting and men talking.

'Let's go back! We won't be able to do anything anyway.' We jogged back the way we had come.

Our footsteps echoed hollowly under the stone arches of the gates. There were low, dense fir trees standing in tight groups along the avenue; we couldn't see the graves and the crosses. Everything here was in ruins. The tall bell-towers of the old white church stood out clearly against the dark background, their gilded domes gleaming. Several blue fir trees stood handsome and erect around a small white crypt with a golden dome. What had we really thought we were going to do?

Stalin was rumoured to visit the grave of his wife Alliluyeva in the cemetery of the Novodevichy Convent. It is quite possible that they had spotted him there.

20 October 1933

Dad has a good friend by the name of Pyotr Ivanovich [*a former colleague and friend of Nina's father who managed the finances of Lugovsky's co-operative*]. **I remember the first time I saw him at the treasurer's desk. And then he was exiled for living under an alias, and sent to the north. He spent six years there and came back at more or less the same time as Dad. Some time in spring, two years ago, he came to our flat. I opened the door and, as he took his coat off, almost as if he were shy or – more likely – embarrassed, he thrust a pair of grey gloves into my hand, a present: 'Here, take them: they'll come in useful.'**

I took them and thanked him. Is he crazy or something? I thought as I looked them over rapidly and rather disdainfully. They were perfectly ordinary cheap gloves with fingers that were too long. Disgusted, I tossed them into the furthest corner of the drawer and piled other things on top of them.

This incident stuck in my mind for a long time. I tried to avoid Pyotr, and the thought of him made me feel uncomfortable. I should really just put that strange episode to the back of my mind. In every other respect Pyotr is a wonderful person. He speaks slowly, drawing out the words as if he is singing. His face is calm and good-natured, even rather phlegmatic.

30 October 1933

Today is not a school day . . . I waited for it, waited a whole five days and then . . . Life's horrible sometimes. The day's absolutely ruined for me. I have to go to school for nine o'clock. Ksyusha will come in ten minutes, and then I'll go. Human life is a terrible thing, such a bundle of contradictions. There's no truth or justice in it, it's all lies and deception. Deception even in the truth, in everything, in everything, and it will always be that way. People will never see a time when everyone on earth will be equal, when nobody will have the right to coerce and humiliate anybody else, when there won't be powerful people ruling everybody else and weak people with no rights.

Life's a battle. In a battle, the strong person always wins, and the strong person is praised to the skies while the weak person grovels at his feet. And what is a woman? A woman is a dog who tries to rise to the level of her master, to occupy the same position as him, but can't get there. What is the liberation of women? It's a mirage, nothing more than a hallucination.

Contrary to what the NKVD man who underlined this passage seemed to believe, Nina did not think women were inferior – she was obviously being ironic here.

8 November 1933

I'd have been better off not having this rest, this break, if they'd kept me in the cage all the time, but they let me out, allowed me to stretch my wings and fill my lungs full of air, and then put me back in prison again. It seems so strange and ridiculous now to remember how I felt about school earlier this year; it all seemed so easy and interesting. I had so many plans and hopes – just imagine how naïve I was two months ago. And now? What is happening to me now? I don't have the strength to get down to studying, but not studying isn't an option.

I feel last year's depression coming over me again, but this year it feels easier somehow, because I don't keep quiet for days at a time, wincing with the pain. Sometimes I even spend ages telling Mum and Dad about school and cursing my entire life to them. **God, it's horrific, being alive! If only the school would burn down and they'd send us all home, I'd be glad, really. I can't do a thing. I've missed homework assignments and I carry on missing them. How can I change this terrible life? Sometimes it's enough to make me long for the good old days, when there was no need to study and I could do whatever I wanted all day long.**

This year's October holidays have been a bit strange for me. On 6 November, Lyalya and I went to the Maly

Theatre to see *Lyubov Yarovaya* [*a 1926 production of a play by Konstantin Trenev (1876–1945)*]. I hadn't been to the theatre for ages and, just recently, I've become so unused to it that I didn't feel any urge to go at all, but now I really do want to go more often. Yes, really and truly, I had never seen genuine actors before today – I've seen good acting, but they never acted like this. It's absolutely fantastic!

It's only possible to live through someone else's life. No longer to belong to yourself or be yourself but to feel and experience what another person feels. I never suspected that people could act like that, with no trace of anything unnatural or artificial. No, I just can't describe what a powerful impression this play made on me! During the interval, I sat there in a solitary trance and **kept picturing Lyubov Yarovaya to myself, and her voice, in which you could hear the tears and the suffering. Oh, my God! How well she [*the actress Vera Pashennaya*] acted the part! And Lieutenant Yarovoi! How his voice trembled when he clutched his head in his hands and said: 'Lyuba! I can't leave you.'**

I suffered twice over as I watched them: I suffered with them and I suffered for them. What were these people struggling for? I asked myself. Why did they ruin their lives, what did they wreck them for? Again and again, I felt a bitter pity for these noble, idealistic people. How cruelly our evil Bolsheviks have mocked them, transforming their ideas and their dreams into an appalling caricature, building their own prosperity, Stalin's wealth and the suffering of the people on these people's lives, which they had invested in such a great cause. And after the theatre, our own lives seemed even more vile and loathsome to me . . .

9 November 1933

I didn't go to school today, and I've been stuck at home the whole day. There's snow outside, and I'd love to go out for a walk, but I can't, I have no time for that . . . Why do I torment myself, why do I sit like this for days on end and get 'excellent' marks; after all, I've forgotten everything that we did last year and don't remember it any better than Alka does. I could just give it all up and fail everything, and then I'd be free all day long: I could go for a walk if I felt like it, play games, draw, write if I wanted to. That would be terrific! But . . . I can tell that I won't be able to give up studying, I won't allow myself to fall behind Irina and the others. It's become too much a part of me, this vague craving to come first in everything – I'm far too ambitious.

I keep thinking about how to arrange things so that I don't study very much and still get good results. I could try doing all the homework assignments in school; it is possible, with more cramming and less playing the fool. In a month or two I'd get into the swing of it and it would feel natural. Last year, at least I could sleep to my heart's content, but now I don't even have time for that, and every day I hate school and studying more. I dream of being free of them but, without even noticing it, I have got so tangled up in this boring, tedious life that I won't be able to give it up even if I do get the chance.

Sometimes I want so much to go out for a walk and roll around in the snow, but I know that in reality that won't make me feel any better at all. I've left all that so far behind. Last year, I was incredibly stupid, those things I wrote about Lyovka – how naïve it all was and how mature at the same time. Now when I read it, I'm amazed that I could write such nonsense. In another two years' time, I'll probably cross those lines out.

I didn't go to the demonstration; I went to bed late the night before and didn't feel like getting up early. In the morning, I listened to the radio: shouts of 'Hoorah!' and an orchestra. And it was a painful and annoying kind of feeling to know that I wasn't involved in the same life as everyone else. [*four lines crossed out*]

11 November 1933

> *Farewell, unwashed Russian land!*
> *Country of slaves and gentlemen,*
> *And you, the bright-blue uniforms,*
> *And you who bow your heads to them.*
> *Beyond the Caucasus, unseen,*
> *May I escape your pashas' reach,*
> *Their eyes all-seeing, bright and keen*
> *Their ears that catch each word of speech.*
> ['Farewell, Unwashed Russia' (1841), by
> Mikhail Lermontov (1814–41)]
> [*two lines crossed out*]

It's all very well to love your homeland and the people in it, but it's very difficult when you live among savages – the uneducated, uncultured mass of the people. Among the coarse, uncivilized Russian people who understand nothing, who know nothing about

anything, as vicious and instinctive as a wild beast, interested in nothing except grub and free handouts, with no sense of honour or pride.

Living in a never-ending rage at everything and everyone, beginning from the very bottom, from the ignorant peasants, hating the stupid, absurdly submissive but sometimes terrifyingly rebellious crowd and striving with all your strength to help it. There's not a single state on earth that is so vast, talented and ignorant as our poor 'unwashed Russia'.

This rant against the ordinary people shows Nina to be a bit of a snob – an attitude inherited from her father – an attitude the Bolsheviks would label 'bourgeois' and abhor.

12 November 1933

It's my birthday in a month and a half, but it doesn't make me happy any more; the time is already past when I used to think about it for ages and count off the days and hours till it came. I try to make myself feel excited about it, and I can't. A few years ago I used to think that 25 December would be a happy day for me for ever, but . . . Until last year I used to love this day and wait for it to come, and then, suddenly, everything changed: I became a different person, unlike the old Nina; I suddenly had new desires and interests, and all the old things that had been interesting before then became repulsive to me.

It's a curse to be an ugly freak and to have a human soul. If only I had money. Money, money! The things you can do! . . . Oh, I would go to the theatre every day and watch all the plays. I would watch other people's lives and live through them. I wouldn't lose anything by it, it wouldn't make me unhappy, and I might even become happy . . . Why did I start reading books and studying? Why was I so anxious to learn how to think and understand? Oh, if I were an uneducated, ignorant peasant girl, then I'd be happy. I might have to work hard, but then I'd really know how to enjoy myself.

The day will come when I will curse the moment of my birth.

Nina seems to be skipping school, probably because she is depressed but perhaps also because she has been teased or bullied about her squint again.

18 November 1933

It's a curse to be an ugly freak! . . . On my last day off school, I got up very early, feeling dejected, angry and ready to burst into tears . . . I was in a terrible state. Then, suddenly, quite unexpectedly, entirely out of the blue, a thought that was enchantingly novel came to me: Give up everything and study at home. My bad mood disappeared as if by magic – *I'm at home, alone, for the whole day*. I imagined how wonderful it would be: playing the piano, going for walks, writing, drawing, reading to my heart's content and, of course, studying.

29 November 1933

How and when it happened . . . What does all that matter! I haven't been to school all five days this week. I've been sitting at home, alone, and every day my mood has been positive and cheerful. I spend a long time laughing, sitting on my own, or I run around the flat, smiling to myself. I play the piano for hours and read a little. Every day Ksyusha comes, bringing me news from school, from the place I want so badly to be finished with. How angry and annoyed it makes me, this slavish bond with that repulsive and disgusting world which I'd like to forget about altogether . . . but at least some of my wishes have been granted.

The time passes quickly and I hardly notice it passing. I'm studying much less now and enjoying it a lot; today, though, my relaxed mood was clouded a little. Zhenya is in that terrible, miserable mood that I often used to be in, and I've been infected with it again – that strange sense of dissatisfaction and anger with life has reappeared. At lunch, Dad said to me for a joke: 'Nina, let's go travelling round Russia. They won't give me a passport anyway.'

'Yes, let's,' I exclaimed, with a shudder of surprise and joy.

And in my mind's eye, the captivating pictures were already taking shape . . . Forests, fields, new faces, new cities . . . Turbulent streams and wide, calm rivers. A dark web of branches and leaves, fragrant scented grass, damp pine needles, a boundless, infinite sea of swaying rye, the wind, the sweet summer wind and, above all of this, the sky, blue, far away, sometimes savage, sometimes tender, covered with clouds or clear, laughing a little in the evenings and turquoise in the mornings . . .

What do I need books and learning for? I wasn't made to be stuck in a stuffy room, to be with people. Freedom! My heart craves it . . . To become one with nature is what I long for, to go soaring high above the earth with the free wind and to fly . . . to unknown countries far away. But they keep me locked up, torment me and torture me and poison my life.

5 December 1933

The second five days have gone by quickly and imperceptibly. The idea of going to school again seems horrible, but I'll have to, and very soon, too. The quarterly tests have already begun, and Mum says that I have to pass them. I don't suppose I'll stay there for more than five days. School doesn't seem so repulsive to me now as it used to, but I'm afraid that soon everything will go back to the way it was. I feel just fine now, my mood is calm and cheerful. After all, I don't speak to anybody, I don't mix with anyone, I'm on my own all the time, and there's no one to remind me about my cross-eyed deformity.

Nobody will ever realize that my monstrous ugliness has made me the way I am. And now I'm a double monster: physical and moral. One monster has created the other. One – the physical deformity – has mutilated and remade my soul after its own fashion, turned it into some kind of terrible tangle of contradictions, quarrelsome and suffering. It has forced me to keep silent and

feel angry, forced me to suffer. But somewhere deep in my soul, the ardent desire to be like Zhenya, Lyalya, Mum and everyone else still sometimes breaks through. And knowing that this is impossible is hard to bear.

The days go by one after another . . . Not so much quickly, just somehow unnoticed. But on 19 December I have to go back to school, and it will be even more hideous than before, now that I am so unused to being with people, so wild and strange. What do I want from life? Only one thing – to live alone, and that is all. It never occurred to me before that for me happiness requires so little. This temporary isolation has done me no good at all, just the opposite: I've become so unaccustomed to people that I feel awful even when I'm with my own family, and I have absolutely no idea what to do with myself.

Everything about me seems laughable and unattractive: the big red hands sticking out of sleeves that are far too short, the stooping figure I try to straighten up, only making it even more unnatural and ugly. All the time I'm with Granny I can't stop thinking about it – about my face, my eyes and my figure. Is this frivolous nonsense? I don't deny it. But it's so hard to accept that the things which cause me such pain and torment are totally trivial.

Often I wonder what other women and girls are thinking – if I knew that, then maybe I'd finally understand myself. We women don't know ourselves because we have no one to learn from. All the great writers are men and, when they describe women, they look at them exclusively from their own point of view, they don't know what we're like. I need so badly to know women's thoughts, their desires and needs.

16 December 1933

Today, Ksyusha suddenly suggested that I shouldn't go back to school before the holidays. I sat and thought about it, and a voice in my heart kept growing louder and bolder: 'Stay here.' I'm almost certain now that I will stay. In any case, I only need Mum and Dad's permission, although I feel a little bit embarrassed to ask them, because I change my mind so much, but then those ten extra days are so tempting. And then, after that, another fifteen days free, with no worries.

Today, I took out my old notebooks with my jottings from 1928 to 1929 and, as I read them, I couldn't help laughing. They're so naïve and childishly simplistic. However, in 1929 to 1930, a certain glimmering does appear to refer to collectivization and the destruction of the peasantry. I begin to speak out against the Bolsheviks, railing at them in the name of my heroes. In general, there's a new seriousness that in some way resembles my writing now.

Nina refers to earlier notebooks than the three which make up this volume. She must have destroyed them, or they were lost, since they did not end up in the NKVD archive.

20 December 1933

I'm staying at home . . . The weather is warm and calm, there's a fine, light snow sprinkling down from the dark clouds, not even cold, but pleasantly refreshing to the face. But I'm staying inside, even though at times I feel so miserable, I long for the frosty air, the distant hazy-blue vista and the bright blue of the sky.

I promised myself that I would go walking every day of the holidays, and I would have gone walking – if only Ksyusha had stayed in Moscow, we would have walked to the ice-rink together and run around on the Sparrow Hills. But she's going away to the country, the only person I could have gone walking with.

Once, by chance, I overheard Mum and Dad talking about me, and Dad said: 'She's so shallow that she's not interested in anything that doesn't concern her, and she's even forgotten how to make conversation.' These words made me feel bitter and resentful. At first I wanted to speak to Dad about it, but then I changed my mind. What's the point of humiliating myself all over again?

21 December 1933

My life is so strange – abnormal even. I'm like a prisoner put in jail for life who, even though he has no hope of release, still dreams of his freedom. All the time I think about the same thing. And that one single thing is me. It's true, if you look in my diary, there's nothing there except me. It's all me, me, me. True, somehow or other I haven't written anything for a long time, not since last spring, I suppose – that is, before this summer.

I flicked through my diary today and read about Lyovka and . . . I felt ashamed. My God! What a fool I was, how could I have been so stupid? The entire business with Lyovka is disgusting, and we were only in fifth class. I think that I created the whole mess myself and, when I remember it, I start to despise myself: both for my stupid infatuation and for not being able to hide it from the girls, from Ira and Ksyusha. Just disgraceful! Running around after him, blushing if he just looked at me and smiling happily at every word he said.

24 December 1933

I have such a strong urge to go out for a walk; I'm bored at home and I don't feel like doing anything. In the last few days I've begun missing homework assignments. I just can't summon up the strength to get down to it – my dissatisfaction and strange, vague desires have come back again. Is it possible to live like a hermit at the age of fifteen? At the very best time of your life, to have no fun or pleasure, nothing but futile, boring and unnecessary learning that stinks like putrefying dead animals? I'm only fifteen!

It's odd that nothing interests me now: not painting, not music, not any area of learning, not writing. Not even sport, my ice skates or gym exercises give me any pleasure.

For some time now, whenever I start to do something,

I repeat to myself, 'You have to,' but I never say, 'I want to.' What I like doing most of all now, not that I didn't like doing it before anyway, is to lie in bed for hours in the mornings, dozing from time to time and dreaming about the same thing in different ways.

Dreaming is so tempting sometimes, although you find yourself thinking: Why are these only dreams? I can dream for ages, hours at a time, making up conversations, playing several people's parts. The one thing I still want to do is to read, read without ever stopping, but even then the repulsive phrase 'You have to' won't leave me in peace. It forbids me to read novels and orders me to burrow through boring, dry history books. And I love novels so much ... You forget about everything ... You live somebody else's interesting life, you are transported into a mysterious, miraculous world.

26 December 1933

At the beginning of this month, I begged Mum to make an appointment for me with the oculist at the hospital. I was feeling wretched about my deformity; the memory of what had happened at school was still fresh. I reminded Mum every day, but she took no notice and kept putting me off, saying that we had no money, when really she thought there was no need for it. She was partly right because, of course, there's no question of any operation, but at the time I was still hoping for and expecting something. Now, though, while I'm at home on my own all the time, I've forgotten about my eyes and stopped talking to Mum about them.

Then, suddenly, yesterday and today, she reminded me about it and even asked my father to make an appointment for me, and Dad, who had disapproved of the idea before, agreed without the slightest objection. Their consideration struck me as very strange: perhaps they've read my diary? That's the only place where they could have found out anything, and it is entirely possible that they have read it, but I wasn't even very upset about it. Who cares what they do! Let them read it, what difference does it make? As long as they don't go on at me about it and, if they do start, I won't keep quiet, I'll give them a really good tongue-lashing.

I'm getting on disgustingly badly with my family. Having got used to solitude and isolation, I've become too independent, and I can't stand it when anybody criticizes me or lectures me. I don't want to be like that, but it only takes someone to point something out to me, and I start arguing and snap back at them. **My relations with Dad are the most strained of all. Why? I don't have the slightest idea. But we're alike, so that's probably where it all comes from.**

I don't talk to him very much at all and, in general, I talk so little it's ludicrous, but if we do start talking about something, then we're bound to end up arguing. I start to feel an incomprehensible, uncontrollably powerful irritation with him. What kind of idiocy is that? I just can't control myself. Dad has always been a bit grumpy, but as he's got older it's got worse. He grumbles at absolutely everything: at the radio, at Mum, at us and, most of all, I think, at me – after all, I'm always within reach. It's something he needs as much as food and sleep.

However, it doesn't stop me respecting him, and respecting him a lot. If I have any authority that I can refer to on almost everything, then it's my father. His word is final for me (I should add a proviso and say only in politics and science) [*one line crossed out*]. I accept my father's words, saturated with spite and sarcasm, as the truth, and the sharper they are, the more I like them. Dad has done really well: going from being a simple peasant to becoming a fully educated, intelligent and remarkably highly developed human being is not easy, and I don't think that we are any match for him.

We may not think too highly of ourselves, but our father's opinion of us is even worse. He runs down the whole of Soviet youth in general; to him, we are totally stupid, undeveloped and shallow in every way. The fact that we are women also contributes to his attitude, as to him all women are trash – and not just for him, but for lots of men. It's a good thing that at least I don't have a brother: the difference between his treatment and ours would be colossal.

The goal of the communist revolution was a society of equals, which should have meant equal rights for women. Nevertheless, there were no women in prominent positions in the government and, generally, women didn't have any power. The ideal Soviet woman worked in the textile industry or as a farmer or pioneer. She was the mother of many children, devoted to her husband and the state, productive and conscientious but submissive. Like anti-Semitism, sexism was a normal way of thinking in the 1930s: Nina's father's views on women were shared by most men in Soviet Russia.

1 January 1934

A little while ago, I went outside with Ira to have a chat –
after all, with her there's no need to think about what to
say, she talks non-stop herself. I wasn't really interested in
what she was saying and found it slightly odd to walk
along with her and listen to her frivolous adventures,
which had absolutely nothing to do with me. Perhaps she
wasn't feeling very cheerful either, but she took great
pleasure in describing her life and the way she spends
her time in the company of her charming friends, her
pretty fifteen-year-old girlfriend, V., and her admirer, a
thirteen-year-old Greek. Their evenings are all foxtrots
and flirting.

If I'd heard this from anyone else, I wouldn't have
believed that this was what Ira was doing at the age of
thirteen and, in that respect, she seems far older than I
am. You can see an interesting, slim and cheerful young
woman in her now, someone who knows what to say to
any admirer and how to dance. And although she
claims that at first she didn't enjoy it, she soon started
liking it.

That's what girls *should* be like! Not ugly freaks like
us, thinking about some sort of equality, insisting that
we should be regarded as human beings. Who put these
stupid ideas into our heads? Why are we ashamed when
men pay for us in the tram, when we have to let
someone else pay for us to go to the theatre? It's
nonsense! It's about time we realized that we're only
women and nothing more, and it's absurd and foolish
to expect to be treated in any other way.

I'm certain that Ira won't be surprised, but only flattered, when one fine day the Greek hands her her coat or dashes to help her button up her shoes. And she'll be right, too. Lyalya already regards it as natural that men should give up their seats in the tram for a woman, although I still find it shameful. The moment I realize that a man is immeasurably superior to me, I'll abandon any aspiration to stand on the same level as them and even be grateful for the petty hand-outs they give us.

In short, I'll become a woman, and I'll look out for that special half-mocking and insulting smile men have when they talk to a woman, that elegantly exaggerated politeness of theirs. Today, Dad made me feel very much a woman when he said, 'How can you compare with the lads? The lads are great guys, but you're just girls.' And I stood there, smiling ever so slightly without feeling angry – of course he's right: how could we possibly be the equal of boys? And I remembered my dreams and aspirations, which are destined to come to nothing.

7 January 1934

I was all alone in the flat, and it was bliss. I told myself: There are two solutions: one is to change your life somehow, but that's impossible; the other is to put an end to your life, but that's impossible, too. There's only one thing left to do. And I laughed at the unintentional illogicality of my conclusion: All you can do is carry on living without changing anything. But that's impossible, too, isn't it? There are three impossibilities, and the last is the most impossible of all. It was so very painful to realize my own powerlessness. I could poison myself, I thought, but not the way I used to think about doing it before, not on the quiet, but in a perfectly legal way. If somebody got the idea of offering me a phial of opium as a joke, I wouldn't refuse and I'd drink it quite happily. But . . . I can't do it so that no one would know. It feels strange and frightening, and what would Mum think, what would it do to her – and everyone else, but especially Mum?

I'm tormented more and more often and more painfully by my face and my sex. I'm a woman! Is there anything more humiliating? I'm a bitch! But I'm still a human being, and it's painful and shameful to serve Dad and Kolya [*cousin Nikolai*] at dinner. What right do they have to sit there talking and laughing, making me bring them spoons and plates and interrupting my meal? Even if I am worse than them, inferior, then so what? I'm still a human being, a free person. I want to be free!

But no, they'll break me, they'll have their way; even now, my father is trying stubbornly to turn me into that kind of humble slave. He probably doesn't want me to ask myself the fateful question that he himself taught me: What gives them the right? I won't give up, surely? No, never.

11 January 1934

I've just been sitting in the kitchen, drawing. The flat is

empty apart from myself and Betka. Suddenly, there's a knock at the door, not one I recognize but a very insistent one. I carry on drawing for a while and pay no attention. I'm already used to it; I have no intention of opening the door, I know it has to be strangers. If it weren't for Dad's legal situation, there'd be nothing to be afraid of, but since he's living with us without a passport, you can expect anything. It could easily be the militia. Now, just before the 17th Congress, they're searching everywhere for people without passports. What are they afraid of? No one knows . . .

The stranger went on ringing and knocking for a long time. I put my pencil and paper aside, took off my shoes and went out into the corridor without making a sound. Just at that moment, the woman came out of the next-door flat and said in a loud voice: 'They're probably not home.'

'Then what's the dog doing there?' a man's voice answered. He went on knocking for a while. Betka climbed on to the trunk and barked loudly, and I stood beside her, my heart pounding noisily.

Eventually, Betka stopped barking, so I thought the man must have gone away. But then, about twenty-five minutes later, there was a quieter knock at the door. I thought someone knocked three times, but I wasn't sure. The dog started barking again, and I stood there, afraid to move a muscle, thinking: I have to get out of here as soon as possible. But I can't make a run for it: Dad could come home at any moment, I have to be here to open the door for him. But, anyway, I'll only wait until four o'clock and then I'll grab Betka and sneak off to Granny's house. I wonder if this man is going to come back again or not? There was half an hour to go until four o'clock. I didn't know how to pass the time. I was really scared; I couldn't concentrate on anything. Those bloody Bolsheviks, how I hate them! All hypocrites, liars and scoundrels . . .

From the summer of 1933, the family decided that Nina's father would use a special knock to let everyone know when he came to the flat on his illegal visits to Moscow.

The 17th Party Congress opened on 26 January 1934 in the Kremlin. Dubbed the 'Congress of Victors', it served to elect members of the Central Committee, most of whom, ironically, were later shot. This was when Stalin began his despotic control campaign, at first focused on political rivals, and can be pinpointed as the start of his Terror.

17 January 1934

Between eleven and twelve in the evening, when we were drinking tea, cousin Nikolai arrived and told us in a low whisper that the housing committee had decided to hold raids that night. 'Go away right now,' he said to Dad. 'This very moment.' Dad was in a calm and even rather genial mood, probably because of his unusual situation. He finished his tea deliberately, taking bites of bread with it, but I could still spot a certain haste and restrained agitation in his movements. And I couldn't help thinking: What self-control and willpower it must take to remain calm at moments like this. Even I was feeling uneasy, as if my heart had skipped a beat.

31 January 1934

What has happened to me? Only three or four days ago I was cheerful and contented, laughing and chatting away at school. And, suddenly, everything has turned upside-down, and again there is boredom and anguish. I want to understand the reason for this change – I want to, but so far I can't. Until the twenty-eighth, everything was fine. I didn't go to school that day, I had to go to the hospital – Dad had made me an appointment with the eye surgeon Strakhov. It's strange: during the holidays, before school started again, I was incredibly upset about my eyes, I was afraid that after such a long break I'd find my deformity especially painful to bear at school. But then . . . it suddenly wasn't like that at all! I forgot all about my eyes, I didn't even feel like going to the doctor, since 'that' isn't bothering me any more.

Strakhov said that I ought to have an operation, and I wasn't surprised or frightened to hear it, because I'd thought about it, but I wasn't delighted about it either. At first, I even liked the idea of going to hospital for several days, and I was in a really good mood: what used to be an impossible dream had become reality.

That dream was good because it was a dream and I had grown used to it, but . . . when the chance came to make it happen, I was frightened. I had the feeling that I shouldn't do it. I imagined myself becoming normal, and

I knew it wouldn't make me happy. It would make no difference whether they operated on me or not. So what was it that spoilt my mood just then? Could it have been affected by the interview at school? No, that's not it at all.

I feel all the futility and ugliness of modern life, and that's a terrible burden. To see this injustice, falsehood and cruelty and feel that you are powerless. But what can you do? Is it really true that man will never be completely free? Is freedom really only an illusion? Can the endless struggle for freedom that mankind has waged over the centuries really have been in vain?

Yesterday, a stratosphere balloon was launched in honour of the 17th Party Congress. Taking no notice of the bad weather, three daredevils risked their lives to go soaring up into the forbidding clouds and disappear into the damp mist. From data received from the balloon, the news was that they had reached a height of 20.6 kilometres. The last data reached earth between three and four o'clock in the afternoon – the stratosphere balloon had started to descend and entered a band of thickening cloud.

And then it all ended. Last night and this morning brought no more news, and it was only this afternoon that we learned that splinters from the gondola and completely unidentifiable bodies had been found. These were no longer recognizable as the three daredevils the balloon had carried up into the distant stratosphere the day before. There they were, far away up high, all alone in airless, boundless space, and then they felt the wind in their ears as they went hurtling down towards earth at incredible speed, their breath snatched away, and waiting for them down below was inevitable and terrible death.

On 30 January 1934, Andrei Vasenko (35), Pavel Fedoseenko (36) and Ilya Usyskin (24) flew to a height of 22 kilometres in the stratosphere balloon Osoaviakhim. *During the descent the balloon was damaged and it crashed. The dead balloonists are buried in Red Square in Moscow.*

10 February 1934

I'm fifteen years old, and they say these are the best years of your life. That's not the way I feel. When I was younger, I was so happy in my childish stupidity and naïvety, because I didn't read books and I didn't know anything then. Now I've realized that happiness is nonsense, it doesn't exist in this world, you can never find it. Sometimes it might seem that it's sitting right there beside you, teasing you, you just have to reach out your hand and you can possess it. But it's a delusion, a mirage.

They don't understand me, they're not interested in me, they don't want to teach me how to live! Everybody is so busy with their own affairs, nobody has any time to take any interest in me. But what do I do about it? Am I too embarrassed, then, to say that I'm suffering, am I ashamed to bare my soul? But who shall I tell? My dad, who despises us, who grumbles all the time and reminds us every day that we're stupid and don't understand a thing, no better than dunces? The person who, when I cried and asked him to take me out of school, tried to soothe my tears by promising to go to museums and the cinema more often? (As if I was crying on a whim, as if unimportant childish things would be enough to make me humiliate myself by crying in front of him.)

I feel ashamed enough as it is for not being able to hold back my tears and giving him a reason to call me an empty-headed, stupid little girl. How can I trust this man with my entire soul, all my anxieties, all my dreams? He'll probably suggest a trip to the Polytechnical Museum this time, too. I could tell Mum everything. But what's the point? Perhaps she might understand how miserable I am, how upset, but she won't understand what's making me that way. She'll pity me, but she won't show me the way forward, and next day she'll forget all about our conversation in the daily struggle to provide us with food.

I won't tell the girls (my sisters) anything at all; they're not very likely to feel sorry for me and they won't teach me anything, they're only eighteen themselves. But I won't find the way forward by myself, I've lost my way in my thoughts and desires, I'm tormented by doubts and I don't understand myself, I only feel that I'm alone, alone in all the world.

Dad says that life is a struggle, that you have to fight, but how should I fight, what should I struggle for, what should I try to achieve? Should I struggle against my anguish, or for money? I don't know. There's only one thing I do understand: I am unhappy, I am terribly unhappy, my heart is exhausted. Ah. I am weary and faint with suffering.

17 March 1934

I've been at home since 4 March now. At times I've felt drawn to write in my diary, but I couldn't bring myself to. My eyes hurt, and they get tired really quickly, and now I have to copy out my hospital notes, too. Yes, and today I won't have much time to write. It's after nine already, and Mum will be here soon. I was in hospital a long time, a whole fifteen days. I got to like, even love, my strange new life. I remember the time I was recovering hazily, like a pleasant dream, lying in bed for days on end with my eyes closed, sometimes listening to the quiet conversations of the patients but most of the time half-asleep, in a state of drowsy weakness.

I quickly got used to everybody, and the other patients, total strangers I regarded at first with hostility, came to feel close to me and comprehensible. We were brought together by a common grief, common fears, the common life of the ward, identical wishes and interests. I now regret that I didn't write anything down earlier, while I was still in the hospital. It has started to fade now – everything has turned into a messy, chaotic heap of vague and unclear recollections.

After being back at home for so long, I've begun to forget the details of hospital life, and the first things that have been displaced from my memory are the unpleasant and painful moments. Immersed in the horror of the situation at home, in the agonizing boredom of doing nothing and wishing for something, I've started to miss the hospital. Every so often I feel I'd like to go back there.

Nina's operation was probably to tighten and correct the eye muscle which was causing her squint. The operation was not a success in the long term.

18 March 1934

Just recently, I said to Zhenya: 'Could you give me a phial of opium, knowing that I'd be poisoned?'

'Why not? Of course I could.'

'But I couldn't . . . Zhenya, do you really mean it?'

'Of course.'

'You'll give it to me then?'

'Yes, only you find the opium.'

'All right, agreed, only don't you trick me.'

Since then, every so often I remember our conversation. I must poison myself, I tell myself. It's stupid to go on living when you know that in the future nothing is going to change, that the whole of this long life will be just like the present and the past, nothing but torment, hopeless yearning for something. It's stupid and absurd to live like that.

But how can I put an end to this life? I still have so much left to do, I still want so much to live, and all my desires are to do with this life. Will I finish this notebook by the end of March? I think, but then a moment later I come to my senses and tell myself: But the end of March doesn't exist for you any longer. Yes, it is hard to die, when you still haven't settled all your scores with life. But I have to get a grip on myself, I've lived long enough and learned everything, and if I don't do this now . . . **I'll really regret it later.**

Mum has just shouted to me: 'Don't write too much, or your eyes will start hurting.' But what do I care, what do I need them for now? But then, why did I have the operation? Ah, yes, I thought it would make people like me! Ah, but no, even there I've been unlucky. Today, when I was looking at the girls, I tried hard to make my eyes straight, and I couldn't stand the feeling that one of them was looking sideways. I've just gone up to the mirror and had a long look at myself: No, I'm still the same! It's time to die . . . Enough, enough. But I don't want to die. Will I be able to make one last, decisive effort of will? **I have to go to Granny's place for the opium.** I'll go right now . . . Oh, it's so hard . . .

Opium was a common medicine, used as pain relief, so it was quite normal that her grandmother should keep opium drops.

21 March 1934

I didn't poison myself that day. Why didn't I? After all, I did go to Granny's place for the opium, but I never got around to asking for it, for several reasons. Actually, I don't think I would have gone through with it, even if I had got it; I could feel that, and I only went there out of some horrible sense of duty, to justify myself in my own eyes. I wouldn't have poisoned myself in any case, I still want to live too much.

But if I'm planning to die, I have to think about the fate of my diary. What will happen to it? Naturally, not finding any note, everybody will go dashing to it as the only explanation for such a strange act. They'll start reading it, judging and making fun of it. And I know how many smiles and laughs will be provoked by my most intimate feelings, the things I've hidden from everybody and loved in my own way, the things that have caused me so much torment.

God forbid that my diary should come in for criticism from Dad. And even though I'll be dead, it's still unpleasant to know that they'll start abusing me and calling me a stupid, shallow little girl, a sentimental dreamer and depressive. It might all be true, but they won't understand me, they won't understand my pining, they won't understand that I really did suffer, even if it was only over unimportant things, perhaps more than most of them have suffered. And in ten or fifteen years' time, my sisters will tell their children about their weird sister Nina with slightly scornful regret.

These last few days I sometimes want so badly to tell someone everything, to open up completely, to shout out to them: 'I want to live! Why do you torment me, force me to study, teach me proper manners? I don't need any of that! I want to live, laugh, sing and be cheerful. I'm only fifteen after all, this is the best time of my life. I want to live, teach me to live!'

But I won't tell anyone this – they wouldn't understand and they'd laugh at me. I don't even need them to understand, but I do demand that they take my thoughts seriously and show them a certain respect. Just recently, when I told Dad that I was feeling bored, he laughed at me and said: 'I hate people who are always saying: "I'm bored, I'm bored!"'

'All right then, I'll never say that to you again,' I said angrily. The same thing happened with Mum, too.

24 March 1934

I'm starting to get drawn into my old ways, once more the same unwillingness to talk, the yearning, the dreams . . . Outside, I lower my eyes again as people go by, and every glance feels painful, sometimes even the chance ones. I try to be unnoticeable; I hunch over and drop my head. When I think that I'll have to suffer all my life because of these eyes, it just makes me feel so terrified. They have ruined half of my life and they'll probably ruin the rest as well. What can I achieve with them? What can I devote myself to? Can I be a musician . . . or an artist . . . or a writer?

26 March 1934

So now my diary is coming to an end . . . At long last. For some reason I've been really impatient for it to happen. The question now is – where should I hide it? What if there's a sudden search and they happen to find it and come across the absolutely unprintable words about Stalin? And what if the police spies get their hands on it? They'll read it and laugh at my nonsense about love. I have to hide it.

Nina realized that keeping a diary was dangerous – the comments she had written about Stalin could have dire consequences for the whole family. Nevertheless, her teenaged mind was more concerned about the 'love nonsense' she'd written being discovered.

THE SECOND NOTEBOOK

28 March 1934

Aha! I did start a new notebook in March after all! The scent of spring is in the air once more. The snow has almost all melted; even out in the country, there's hardly any to be seen. The market gardens are covered with spring floodwater, and dried-out cabbage stalks from the year before are jutting up out of the brown vegetable patches. Last year's dry grass is a faint green on the drying humps and tussocks. The river has become turbulent and wide. The ice that remains glints through the water, giving it a steely tint. It heaves restlessly and rolls long, low waves with slightly raised crests on to the damp clayey bank.

There's school in three days, and I'm very glad that I'm not thinking about it; I'm acting as though I still have two weeks left to enjoy myself. These last few days, I've been obsessed with plants: Mum and I planted some seeds, and now I glance into the plant pots about ten times a day, looking for the shoots. I'm making all sorts of grandiose plans (even here I don't stop my daydreaming) for the future of my plants and vividly imagining an oak tree reaching right up to the ceiling and a big bushy thuja. That'd make the room look fantastic. But it's only a dream.

Just now I'm reading a book which I've been forbidden to read, *Behind the Closed Door*. They have taken it away from me once already, and after that I didn't see it for a very long time; but now I've come across it again by chance so, of course, I'm taking the opportunity to read it. Actually, if it was just an obscene novel, I wouldn't be so stubborn about it. But this book is written from the notes of a venereologist, and it contains a lot of things that are new to me and give me insight into life, which I'm still so ignorant about. It makes me feel disillusioned about a lot of things.

The book Nina was reading was written by Lev Friedland (1888–1960) and had been a bestseller six years earlier, going through five editions. It was an account of venereal diseases written for the general reader.

11 April 1934

The second six-day school week is over. It's not really so bad, fairly tolerable, in fact. I'm studying much less. I've decided to take a little break and then put the pressure on again a bit from 1 May, just before the exams. School has drawn me in and is carrying me along.

I try not to think about the exams. They're not even coming up any time soon and I'm worried. School has taken a firm grip on me, I can rest from myself there, I stop obsessing about happiness and having to study like this for years and years to come ... Nothing horrible is happening. I'm on excellent or at least good terms with all the girls, but we don't have anything at all to do with the boys.

But they're a good bunch. The two troublemakers, Leidman and Gorelov, were expelled a long time ago, so the only boys left are Lyovka P., Budulya, Antipochka, Tolka, Filya, Timosha, Zinok, Linde, Sakharov and Uklon. Mostly, they're quite civilized, not hooligans but good, quiet boys. They keep to themselves and don't bother us girls.

Budulya, Lyovka's friend, is a small boy who has a ringing, infectious laugh you hear a lot and clear blue eyes. Antipa is an intellectual from head to toe, a good student, and witty too; he has quite an ordinary face and speaks through his nose a bit. Tolka joined us this year (he's repeating a year), but even so he's nice. When he laughs, his smile makes him seem handsome, it suits him so well – long dimples appear in his cheeks and there is a sly, cunning look in his eyes.

I don't know Sakharov at all, he joined us halfway through the year. He's not very talkative and a little strange; he gets a lot of 'unsats' for being so quiet. He speaks in a deep bass voice, and his swarthy face and jet-black eyes make him look like a gypsy. Uklon is a thin boy with a long nose and, because his nose is always red, he's been nicknamed 'the drunk'. He's a bit of a namby-pamby and not very bright but, for some reason, he's Linde's best friend. I've kept one boy to the end, because I've got a lot to say about him.

12 April 1934

While I was getting ready to go to school, I pondered on two people who interested me: Lyovka and Dima Linde. What was it that made me feel so attracted to Lyovka last year? He is Yulia's son, blue-eyed and handsome. I was attracted to him instantly – he seemed so different, not like the others and, at the same time, so cheerful and unaffected. My special interest in him became something more, but then a month or two went by, I took a closer look at him and saw that he was just an ordinary boy and, though my heart carried on pounding for a while from force of habit, I no longer felt the same way.

Now I'm interested in Linde. Now, he's an original, he's unusual because, although he's not particularly good-looking, he captivates you with his mind. I watch him closely, and I don't understand him at all. Sometimes I think he's just obnoxious, always with that disdainful and haughty smile of his, directed particularly often at the girls, but that's precisely what makes you want to earn that other, simple smile he rarely gives. Even less often, he gives a genuine laugh. His smile raises his upper lip a little so that you can just see his gleaming white teeth, like those of some small animal. What is he really? I often ask myself. Some kind of extraordinary genius, or an extraordinary fool? That's what I want to find out.

18 April 1934

I can't wait for summer! That's all I want. Kolya and Granny call me a lazybones because I'm thinking about the holidays again. But they're wrong. You have to dream about something and want something.

I'm alone in the flat now. **Mum's gone to see a friend, and Dad's out, too. I'm getting on very badly with him at the moment. Sometimes I just can't stand him and quite often I hate him. It's hideous when he suddenly starts hassling me. Yesterday, he and I had a row about** something; he called me a fool and something else too and then pretty much every name under the sun. And I promised myself that I'd change the way we behaved towards each other, which had somehow become so unbearable. I decided to be less rude and stop being so sarcastic, but still not to ask him for anything or be affectionate.

His petty tyranny drives me crazy. And I often thank God that I don't live in the eighteenth or nineteenth century, when the father of a family was the absolute lord and master. Life would be none too sweet for us under the rule of *my* highly esteemed parent. My antipathy towards Dad has grown so strong that sometimes I'd prefer it if we had no father at all. At least then I'd be able to imagine him as kind and good.

Zhenya and Lyalya are away at college for days at a time, drawing and writing. Lyalya seems to be doing well, but Zhenya is falling behind a bit. I feel sorry for her. I'm getting on relatively well with my sisters. Probably because we don't see each other very often. Two or three days ago, I really wanted to tell Zhenya everything, to be completely candid and be understood. But I can't make myself, I can't call myself squint-eyed . . . It's so painful and embarrassing. That evening, I even cried, secretly.

Some undated letters from Nina's father to his daughters are included as an appendix to the diaries. It's clear upon reading them that he was a very exacting man with high intellectual expectations of his children.

18 May 1934

I'm sinking deeper and deeper into laziness and apathy. Yearning and boredom, the same as before. I really don't feel like doing my geography, but the exam's tomorrow. Mum asked me out for a walk, but I didn't go. I really didn't want to at all. What would I do with her and Dad? **And Dad will start in with his painfully logical exhortations. Just recently, I simply can't stand him. Every word he says makes me angry. I make rude and caustic comments and, no matter how much I promise myself I'm going to behave better, it makes no difference.**

That's part of the reason I'm so sick of everything: I can't stay at home, I feel I need to get as far away as I can. I'm not studying very much at all now, I hardly read anything. I'm bored and angry all the time, I feel I've been unlucky in life.

I've just been outside. It's a hot summer's day today. The air smells so hot and so good. Zhenya and Lyalya are out in the country. **Mum and Dad are at the Sparrow Hills. I don't really feel like going anywhere in particular, but it's unbearable staying at home, sitting here, on the alert, listening for footsteps and voices on the stairs. Any moment they could come from the house administration or the militia to make enquiries about Dad. It's not a nice feeling.**

I was all ready to go and call on Ira, but then I changed my mind. Why? Everything there feels alien and unfriendly somehow, and Ksyushka, my best friend, is away. Why do I feel bored with Ira? Why do I find the things she does repulsive? I think I've risen above her level: I'm not interested in dancing foxtrots, imagining things about boys and passing my time with chit-chat. I want serious company, interesting conversation. I'll never find it, but what I dream about is a beautiful love. How stupid!

Lately, Ksyushka and I have been very friendly. What has made us so close? She's cheerful and I try to be cheerful. We're both very critical of other women. I have a very low opinion of women in general and, first and foremost, of myself and, although I often hate men and think they are scoundrels, I still respect them for their practical turn of mind, because they are quick-witted and know how to live.

27 May 1934

Only two exams left . . . and that's it. Then it's summer. I'm looking forward to it, but what for? Today and yesterday, when I didn't study at all (although I should have), made me realize what the summer will be like. Miserable yearning for things I can't have and do and boredom! It'll be terrible, spending the entire summer in Moscow! What will I do? For the last two days, I've really understood how painful it is to be alone. Ksyusha's going off to the country, and she came to see me today. Well, we had a talk about all sorts of unforgivable mean tricks and then we parted. It's amazing how much I submit to her influence, or not actually submit but feel it every time.

1 June 1934

It doesn't seem long ago that I was wondering bitterly when I would ever reach the seventh class and finish the seven-year school; it seemed like a distant, almost unrealizable dream. But now it's reality: I've moved up into the seventh class. But it doesn't make me feel happy or excited any more; not even the fact that I'll soon finish school makes me happy. What's the point? I ask myself. Next comes more of the same tedious studying: first the ten-year school, then college . . . And what's going to happen when I finish college? Will I get a job? Things will be even worse then – after all, when you're studying, you're still hoping for something . . .

Yesterday, I went to school for my report card. My marks are almost all excellent, but I wasn't made a top student because I didn't take part in any social activities. A pity. Next year, I intend not to do any studying at all, and it'll be a very good thing if I don't change my mind about it.

I have a quite different feeling now for Linde. I often simply dislike him. I don't want to meet or talk to him at all but, when he's around, I always feel I want to behave in a way that will make him think well of me and see me as better than the other girls . . . I'm beginning to change fundamentally now: I no longer find solitude attractive but a burden, I want life and action, dreams no longer satisfy me. But even here, in my passionate aspiration, I've run up against another obstacle – a lack of new friends. I have absolutely none at all. Ksyusha, Ira, and that's it. So few, in fact, that it's ridiculous.

Today, Ira brought me a young sparrow, still with a yellow beak. I was as delighted as a child. I spent a whole hour fussing over the nestling. I tried to give him something to eat and drink. He doesn't eat anything and, if you put any food in his mouth, it just lies there. Either he's still very young or, more likely, he's become weak. He sleeps all the time in the little nest I made up for him, and he'll probably die by morning. But I would have liked so much to raise him.

A few little joys and cares like that and I'd be happy. I've turned out not to be anybody special, just a perfectly ordinary woman. Now I understand why women want to have children – it's simply the urge to create happiness for yourself, somehow to fill the oppressive, unbearable emptiness in your soul.

14 June 1934

For the last few days I've been having quite a good time. Every evening, I've been going to Ira's to play volleyball, and I play around with Alyonushka. Not long ago, Ira came to see me and, in a fit of candour, I gave her a bit of my diary to read, something that was so innocent I don't believe I'll regret it. We spoke for quite a long time after that. We talked about Linde, and Ira told me that next year she was definitely going to get to know him. Close, friendly conversations like that always give me a light and easy sort of feeling.

I'd love to go out to the countryside, and the better the day is, the more joyful and vivid my memories of the fields and the woods are. Oh, I want to go so badly. At the beginning of this month, Mum and I went to Bogorodskoe, where my aunt Sophia and her family live. We walked the whole day long. And there was a forest there, a genuine forest with big fragrant pine trees and impenetrable bushy undergrowth.

20 June 1934

Every day, I've been meaning to get my diary out, but I haven't done it until now. And the days that at first glance seem free are slipping by imperceptibly in trivialities. Just lately, I've started knitting socks, and whole hours have passed in this joyless occupation. I spent ages getting the thread tangled, unpicking it and knitting it again, but I carried on stubbornly, to finish the job. Today, however, I'd had enough: I gave up knitting, and I'm glad I did.

Yesterday, we met some of the passengers from the steamship *Cheliuskin*, which got stuck fast in the ice; people spent dozens and dozens of days working like mad on the drifting ice, tormented by the expectation that the passengers would die out on the ocean. The whole world was watching them ... And many of them, very many, didn't even dare hope that they would get back to land. But they did get back, and they got back thanks to a small group of bold pilots who took the risk of flying in terrible conditions out to an ice floe lost among the tall hummocks of ice.

Moscow has prepared a triumphant welcome for the

people from the *Cheliuskin* and the pilots. Never before, on any happy occasion, had the crowd shouted, 'Hoorah!' with such enthusiasm as it did when it greeted these people. I wanted so much to go to Red Square, it was painful and, as I listened to the radio, my happy, warm feelings for the great heroes made me feel like crying; and another, incomprehensible feeling – the desire to take part in the general rejoicing; to fuse with the united, excited mass of people; to shout a passionate 'Hoorah!' together with everyone else – came over me, as did the realization that all this was impossible.

All day on the radio they talked about nothing else. In the evening, I decided to go to see the pilot Slepnev, who lives close by. A tall arch had been built in the street, decorated with garlands of red ribbons and flowers, and a portrait of Slepnev had been hung on it. At eight o'clock in the evening, the people began gathering. A lorry arrived and they set up a table covered with red material. By about ten, there was a huge crowd there, a solid mass of bodies squeezed together, stretching along the sides of the streets, leaving a wide passage in the middle. The crowd kept surging forward in a wave and then falling back, and there were no soldiers or militiamen there to control its movement. They set up a floodlight on one of the balconies. Everything was ready for the pilot's arrival but . . . he didn't come.

I went away feeling annoyed but, at the same time, I couldn't help feeling glad in a way. Why? I was beginning to feel afraid that there might be a crush, caused by the unorganized crowds of people. There were bound to be accidents. The reception for Slepnev was put off until today.

145

The new 7,500-tonne steamship Cheliuskin *had set out in an attempt to sail the entire Arctic Sea route from Murmansk to Vladivostok non-stop. The expedition was led by Otto Schmidt. On 13 February 1934, the steamer was trapped in the ice in the Sea of Chukotsk. The passengers were rescued by several pilots. Those who flew the rescue planes to the* Cheliuskin, *including Slepnev, were met with a hero's welcome and were the first to be awarded the order of Hero of the Soviet Union.*

Soviet news coverage often suggested that the entire world was transfixed by Soviet industrial progress, its heroes and their exploits. Nina, unusually for her, seems to have been swept up in the general mood of patriotic celebration – or was she perhaps just suffering from a typical teenage crush on a celebrity?

21 June 1934

Yesterday, I ended up going to Slepnev's reception after all. I dragged Zhenya, Lyalya and their friend Pokrovskaya along with me, and so we had quite a good time waiting for it all to start. Again, people were jammed together in a terrible crush, but until Slepnev arrived, standing there was at least tolerable enough. At about nine, voices from the platform shouted: 'He's coming, he's coming! Quiet.' The crowd whispered and fell silent. Two cars drove between the two rows of people and stopped not far away from us. The expectant crowd flooded forward.

To the strains of a well-known song, the pilots got out of the cars and walked to the platform, accompanied by cries of 'Hoorah!' and applause. Flowers went flying into the road. I only spotted the pilot Slepnev when he began to speak. I couldn't hear what he was saying, but I craned forward eagerly in order to get a glimpse of the short, stocky figure in the blue suit. Occasionally, he turned his face in our direction, and then I saw his firm, manly features and his white uniform cap.

The reception was soon over, and Slepnev went home. I didn't run after the crowd following him to his house, but somehow I was desperate not to go home, and I couldn't go to Granny's place either. I was in a terrible mood without knowing why, and I walked round the streets in a state of vague, annoying unhappiness. Several times, I went up to the gates of 'his' house, looked at 'his' portrait, read the words written in flowers on the lawn: 'Greetings to Com. Slepnev.' It was all touching and moving, somehow.

Eventually, I went into the courtyard, and there were still cars decorated with garlands of leaves and flowers parked at the front entrance. There was a bustling crowd of boys and women standing there. I jostled with them for a while and then set off back home, concentrating on my thoughts: Why am I bored? Why am I sad? All sorts of things came into my mind. My everyday interests seemed so petty and ridiculous, my whole life was so stupidly, repulsively banal. I felt it was impossible to live like that, I had to do something heroic, I had to make myself famous . . .

But, really, I didn't know what I wanted just then. Fame? No, I didn't need it. Travel? Heroic deeds? No. All I wanted was to get another good look from close up at Slepnev, the man I'd put up with so much for and thought about so much. When I calmed down a bit, I began to feel both sad and resentful.

23 June 1934

I often think of the Cheliuskinites and the pilots. Remembering them makes me feel incredibly happy. I stop at every shopwindow to look at pictures of Schmidt, Slepnev and the others. I carefully examine the face of this pilot, and every time I like it more – it's a manly, handsome face with large bright eyes with a wide-open, startled look to them.

One evening recently, I was listening to a broadcast of the film *Moscow Welcomes the Cheliuskinites*. Red Square echoed with endless 'hoorahs', speeches rang out from the podium, and Zhenya and I, smiling enthusiastically, hung on every word the heroes said. But, afterwards, I remembered those three men who flew up into the stratosphere on a cloudy day in January. They have been forgotten. Our government doesn't like to talk about failures. It only likes to boast, and the glorious names of Vasenko, Fedoseenko and Usyskin will not be remembered any time soon, perhaps never.

I'm leaving Moscow on the twenty-seventh. My delight at going has given way to doubts and apprehensions. And something is telling me more and more insistently that, even there, I'll find no refuge from my anguish. But, even so, I still want to go.

8 July 1934

As usual, I don't really feel like making entries in my diary, and so they are all odd fragments and say almost nothing. If I start writing a detailed description of my arrival in the village and the journey on the train, it will probably turn out too long and boring. But I'll try anyway.

I remember that the day we left Moscow, 27 June, was terrible, because I was in such an agonizing mood. In the morning, I went to the shops in the centre to buy paints and a few other things with Mum. A single obstinate thought kept nagging away at my mind: the Cheliuskinites. I kept glancing eagerly into the shopwindows to get one more look at the portraits of the heroes – especially, I must admit, Slepnev's.

I used to laugh at sentimental girls who fell in love with attractive heroes and celebrities. But, now, what makes me any better than them? If this feeling is not love, then it's something very close to it. The passionate longing to see him in the flesh and not just in his pictures has been growing stronger inside me with every day that passes.

On that final day in Moscow, I looked closely, with a peculiar, shamefaced kind of hope, at every man in a tall white peaked cap with a badge I couldn't understand, so that I took in sailors and pilots and a whole load of men in other specialized services. In the busy streets – Petrovka Street and Kuznetsky Most – white caps kept appearing, and I gazed intently into the men's faces with my short-sighted eyes, which see nothing from even three steps away.

I scolded myself and promised not to do it again but, still, blushing with embarrassment, I kept on stubbornly turning my head this way and that. At the Smolensky Market, when Mum and I were running fast to catch the tram, a tall man walked past us in a blue uniform jacket and the familiar white peaked cap. I was overcome by such excitement at the sight of his handsome profile and big blue eyes that I forgot everything for a moment and turned sharply towards him, almost knocking a little girl over.

He was walking fast and, very soon, all I could see was the bright white cap. Run after him, I thought suddenly, but Mum was walking beside me. It would have been impossible to explain to her, and the tram was already moving away from the stop. Who was he? I still don't know, because I only knew Slepnev's face from pictures, so really not at all.

Mum came home at about seven in the evening, and we only started packing then. I was almost sure we wouldn't get it done in time, but we did, and we set out for the station shortly after nine. **It turned out that the train was due to leave at one in the morning. An interminable wait in the foul-smelling, dusty roadway . . . Standing by the tall stone wall, I scrutinized the people walking past and those who had taken their places in the queue. They were wretched, ragged, simple folk, peasants, and in their company I felt especially out of place, although I loved them. There were quite a lot of drunken foul-mouthed individuals using bad language.**

While she was walking round the station trying to find

out what was what, Mum discovered by chance that children up to the age of fifteen had to board the train from a special children's queue. I was more than happy to have the unexpected opportunity to settle into the carriage properly, without any pushing and shoving. That day, we had our first stroke of luck. Mum took the top bunk in the carriage and slept on it for the first half of the journey.

I sat underneath by the open window and listened to our neighbours' simple conversations and, later, when the carriage was sleeping, I sat up on the small table, stuck my head out of the window and gazed around, sometimes dozing a little, hardly thinking about anything, with a strange relaxed and peaceful sort of feeling.

I didn't get on to my bunk until it was almost morning, and I didn't fall asleep at all but just lay there with my eyes closed, listening to isolated voices. **Of all the passengers in our carriage, I think we were the only members of the intelligentsia on the way 'to the dacha', and I felt painfully ashamed in front of these half-starved people who never know a moment's rest.**

Dachas were the country houses which bourgeois families traditionally used as a holiday home during the summer months. It was common to grow fruit and vegetables at the dacha, and this became increasingly important during the food shortages.

13 July 1934

A third of a month has already passed . . . in another two weeks we return to Moscow. Well, it's still too early

151

to think about that. At the moment, I'm living in the present – if you don't count the usual daydreams, which won't leave me alone and aren't worth mentioning. It's not hugely great fun here but not so very boring either. The day is taken up with the small tasks that fill peasant life. I stay at home all day long, and we've only been to the forest three or four times. There are open fields and space all around here, and I don't feel the urge to go anywhere.

At first, I felt shy of the peasants, but now that feeling is passing and I find it interesting to listen to the country-men and -women who call in to see us. The owners of the house have almost become part of the family, not to mention their children. There are four of them: Katya, an eleven-year-old girl with a round face and mischievously smiling eyes; Sanya, a nine-year-old boy, calm, with a thrifty, sober-minded attitude; stubborn Misha, seven years old; and the youngest, Petya, a little four-year-old, fat and red-cheeked, childishly wilful and a bit spoilt.

I don't see any other children, apart from the boy next door, Khorkov's son, Yegor, very lively and jolly, with dark eyes. They're all light-haired and blue-eyed – typical Russian children. I'm astonished at how independent the peasant children are and how early they develop. They can manage very easily without the grown-ups and most of the time they don't need their help. And that's entirely understandable; after all, the grown-ups are busy from morning till night, and the children are used to being on their own.

I spend my time observing. I watch everything that happens and try to engrave it all on my memory. I listen avidly to what the peasants say about the way they live,

and now that I've heard a lot about it, I'm beginning to hate the Bolsheviks more and more.

I remember what stupid dreams used to creep into my mind back in Moscow when I thought about the country. Of course, the reality has turned out to be nothing like them, but I've got so used to the constant unreality of my dreams that I don't notice it any more. My artistic frenzy has proved a total flop. In all this time I've only done three feeble sketches. But it couldn't have been any other way. I've no one at all to sit for me, and I don't draw so well that I can capture a likeness on the wing.

Tikhon Ivanovich Khorkov, a member of the Anthill workers' co-operative, was arrested together with a group of the co-operative's members and exiled in 1929. When he was released he returned to Moscow, and in the summer his family used to go to the country.

29 July 1934

We were supposed to go to Moscow yesterday, and I was already making all sorts of laughably impossible plans concerning life in the city and, more especially, on the collective farm that Zhenya and Lyalya were planning to go to in August, with me to keep them company. My sisters were really impatient for the time to come. They wrote to me that they were finding it really hard in Moscow and that they just wanted to get away as soon as possible. And, suddenly, they changed their minds. I couldn't understand it . . . Anyway, that's not the point, the point is that their decision not to go to the collective farm totally changes my plans too. I'd almost completely said goodbye to the life here; all I was thinking about was that soon my life would change abruptly again. But now what? We stay here until the fifth, and after that . . . to Moscow? Back to that dingy, disgusting Moscow? How awful!

In the last few days, I've started feeling unbearably bored here but, even so, I feel sorry to leave when I remember the dust and stuffiness of the city streets. But I have to make my mind up. Mum's given me the choice: either the twenty-eighth or the fifth . . . And here I am, tormenting myself, not knowing what to do. If I force myself to hide away for the whole day to write, then it makes sense to stay here, but if I'm going to carry on with the same old boring life again, then . . . it's better to go.

Nina mentions her sisters planning a trip to a collective farm (or kolkhoz), possibly as temporary workers. By 1934, around 60 per cent of peasants worked in collective farms, with output slowly starting to improve after the initial drop earlier in the decade. The following year, the law would change and peasants would once again be able to own small plots.

30 July 1934

Our arrival in Moscow was unexpectedly bad. From the moment I stepped on to the platform, the old familiar anguish began creeping up on me. **At the exit from the station we were stopped because of the size of our luggage, and we would probably have had to pay the** state a fine if a porter hadn't happened to come up and managed to get us out on to the square. Mum and I laughed together at how the craving for easy money was shared by the state and the porters. I felt hurt and annoyed for my homeland and because I have to live in such a country.

We were standing outside the station when there was an awful hoarse, drunken yell from the platform. It was a young man with a horribly distorted, drooling face. He was swearing obscenely and trying to break free from the grip of a militiaman, who looked small compared to him. In his drunkenness, he tore off his shirt and waved his strong, muscular arms about. That's Soviet citizens for you, I thought.

The stone prison of Moscow was throbbing with anxious life. And I found that life, so unlike the life I had left behind 280 versts [*448 km*] from here, repulsive and alien. And I found the people, the elegant city people in clean clothes, with white pampered faces and hands, repulsive as well. I looked at the women in bright low-necked dresses, with their made-up faces and dyed hair. I heard drunken songs and the sounds of a foxtrot coming from a little restaurant . . . And I remembered the people, dirty and ragged, with faces that are rough but still attractive, who work for days on end for a piece of bread.

31 July 1934

As I should have expected, the first hours I spent in

Moscow were painful. It was after one in the morning when I got home and knocked on our door. After a while, I heard Lyalya's voice: 'Who's there?'

'Nina,' I answered.

'Nina?' The exclamation was full of surprise and annoyance, there wasn't a trace of warmth in it. I felt hurt. And when I was left on my own and got into bed, I suddenly had such a heavy, bitter feeling in my heart . . .

Was I feeling sorry I had left the village? I don't think so but, when all's said and done, it was a little bit better there, I only started getting bored during the last few days. But here, lying in the darkness, I cried. Moscow seemed so disgusting, and so did my room, and the big squares of the buildings. I remembered the blue, dark country nights that I'd enjoyed so much, the quiet and the freedom, the round, white moon. In the silence you can hear even the slightest breath of wind rustling the ripe ears of rye and see them bending over smoothly. The night is alive . . . And things feel so easy and so good.

11 August 1934

We've been staying with my aunt for a week already, and I haven't made a single detailed entry in my diary yet. I never have time: my sisters and I spend whole days writing and drawing, and we do all the housework, too. Everything that was once so alive in my memory has faded away. Sometimes this dacha reminds me of Mozhaisk, the little smoky dacha where we also ran the household and

called each other names and argued, except that then I
think it was even worse. We're older now, even if only by
a year, and that shows.

*Instead of going to the farm, Nina and her sisters had decided to
visit their aunt's dacha in the country.*

15 August 1934

For the last few days, I've been in a bad mood for some
reason. In the evenings, Zhenya and Lyalya go to **the
Anosovs'**, and I tag along. They have an accordion there,
people sing and have fun. And I feel bored and miserable
because I can't join in the general merriment; I sit there
gloomy and angry. Zhenya and Lyalya are learning to play
the accordion now, and they're obsessed with it.
And I watch them, feeling slightly envious. I'd like to try,
too, but they won't let me and, anyway, I won't have a go
in front of the boys. It's painful to see that people like me
far, far less than my older sisters and, worst of all, that
some don't like the way I look. But I can't pretend to be
like them or the person I could have been under different
circumstances any more. What can I do to make myself
cheerful and not sad? Everything's against me. Right now
I feel hungry, but there's no bread. And I feel an urge to go
to Moscow: I badly want to see Mum.

At least we've escaped from that horrible, nightmarish
house, where we have no control and are scolded and
abused. Today, there was another of those unpleasant scenes
between Aunt Sonya and us. She came home from work,

and Lyalya and I had already started eating lunch. Every day we wait for her to come back with a feeling of depressing apprehension and can't help looking into her face and wondering anxiously what mood she's in this time. Today, she was in a fairly good mood. 'Ah, girls, I feel really hungry', she said, and I quickly got up to pour her some soup. She started eating, and we carried on, feeling pretty relieved.

Suddenly, someone knocked at the door, and a peasant girl and boy stuck their heads inside: 'Can we come in?'

'Yes,' I said, without thinking.

It turned out that they'd arrived late for an appointment. Sonya got angry, scolded them and sent them back to the hospital. That was what started it all: 'Why did you let them in? Always send them packing. That's what I told you.'

'You didn't tell us anything.'

'Why should I bother to see them here?' she shouted, paying no attention to our timid attempt to defend ourselves.

17 August 1934

I'm hungry, and I think I want to go back to Moscow. I'm fed up with drawing, I'm fed up with listening to the accordion, I'm fed up with everything. Tonight, we're going to spend the night in the hayloft, but even that doesn't really cheer me up. I know that the boys will get up to their tricks, I just know it. But never mind. I wrote to Mum today to get a few things off my chest. The gypsy in me is stirring again. The moment I get used to anything, it instantly becomes uninteresting and dull. It's school again soon, but I'm not planning on studying particularly hard this year, so I'm not dreading it too much.

All three of us are sitting in a field. Right here beside us there are yellow, large-grained oats growing and, beyond them, we are surrounded by a ring of young, dark fir trees. The sky is clear and blue, covered with fantastic bulks of cloud with snow-white edges. Zhenya and Lyalya are writing. A lively, grey-eyed peasant boy has been sitting next to us for a long time, making witty comments in an odd accent. I'm waiting for him to go away, so that I can stretch out more comfortably in the scented grass and lose myself in stupid but happy dreams.

25 August 1934

I'm counting the days until we leave for Moscow. Three left. Ah, another three whole days and, at the same time, only three more days. I'm waiting patiently and fairly calmly, knowing that I won't find Moscow interesting for very long. After two weeks, or a month at the most, the anguish will return. Or perhaps it won't?

There's half an hour left until lunch. I'm counting off the minutes not so much in order to eat as to be able to say that now another half-day has gone by. Why do I want to go to Moscow so badly? No, I don't want to go to Moscow. I just need to get away from my boredom and misery. And there's nowhere else to go but Moscow.

2 September 1934

The thing that I've hated for so long and with such passion, liking it only so rarely – school – has started. Yesterday, I walked in with Ira, who has grown up even more and become even prettier – she looks like a young woman now. We were surrounded and enveloped by a succession of familiar faces which we had said goodbye to for the summer, some likeable and attractive, some repugnant, some new, and now we would be together for months and months.

And the daily boredom has passed, life has begun again – at least, some kind of life, anyway: a living, close association with other people. There are my classmates – grown up, jolly, full of life, with kindness in their eyes. It's fun, bonding with them, all of us doing the same work. As always, the boys keep themselves to themselves. They're shyer, but they still have smiles on their nice suntanned faces.

I feel that liking for Lyovka again, with his swarthy olive colouring. He's so tall, and all springy muscle – I feel the desire to gaze endlessly into his blue, glowing eyes. And the others, light-haired and blue-eyed, with faces so much alike, make me feel warm and good inside. The long, thin, one with a dark-tanned face was the only one among them I wasn't pleased to see. I don't know what I was hoping for from Linde, but I didn't expect to find him so much less good-looking. And when I listen to the pompous, deep tone of his voice, I feel a dislike for him that stifles my interest, almost a feeling of spite. He is ridiculous and repulsive.

5 September 1934

Extraordinary things happen in life, and today was an extraordinary day for me. It began, I must say, in a perfectly ordinary way. As always, almost an entire hour before classes, I called round to Ira's place, and the two of us set off along the stiflingly hot street to walk to school. The usual weary boredom before class, the haughty strolling in pairs around the yard and the stealthy, almost involuntary and shameful observation of the boys.

The second class was singing. We were cheerfully impatient for the new teacher to appear; we still didn't even know what he looked like. There was speculation that he was the young, blond-haired man who'd been seen around the school several times. The boys were sitting at the front beside the piano that doesn't work and throwing bits of bread at each other out of boredom, but soon we were asked to go into the classroom, and there we saw our singing teacher.

He was a short man with short legs and a large, odd-looking head covered with thick, stubbly hair, which earned him the nickname 'porcupine'. He looked very like the kind of caricatures our Soviet newspapers use so often to represent former members of the bourgeoisie and foreign capitalists. The laughter continued pretty much without stopping throughout the singing lesson.

During the break, we went to the Devichka Park. The next lesson was supposed to be geography. They still hadn't found a teacher, and we were prepared for another whole hour of entertaining ourselves without one. On one of the paths, we met Lyovka and Sigaev, smoking cigarettes as if they really thought they were something. With a mad determination to do something stunning and amusing, I went up to them, looked into their smug faces and asked with careless indifference: 'Got any to spare?'

Of course, they didn't get it, and Lyovka glanced at me, slightly surprised.

'Got any more cigarettes?'

'Yes, yes, we have,' said Sigaev, tugging one out of the side pocket of his shirt and handing it to me, then striking a match.

I leaned over, screwing my eyes up to look at the flame, lit up and walked on, inhaling a few times. People going by saw the whole thing and were shaking their heads in amazement, the other girls were laughing, and I had a slight smile on my face but, inside, I was shaking with irresistible, insane laughter. We walked back in a jolly mood, smelling of smoke.

We couldn't go into the classroom like that. We dashed to the toilet to rinse our mouths out over the sink. When we went to the classroom and I opened the door a bit, I was amazed to find silence and see the boys sitting at their desks. Another few steps and I saw the long, stern face of the German teacher peering out at me from behind a book: 'No, no, I won't let you in.'

I turned round to the left without answering and retreated, colliding with the astounded Zinka (my friend in misfortune), and then scooted out into the corridor. At first, she was upset and horrified.

Wandering desultorily around the school looking for the head of studies or the director, we ran into our Timosha. It turned out that he was looking for Linde, who the German teacher had thrown out just before us, and now she wanted him to come back. Ah, so Linde was thrown out as well, I thought. Knowing that we weren't the only ones immediately made us feel more cheerful, and we dropped everything and went off back to the Devichka.

We strolled along the wide paths, laughing and fooling about. Suddenly, I heard Lyovka's familiar voice calling my name from somewhere off to one side. Coming towards us were Lyovka and Sigaev, with Linde walking beside them, looking just like a little boy.

'Ah, friends in misfortune,' Zinka shouted.

We were killing ourselves laughing. Damn them all, and the German teacher, too. When here . . . ha, ha!

'Did you get thrown out too?'

'We didn't even get in.' Lyovka laughed in a low voice already so like a real man's, and looked down on us from his lofty height.

It felt weird. I just can't get used to the idea that the boys aren't little boys any more but adolescents, and the difference between us gets bigger every year. Lyovka broke off what he was saying and shouted out: 'Look at the great way that guy's sleeping!' Then, he burst into laughter, which was joined by Sigaev's cackling and Linde's bellowing bass. Zinka was dying laughing. She hung on to my arm and squealed. It was impossible not to laugh. There was a pair of legs lying on the bench at the corner, and then we saw the head and body of a seedy, crumpled-looking drunk. Lyovka began diligently cleaning the dust off his jacket, until the man unconsciously fluttered his sleepy, stuck-shut eyelids.

'Enjoying yourself, Lyovka?' Zinka commented.

'It doesn't matter, I won't end up like him anyway!'

At that, we left them and spent the rest of the hour wandering around the park.

7 September 1934

I really ought to study this year – after all, they only take top students into the eighth class. But I don't feel like thinking about the future yet, when the present is so enjoyable and amusing. It's fun being at school, despite my impossible, vague longings. Linde, who seemed so repulsive at the beginning of term, has started to seem interesting again, with his casual contempt for girls and for studying. I really liked his reply to a note from Ira asking which of the girls he fancied; I suppose it aroused my female vanity. 'Fight! The one who wins shall have me': that was his answer. The female mind really is remarkable! I only fancy Linde (if I can put it like that) because he doesn't fancy me; if things were different I'd probably hate him. But now I'm giving him those furtive, curious glances again.

It's strange: I sleep a lot and don't study much, but in lessons (during some of the explanations), I sometimes suddenly feel so drowsy I can hardly lift my head up, and my eyelids keep getting heavier and heavier, until they close.

13 September 1934

Our whole group was split into two ages ago. One half consists of well-behaved, quiet girls, the other of rowdies, both girls and boys. Last year, this split wasn't so noticeable. We were all united by our little strikes, we didn't fool about and play wild pranks so much, we didn't have such close ties with the boys. Now, it's become only too obvious.

The others – the Usachevka Street group – have gone completely quiet and got bogged down in cramming, while we – the Devichka group – have really let ourselves go, stopped studying and are worse hooligans than the boys. The animosity's growing between the Devichka group and the Usachevka group. They go around grumbling and scowling at us (maybe they're going to complain). But to hell with them, anyway: we want to have fun, we want to live. The exchange of notes with the boys gets livelier every day. But out of some strange sense of pride, I don't actually join in, I only ask the girls about it sometimes.

1 October 1934

I stayed at home today. I had to wash the windows and do the ironing . . . There are two personalities battling away inside me: one, a woman who yearns for the never-ending concerns of keeping a home, for order and cleanliness; the other, a person who wants to devote her life to some other goal, something more interesting and elevated. This struggle can be very painful. I have to make my mind up one way or the other, to decide on something. I know I ought to subdue the woman in me, but often it's not possible. I think it's only fair on Mum to help out, and that often makes me accept the way things are.

12 October 1934

Yesterday: tedious, boring lessons, incomprehension, anger and fear, wearily monotonous breaks in the cramped hall with the young riff-raff jostling and swearing, sleepiness and exhaustion in the final lessons. All day waiting for something to change, for something clearer and more interesting to emerge. The physics teacher, a tall, frightening old man with a yellow face overgrown with hair like a monkey's, explained something or other, stammering slowly. Then he took his time asking questions, tormenting his pupils and sending us to sleep.

On the way home, I think I brightened up a bit, but I was still thinking about somehow getting out of school the next day, about taking things in hand. What could I do? **Poison myself? Somehow, it didn't seem a frightening or terrible idea, and I had no regrets about my life. And I couldn't think of anything else. I stole a phial of opium from Granny. But what if I change my mind? I wondered. After dinner, I went home. I put twenty dark drops into a cup and drank them before I went to sleep. I drank it!** It felt acrid and bitter in my mouth, and the taste went up my nose.

Pleased with my own resolute action, I snuggled up in the blanket and got ready to go to sleep. But I couldn't sleep. I kept thinking in a dreaming sort of way about what would happen the next day, and I didn't believe that I was really going to die. It was strange: part of me was glad that I wouldn't have to go to see Dima M. [*a boy she was supposed to go up to for a bet*], and another part was quaking like a timid coward. I'm going to die. When I began sinking into a drowsy, dizzy state of weakness, I felt like my head was being twisted backwards. I jerked upright convulsively and writhed about.

I woke up when Mum came into the room to get something. I tried to open my eyes. I thought: What if I've given myself away somehow? I looked at the bright light through my eyelashes. When she switched it off, I calmed down and said something to her. A few moments later, I looked at the clock, and it was twenty to one. Two and a half hours have gone by. What does that mean? I woke up again in the night: darkness, bright moonlight on the wall. This is cruel! Is it a trick? Isn't it really opium? I lay there for a long time with my legs drawn up, trying to get to sleep. I'm so unlucky! I decided simply to poison myself, but even that didn't work. In the morning, I got up as usual and went dashing round to Granny's. What was in that little phial? It turned out to be opium mixed with some other kind of drops.

18 October 1934

Today, Ksyusha and I went to the Bolshoi Theatre to look at the body of the tenor Sobinov. We waited in line for three hours and, when we finally got inside the tall doors hung with black wreaths, there were fir-tree branches adorning the steps and a smell of warm, fragrant evergreen needles. The huge carved chandeliers glowed a warm yellow, and the militiamen in the guard of honour stood there like stone idols. A quiet, dark row of people filed soundlessly through the hall.

The coffin was standing on a dais covered with flowers, and we could see the yellow hands lying high on the chest and the oval form of the head from below and just off to one side. A choir was quietly singing a funeral march in powerful harmonies . . . Standing by the wall was a little girl in a white jersey suit with a serious look in her black eyes and, beside her, a woman and a grey-haired gentleman.

Leonid Sobinov (1872–1934), who died of a heart attack aged sixty-six, had retired from the stage three years previously. He had been an internationally renowned opera singer, performing at La Scala in Italy as well as in London, Paris and Berlin, and was one of the first major artists to be recorded. He sang most frequently at the Bolshoi and had been ranked People's Artist of the New Soviet Union and Officer of the Red Army.

22 October 1934

My bewildered, tense, bored mood seems to be passing. Today was quite enjoyable: the German teacher didn't come, and we got the idea of swapping notes with Lyovka during her lesson. At first, everything went well, but then he abused us in such filthy language, wrote such nasty things . . . The bastard! We cut the exchange short. But, even so, it was good fun. Lyovka's our top hooligan now. No one else can shower you with obscene abuse so frankly and say such disgusting things, but no one else laughs so infectiously and charmingly either.

I was seriously angry with him today but, when he was talking about something with Ira after lessons, I couldn't help admiring the slight tilt of his head and the thick mass of dull gold hair above his incredibly handsome forehead, and his smile, so often disdainful and insulting but so attractive. Oh, he's really something! And always so cheerful. I just can't understand how a person who has read so much, is so cultured and from a good family can be such a loathsome hooligan at the same time.

Musya said to me a while ago: 'You know what, Nina? A certain boy fancies you.'

'Me? . . . That's nice . . . No, don't tell me who. I'll start looking at him differently.'

'That's really stupid.'

'Well, who is it then?'

'Margosha.' [*a new pupil*]

'Margosha? Where did you get that idea?'

'He told me himself.'

'Oh, sure. I don't believe you. When?'

'Yesterday. Zina and I were swapping notes with him, and we asked who he fancied. He wrote: "Lugovskaya".' She told me some other lies, too, but I didn't really believe any of it, and I wasn't really interested. Why on earth Musya got the idea of telling me about their notes then, I don't know, but now I can't relax. It's put me so on edge, the uncertainty of it all. I want to know if 'it' is really true or not.

25 October 1934

Musya is a small, elegant, plump Jewish girl. She has round shoulders, round, plump hips, rounded breasts and a slim little waist, soft black hair, brown eyes that sparkle warmly and smooth, even rosy cheeks. I never thought she'd become so pretty. She's unusually lively, talkative and witty. I think the boys like her a lot, and she herself likes passing the time with them.

One ninth-class pupil with dark sheep's eyes and a chubby, attractive face is very keen on her; he picks on her and teases her a bit in fun and calls her his dark little girl. She's definitely attractive. I think that lately Margosha's been completely crazy about her.

She and I are on excellent terms now. She's very frank with me, and I'm very grateful to her for that, although I don't repay her in kind, since I can't be frank with anyone at all. But she doesn't ask anything from me. Yesterday, on our day off, Ira was over at her place. While they were talking, Ira kept teasing Musya about Margosha and then, all of a sudden, she showed her the end of a note that was signed B.M. [*his initials*]. Musya, intrigued and, in her heart of hearts, perhaps even hurt, later told me about it excitedly, and we both started wondering how to explain it all. In school there are no signs that there's anything between them at all; there haven't been any unnecessary glances or words. Are they really able to restrain themselves that well?

26 October 1934

If I were in love with Margosha, I wouldn't think about him any more than I do at the moment. But I still tell myself that I don't fancy him. I recall my infatuation with Lyovka, when I used to stare at him for hours on end, turn pale and tremble at every word he spoke and admire every movement he made. That was quite different. Margosha interests me: I can sense him. There are boys that you don't notice, but I sense him with my entire being, I can't help it – without even looking, I watch him and listen closely to what he says.

But Margosha fancies Musya, so what am I thinking of? I'm sure he does, and even despite that, every day I wait impatiently for some word addressed to me, or a smile. It's hard but it makes things interesting, completely hiding the way I feel from everyone. Not showing too much interest in Margosha, not looking at him more than is acceptable. I've managed it so far. But the constant tension and hope are making me dreadfully nervous. Sometimes, I can't help myself and I steal a look at him, and then I feel very upset and ashamed of myself.

Margosha is as clumsy and awkward as a bear, laughable and not handsome. I realize all that. And yet it gives me a strange pleasure to watch him, to suddenly see his shambling figure in the hall, to catch an indifferent glance from him. I need to distract myself, move to a different seat and try to forget it all, but I . . . only intensify what I need to cut short. But it will soon pass, it must pass. When I'm at home, I wait impatiently for the next day and school but, in class, I feel I want to get away, to go home.

We are being taught literature by E.V., an elderly woman with a very attractive face and lovely dark eyes. I think everyone likes her and is pleased with her. E.V. hardly ever tells us off, and she's always conciliatory, calm and kind. Somehow, the girls have got the idea that she likes me. They've taken a series of coincidences and chance incidents and made them into something serious. They keep pestering me to resit the literature exam to get 'excellent', and they get angry with me for being so obstinate.

So now I'm beginning to develop a sort of ill will towards her, something like resentment and spite. But she came up to me at lunch and asked: 'What about you, Lugovskaya, won't you resit the exam to get "excellent"?'

'No. I wouldn't get it anyway,' I replied categorically and stuck my nose in my plate.

But today, after classes, Musya came up to me beaming brightly and said: 'All settled and signed. Congratulations!'

Thinking that she was talking about her bet with Margosha, I shook her firmly by the hand. But it turned out that she'd gone to E.V. and told her that I knew the subject much better than just 'good' and I ought to resit for 'excellent'. Of course, E.V. agreed to examine me again. So now I'll have to spend all tomorrow morning cramming Tolstoy's *Hadji Murat* [*a story by Leo Tolstoy written in 1904, but not published until 1910 because it was banned by the censor*], because you can't take any chances when you resit an exam.

27 October 1934

Study *Hadji Murat* again? Oh, God, and I still won't get 'excellent' anyway. I can feel it, I can't string two sentences together properly, and for this I have to prattle on for at least five minutes without stopping. I'm not nervous, it's just depressing to resit and not get the mark. Why did Musya have to go and say that to E.V.? I'm in such a vile mood now, I can feel how untalented I am, I'm full of resentment and anger because I can't get anything right. I'm a perfectly ordinary, commonplace person, and the only problem is that other people, and even I myself, used to claim that I had some kind of talent. A stupid and sad mistake. I really ought to have come to terms with it and calmed down ages ago, but I keep getting angrier and angrier. Look at Ira: how come she's so good-looking and witty, and an excellent student to boot?

30 October 1934

Dad came home this evening. And again I could feel my fury with the Bolsheviks rising in my throat, my despair at my own powerlessness. And pity for him, a sick and homeless tramp.

Later, after I'd read a lot of Lermontov, I got the idea of writing some poetry. I smiled as I pulled out a pen and paper, and some meaningless drivel came out. At first, I wanted to tear it up, but I decided to copy the best bit into my diary.

I hate the light but love immensely
What in these parts is known as light.
I am sick of life's regularity,
That strikes me dumb in dreadful fright.
My fate is quiet and unseen
To live within my close, dark shell,
And none shall know my secret dream
Of things that only I can tell.

12 November 1934

Yesterday, there was a performance at Zhenya and Lyalya's student hostel. Their group was putting on a short vaudeville show, and the girls invited me to go. Ksyusha and I set out to join them at about nine o'clock. By accident, we got off one stop short of 2nd Donskaya Street, and we laughed nervously as we ran along the dark, empty side-street. Somehow, we managed to reach the student hostel and went in, gazing around in confusion. People we didn't know, faces that looked hostile!

Eventually, I found their friend Zhorka at the door of the hall, where Zhenya and Lyalya had asked him to wait for us. He led us to the front row and sat us there. I was surrounded by the noise and chatter of the student life I love so much. I looked around, keen to catch every movement and word. 'Sokrat' came, a blond-haired, interesting man with the dark stripes of sideburns on his pale face. He sat down beside us, and I listened to his conversation with some girl student, all the time feeling rather sorry for him.

Feeling a bit more at ease, I went backstage and . . .
suddenly I found myself in the women's toilet. Standing
in front of me were some of the performers but not a
single familiar face. Several awkward moments passed as I
goggled at them without speaking, not knowing whether
it was the make-up that had changed them so much. But
then a girl in a blue dress and light wig came in and, from
her voice, I realized it was Zhenya. Even after I got a bit
more used to them, quite a few times I found myself looking up at made-up faces I didn't recognize.

But then the show started. The director, Zhenya G., had
had the clever idea of presenting the performers in
absolute darkness and lighting up their faces with pocket
torches. There were frequent hitches behind the swaying
folds of the curtain, and I was very upset by the nasty,
mocking laughter from the audience. But I felt even more
nervous when the curtain rose and there on the stage were
my sister Zhenya and Nina K. I felt terribly anxious for
them and, all the way through the play, I was afraid that
they'd mess things up somehow.

But everything went off well and, after the thin
applause, everybody started to leave, and Ksyusha and I
went backstage. Everyone was feeling elated and excited.
Andrei B., looking frightening with powdered hair and a
false nose, jested wildly and then, leaning down over
Lyalya, he began wiping the make-up off her face. Zhenya
and Lyalya got changed, then gathered up all their
bits and pieces and set off through the long, bright
corridors to room 208, where Zhorka, Kolya N., Ozerov
and Zhenya G. live. For some reason, I'd already started to
feel a liking for Zhenya G. during the performance and felt

happy drinking in the wonderful intonations of his voice.

Ksyusha and I walked up and down the corridor near room 208 for a long time until Kolya N. invited us to go in. Inside, it was a terrible mess. All the beds were piled high with coats, costumes and papers. We sat on one of them. The girls didn't start dancing; they sat there for a long time, talking to Zhorka and Zhenya G. They turned the lights out, and the outlines of figures drowned in darkness were suddenly lit up by torches.

Everybody was laughing and joking, and I took advantage of the darkness to look at Zhenya G. I was liking him more and more, and a positive feeling of gratitude towards him was growing stronger. He sat there looking tired and, I think, drowsy, his shirt slightly open on his chest, kind and gentle, with a really, really lovely smile.

13 November 1934

I'm completely unsettled again. I don't know what to do with myself any more: thoughts and desires, inexpressible and naïve, keep coming into my head one after another. Yesterday, Zhorka and Andrei B. came to see my sisters. Andrei came to learn how to dance and, as I watched him practise, I couldn't help laughing at his clumsy, tall figure. In the dance, he and Lyalya held each other close, he leaned his handsome, narrow face down over hers and lifted her petite body, her head raised towards him.

They were so free and easy with each other, joking and teasing. Andrei pressed her against himself and stroked her hair so often that I began feeling embarrassed for them. Lyalya was flirting with him, perhaps unconsciously, but she screwed up her cunning eyes at him mockingly. She's already made Zhorka crazy about her, and now he comes round every day, and I think Zhenya G. likes her too – and Bart was being too affectionate with her yesterday.

I'm almost delirious about going to college and . . . I think . . . about Zhenya G. too. Dad told me just the other day that they'll be taking on students for the Textile Institute in January, and even though I'm sure they only take people after the eighth class, I still begged (our) Zhenya to find out all the details. What if I could finally escape from stifling, repulsive school, break free, this time for ever! And life's quite different there. There's really no point at all even thinking about college, but I can still dream!

I'm not interested in school at all any more; there's nothing there for me: Margosha barely interests me any longer, and I've stopped thinking about Linde altogether. And Lyovka? No, his charm hasn't faded. Just like before, I can't help smiling when I see that funny, long-legged figure and that shaggy, cockily poised head which looks so young, even childish, and those eyes that are so cheerful, arrogant, all-knowing. He sometimes reminds me of Lopukhov in *War and Peace*.

But today I heard some astonishing news. Lyovka, this boy who's been going around swearing at everybody and laughing crudely and vulgarly at the girls, has written Ira a note: 'Irina, I like you and would be grateful if you would please agree to stay behind after school. I would do anything for you.' I was astounded and, I must admit, upset.

Nina mentions applying to the Textile Institute, so it seems she was still thinking of following an artistic career, despite the lack of artistic freedom at the time. The Constructivist art movement, which had grown up in the aftermath of the 1917 revolution, had brought new life to textile design. The Constructivists were an abstract avant-garde group who sought to 'construct art' using 'real materials': they created collages, sculptures and textiles. Nevertheless, under Stalin, independent groups were banned and abstraction was forcibly replaced with social realism. Many artists, most famously Marc Chagall and Wassily Kandinsky, had already left Russia in the 1920s, aware that their creative freedom would be hampered by the regime.

18 November 1934

By some miracle, we only had two lessons at school today. And it came just at the right time, too, because I barely managed to sit through even those two. I've become a complete outsider there; school life flows right past me. Occasionally, lively little Musya will turn up and say something to me, her black eyes glowing. When Margosha had to answer her question about who he fancied after he lost a bet, he wrote: 'You.' She looked indifferent but surprised, and I said: 'You should have expected that.'

It hardly bothered me at all – I was so absorbed in other thoughts. Covering my face with my hand and ignoring what the teacher was saying, I tried to picture

Zhenya G.'s face. And I walked home hoping that he would be there. There was light coming through Zhenya and Lyalya's window, and it threw sharp shadows from the cross-pieces on to the protruding ledge of the wall. They must be drawing up there, I thought, climbing quickly up the stairs.

I stopped outside the door. Someone, apparently Zhenya, was playing a serious piece on the piano. That means there's no one else here, I said to myself. No, of course, I can't be lucky every day. But, even so, everything inside me somehow collapsed. I sat in my room for more than an hour without taking my coat and hat off. I sat in the same armchair I sat in yesterday and struggled painfully to remember him. But everything kept blurring.

It felt strange to think that perhaps I might not see him for a month. I dozed a bit and started dreaming. Is it true that Zhenya G. likes Dusya? Yesterday, when Lyalya asked him: 'Is Dusya definitely going to come?' he didn't say anything and just twirled a notebook in his hands, examining it closely. Then Zhenya asked him the same question when they were drawing me. 'She must have found some good reason,' he said, stressing the word 'good' ironically, without looking up from his book.

When I went into my sisters' room Zhenya glanced at my sullen face and said cheerfully: 'We're going to invite Zhenechka G. round tomorrow!' I went back to my room, clutching my head and thinking: Oh, that's really given me something to look forward to tomorrow evening! But what if my sisters end up meeting him in the student hostel instead?

23 November 1934

I didn't go to school again today. This is my love's swan song. After this, I'll have to put an end to it, try to forget, try not to expect anything. Right now, I'm deliberately not doing anything, not even reading. I want to suffer the torment of anticipation and disillusionment and dream to my heart's content. The hours go by drearily but not unpleasantly. Zhenya and Lyalya will be back late today – they've got volleyball – and after that they'll go to room 208. There's no point even thinking that Zhenya G. might come here; the girls simply won't invite him again, out of pride. They know now that the only person he needs is Dusya.

24 November 1934

And, of course, Zhenya G. didn't turn up. I waited for a long time and, even when there was no hope left of him coming, I carried on waiting. Zhorka and Lyalya arrived here at nine o'clock. If only Zhenya would come – she'd probably know something. But what a terrible mood she was in yesterday evening! And I know why – because Zhenya G. refused to come to our place without Dusya. I remember Zhenya pacing about all evening, so gloomy, silent and intense. When the two of us were alone in the kitchen, I sat down beside her. 'Well, is there anything you want to tell me?'

'Nothing. I don't feel like talking today.' And she was quiet for a long time, then, suddenly, she brightened up and said: 'I've dreamed about Zhenya G. for two nights in a row.'

Ah, that's who you're thinking about, I thought.

Zhenya came back at twelve, cheerful, her eyes gleaming. She winked at me and laughed. She's happy, I said to myself, and felt miserable. She didn't tell me anything; maybe she was afraid that I'd get the wrong idea. I couldn't bring myself to ask her a single question and went off to bed feeling angry and depressed. Tomorrow they'll go to college, and then to the library ... with Zhenya G. They're so lucky, I thought.

I fell asleep quickly, because I was totally worn out, mentally exhausted from constantly focusing my thoughts on Zhenya. In the morning, I only woke up when the girls were already drinking tea. Maybe they'd invite him over today? 'Zhenya!' I shouted loudly.

'What?'

'Will you be back late today?'

'I don't know, probably fairly late.'

'Where are you going now?'

'To the studio, to paint ... do you want to come along? You could take a look around.'

I sat up in bed: 'With you? I'll be right there!'

'But be quick.'

Oh, they needn't have said that! I'm going to see him! That's what the studio and all the pictures mean to me. What a stroke of luck! I forgot my previous two days of torment so completely that, from then on, they were just a blur.

The chaos in the studio was extraordinary: easels with paintings and without stood all over the place, pointing in various directions; the walls were hung with pictures; unfinished pictures and pictures barely begun lay on the floor and in the corners. There were two thick columns in the centre with still lifes laid out on little tables beside them.

The girls showed me everything and told me about everything. Soon, Zhorka arrived. Alone! While they were choosing a place to work, Zhenya asked: 'Is Zhenya G. going to come?'

'I don't know.'

I can't even remember what state I was in at that stage. But sitting there drawing was a lot better than pining away at home. I settled down behind one of the columns and began sketching. It was quiet. Far away, at the end of the corridor, there was the muffled bang of a door. That corridor frightened me, with its long emptiness.

Lyalya looked through the keyhole: 'It's Zhenya.' I quickly closed my sketchbook and started looking at Zhenya's drawings, waiting, and feeling slightly anxious. There were footsteps at the door, and he came in: 'Hello.'

'Cheers.'

'Hello.' I glanced at him furtively for a moment, but he didn't seem to have noticed me. Then, as he was walking between the easels and the benches, he saw me and said: 'Ah, Nina, hello. What sisterly solidarity.'

'Yes, I came to watch.' And I hid my face in my book quickly, so as not to blush, but I still just glimpsed a slight smile on his face.

He walked round the studio, looking for something, moving something else, talking about this and that and laughing, before stopping behind me by the window. I felt angry, sensing that he was dawdling behind my back, afraid that he would glance at my work; I just felt uncomfortable. I wasn't entirely satisfied: I wanted to see him from closer up, wanted him to say something to me. Then I stopped drawing and picked up a book to read.

At that moment he was walking round the studio, eating something: 'What are you reading, Nina? *Hamlet*? Aha!' He stopped at an easel close to me. That bothered me, because I'd moved to the other side of the studio so that he couldn't see me but I could occasionally glance at his outstretched arm and lovely head. He sat there quietly for a while, then lost patience and jumped up, walking past me and stopping to look at my book. Half-covering the page with my hand, I turned round – there were those blue eyes looking at me. 'Show me, Nina.' I shook my head, but he suddenly took hold of my hand, gently moved it aside and said in a tone of gentle reproach: 'We-ell?'

'I haven't read anything yet. I've only just begun,' I said, blushing as I drowned in his laughing eyes.

'Let's go to our place. Let's all go and have lunch there,' Zhenya G. suggested.

'Oh, no, we're not having lunch at your place!' said (our) Zhenya.

'Oh, come on, Zhenya!'

'No.'

'Nina, will you come?'

'How can I come on my own?' I said, smiling (it wasn't a refusal). As they said goodbye, they shook hands, but I looked away and then bowed to everyone and said: 'All the best.'

The bow was to everyone, but I was looking only at Zhenya G. I'm a fool! It's becoming so obvious, but I only realized it too late. At the door of the studio, as I was giving the book back to Zhenya G., I said: 'Take your *Hamlet*,' putting the stress on the second syllable.

The girls laughed: 'Ho-ho! *Hamlet*,' they said, echoing my pronunciation.

'Yes, *Hamlet*,' I repeated, deliberately this time, and looked at G. with a laugh.

'*Hamlet*,' he said, correcting me by emphasizing the first syllable very gently, as if he were afraid of offending me. How kind and sensitive he is!

25 November 1934

School wasn't so hideous today – perhaps because I've had a chance to get a bit less used to it – but, even so, the thought of studying like this right through the winter frightens me. Ah, why did I have to notice Zhenya G.? Now, the only thing on my mind is to arrange my life so that I can see him more often.

Linde was there today, but I don't care one way or the other about him now, so I joked at his expense and tried to wound his pride. He makes me angry, the way he obstinately ignores the girls. And I take a more sober view of Margosha now as well. He looks handsome, I suppose, and I wouldn't have minded having the kind of relationship with him that Musya has. But he no longer makes me feel that old excitement and heartache.

26 November 1934

I have to leave school. But how? In January, students are selected for the colleges and universities. I've given up thinking about the Textile Institute, but anything will do, as long as it's not school. The *rabfak* perhaps, foundation courses . . . This morning, I was thinking really positively about how I would go to see Kolya [*cousin Nikolai*] today and study physics with him, how he would give me some new assignments. I'm going to study, study, study.

I can sense that I have the strength to work long and hard, but I need to know for definite what all the effort is for. Most important of all, I need someone to supervise my work, someone who will check it and help me. I can't do it all on my own, without any support. I can't put up with taunts all the time. I was hoping Kolya would lend a hand. Surely I could prepare for the exam in a month with his help? I had a work plan, and I looked through what has to be covered: it all seemed possible, so I went to Granny's to meet Kolya feeling that I had the strength and commitment for the struggle ahead.

But then I began feeling timid. Nikolai just sat there, looking indifferent, absorbed in some technical drawing. I was afraid he'd laugh at me and, at one point, I felt like sorting it all out through Mum. I walked around the room for a long time without saying anything, thinking: No, I'll never be able to say anything, I can't or I don't know how. I'll tell him myself.

Glancing out of the window, I asked Nikolai: 'What course do people get on at *rabfak* if they join after the seven-year school?'

185

He said: 'What's this, do you want to cut your education short?'

'Yes.'

'It can't be done. You'll never cover the course in a month.'

Not only did I not ask him to help me study, I was even afraid to ask him for a little bit of advice, and I went home feeling angry, with a more sober view of things.

Will I be able to get through it all on my own? I have no one to set me assignments in physics and chemistry, and that's essential. What can I do? I have to get through it. I must be able to, surely? I felt miserable and depressed. I waited for Zhenya G. to come again, despite myself, and then for (our) Zhenya and Lyalya. I'm determined to do it after all, I've got to make my mind up and go for it. Nothing ventured, nothing gained, and there'll always be time to go back to school.

30 November 1934

I've been studying for the last few days. In the evenings, I go to Nikolai. He sets me assignments, asks me questions and tries to persuade me to stay at school. He doesn't believe in my desire to go to college, and he doesn't believe that it's possible. But I'm still positive. Yesterday, Mum started talking about the preparatory faculties for the Foreign Languages Institute, and it made me so happy.

It's all right if I can't see Zhenya G. or have the entertaining life that my sisters have, which I've created so many beautiful fantasies about in my head. It doesn't matter! I'll find my own interests, start my own life. It's frightening to think that these are only dreams and that I'll have to go back to school. The thought of the long hours of study scares me, yet I know for certain that I'll do it. Only I need to find out the precise details quickly – perhaps I'll be able to get into the Textile Institute!

1 December 1934

I'm dreaming about Zhenya G. again. I got his photo from the girls and spent a long time examining it excitedly. Oh, God! If I could just see him for a moment! I remember him reclining on the bed after a wild waltz, that charming smile of his.

2 December 1934

What should I call it, happiness or unhappiness? Zhenya G. came yesterday. My heart was pounding, and my hands suddenly started trembling. He gave the secret knock, and I opened the door, certain that it was Lyalya, so it was a surprise for me to see the vague outline of his figure in the semi-darkness of the staircase. I don't think he replied to my timid 'hello', speaking to Zhenya without noticing me. I stood in the kitchen, biting my lip. And I was hoping, thinking that these dreams were real.

At about eleven o'clock, they announced on the radio

that Comrade Kirov, a member of the Politburo, had been murdered in Leningrad. 'Oh-oh, my God!' Zhenya G. exclaimed, clasping his face in his hands, his voice full of tears. I felt a bit ashamed that I wasn't at all shaken by this announcement; on the contrary, what I felt was joy. It means our struggle is still going on, we still have an organization and real people. It means we still haven't completely sunk into the slops of socialism. And I felt sorry that I hadn't been a witness to this terrible and significant event. Now, there's going to be a real uproar.

The boys talked about it for the rest of the evening. As they were leaving, I was standing in my sisters' room, and Zhenya G. did in the end manage to give me a nod over Lyalya's head from the corridor and wave his roll of paper. His affectionate attention makes me feel confused. Perhaps it's only because I'm still a child that he treats me like that. Damn it! I do love him.

On 1 December, Sergei Kirov (1886–1934), the First Secretary of the Leningrad Regional Committee of the Communist Party and member of the ruling Presidium of the Central Executive Committee, the Politburo, was murdered. Immediately after the event, sixty-nine White Guards (anti-Bolsheviks) were arrested and shot in Leningrad without any investigation or trial. The assassin, Leonid Nikolaev, who was said to be disturbed, was executed the same month, and thirteen other people were convicted and shot with him, although they had no clear connection with the crime. Nina clearly took the assassination as a sign that the anti-revolutionary movement was still active. Although Stalin was said to have orchestrated the murder himself, this didn't stop

him representing it as political terrorism against the Soviet state.
On 1 December, a new law was drawn up against 'terrorist
organizations and terrorist acts against employees of Soviet power'.
No appeals were permitted, and execution was the most likely sen-
tence. Kirov's death was a pivotal historical moment, since it
sparked the first of Stalin's great purges, which would lead to about
a million deaths.

8 December 1934

Zhenya G. was here again on the fourth or the fifth. He
came with Zhorka, so it wasn't really convenient for me to
hang about in the room. But yes, I put any feeling of
embarrassment to one side and spent the entire evening
sitting in my sisters' room. Only, strangely enough, I
didn't enjoy it at all. I think about him a lot more calmly
now, and sometimes I think that the infatuation is passing, or that at least it's got weaker. But that's only because
I very rarely see him and, when I do see him, I don't
glance at him even once. I try not to pay any attention to
him (that is, to appear not to).

That evening, Zhorka and Zhenya G. left unusually
early, and I couldn't stop myself from going out into the
corridor to see them off and standing there while they put
their coats on, although I felt like a fifth wheel. And, after
that, I waited for him again every day. On our day off,
Zhenya asked me to copy out a study programme for her.
I agreed and thought with satisfaction: I'll copy it out
when he comes. There's so much in it I don't understand,
I'll have a reason for going into their room.

I was so pleased with this idea that I kept smiling in anticipation of his arrival and felt quite cheerful. One evening, Zhenya asked me: 'Well, how do you like Zhenya? Handsome, isn't he?'

'Zhenya? Yes, he's a cheerful boy,' I said carelessly, but somehow it sounded wrong.

That same evening, she said: 'You know, Nina, you blushed when he started talking to you.'

'When was that, the last time?'

'No, before that.'

'Aah, when he asked me how it was going? Yes, I remember. It was because it took me by surprise.' And I watched myself carefully, to make sure I spoke evenly and didn't blush again.

What the hell is going on? How could they know that I like him? Have they read my diary? No, I wouldn't expect that kind of dirty trick from them, it would be too mean. And yet they do suspect something; every evening, when Lyalya sees that I'm bored, she asks: 'Not fallen in love, have you, Nina?'

'No, not with anyone,' I reply indifferently.

'But really, you should fall in love. Would you like me to pair you up with Zhenya G.?'

I was talking to Zhenya at the same time, and I answered her before turning to Lyalya: 'Yes, if the feeling's mutual, but so much the worse for him.'

10 December 1934

I was hoping that this evening would be like when the

three of us were together before – me, Zhenya and him. But, precisely because I was expecting so much of it, nothing worked out. Yesterday, Zhenya told me that she was going to invite him round today to rehearse a play, and I was so looking forward to it. He was here yesterday, but so was Dusya, and that was why he came. I watched him closely and suddenly began to feel disillusioned and frightened that love would slip away. But the moment he started whirling round in a waltz, he smiled and, once again, it intoxicated me. And, once again, he started playing the fool, glanced at me and laughed, and I waited for that glance, longed for it.

11 December 1934

Today has been a strange day. Zhenya and Lyalya came back late yesterday, when I'd already gone to bed. What on earth made me decide to get up again? I was hoping they'd have something to talk about and mention his name, at least in passing. But, it didn't happen. **Somehow, our conversation turned to the most dangerous subject: Soviet power, the Bolsheviks and modern life. We were at opposite poles; we were like a blind man and a sighted man who is trying to explain colours to him. We just couldn't understand each other . . .**

Well, what objection could I make to phrases mindlessly learned by rote like 'Anybody who is not for the Bolsheviks is against Soviet power' and 'Things will be better in the future'? Are the five million deaths in the Ukraine temporary? And the sixty-nine people shot?

Sixty-nine – are they temporary? What state, under what system of power, has ever issued a sentence like that with such cold cruelty? What nation has ever assented with such slavish submission and obedience to every atrocity committed?

We spoke for an entire hour and, naturally, no one was persuaded to change their mind. I was so angry with myself: how can I be so stupid, so unable to express myself and to prove to my sisters, even with the facts on my side, how totally false the Bolshevik system is! That's some lack of talent!

Zhenya and Lyalya are busy with their own stuff and their art; Mum with her job. No one will give me any advice about what to do, no one understands how miserable and afraid I am. **Dad came today. He brought some news from the Polygraphic Institute. There's a faint hope I could get in.** But when this dream began to come true, I suddenly felt nervous and even felt I didn't really want to go there any more.

And I couldn't help laughing when I realized that all my thoughts and hopes were directed towards 'him', in order 'The smiling mouth, the shifting eye/ To seek with bright, enamoured eyes' [*from Pushkin's novel in verse, Eugene Onegin*]. I can't get into the Textile Institute, and I'm beginning to lose interest in the other places. I've only just understood today that all my motivation, all my energy, is nothing but love. How astonished and shocked my parents would be if they found out that their daughter indulges such stupid feelings and is planning to destroy her entire life for the sake of love.

Nina's school class, photographed in 1933.

A May-Day parade like the one Nina refused to attend in 1933.

LEFT: Child victims of the devastating years of famine that gripped the Ukraine, mentioned by Nina in her diary.

BELOW: Members of the Young Pioneers, which Nina eventually left, marching with a banner of Stalin.

ABOVE: Nina was disgusted by the way the newspapers reported the funeral of Stalin's wife, Nadezhda Alliluyeva, in 1932.

ABOVE: Stalin attending the funeral of Sergei Kirov, whose murder was to Nina a joyful sign that the anti-communist movement was still alive.

LEFT: The eight-engined aeroplane *Maxim Gorky*, a source of immense Russian pride before it tragically crashed in Moscow on 19 May 1935, as reported by Nina.

Newspaper article celebrating the pilots who rescued the crew of the steamship *Cheliuskin* in 1934, including Nina's heartthrob, Slepnev.

This desolate prison camp located in Siberia was in the same region as Kolyma, where Nina and her family were imprisoned.

Police mug shots taken of Nina and her mother [left] and Eugenia and Olga [right] after they were arrested in 1937.

The NKVD headquarters, the Lubyanka, where Nina's diary was held in archives after her arrest.

Nina after her release from prison camp.

ABOVE: Nina and her mother pictured at the end of the 1940s.

BELOW: Eugenia and Olga, Nina's identical twin sisters,
photographed after their release from Kolyma.

Self-portrait.

Nina as a painter, her chosen career following her imprisonment.

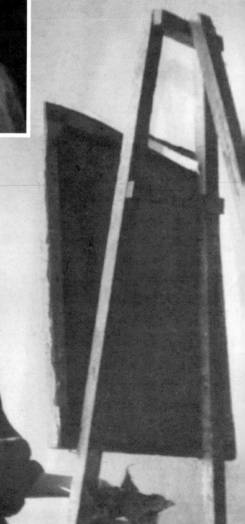

14 December 1934

It's amazing: why does everything have to end in tragedy for me? 'The End,' I write. Yes, because this is the end of my love for him, the end of my dreaming. It seems absurd now to think that only two or three days ago I was afraid that my infatuation would fade. I enjoyed it, it brought me new, intense feelings, it made my heart beat faster and made me feel excited and experience a kind of joy I'd never known before.

I joked and played games with love. It tickled me gently with soft paws that suddenly revealed sharp claws. And, until the moment those claws appeared, it was fun. How is it possible to experience so many different feelings totally unlike each other in two or three hours in a single evening? Well, that's the kind of evening I've had.

It started just like any other: with the cautious, delicious hope that he would come. From six o'clock, I sat waiting for him, but calmly and patiently, as I do these days. There was one question in my mind: was I beginning to fall out of love, or was that love still there, the same as before, but settled into habit? It wasn't tormenting me or giving me any pleasure. Some time after six, Zhenya came home, and I followed her into the room with my now usual feeling of anticipation. 'Let's go for a walk!' said Zhenya.

That means no one's coming, I thought, but I agreed to go. I put my coat on slowly and reluctantly; my cheerful mood, energy and excitement had instantly disappeared. My heart felt somehow sad and empty, hope had been replaced by disappointment.

When we called round at Granny's to return the key,

Zhenya told me: 'Nina and Zhenya G. are supposed to come round at about eight.'

'We'd better not be late, then,' I remarked and smiled happily. That's wonderful. Now the whole evening will be happy, I was thinking.

But why is he coming? Dusya won't be here. Nina? No. Zhenya. No. Somehow I couldn't believe that he was attracted to Zhenya, although it could seem that way. Lyalya? But she was at the skating rink, and he knew that. And some spiteful, malicious little imp started stirring and muttering inside me: That means . . . that means . . . It wasn't even a definite thought, but I understood exactly what the imp was saying.

I felt as if I was floating on air. I didn't really believe that he liked me, but even the knowledge that he didn't like anyone else was pleasant. Zhenya was playing the piano, and I kept looking at her back, smiling blissfully. Then, Betka began barking gently and lazily, and I went out into the corridor. I could hear voices downstairs. Nina? Yes, of course, him and her. And I managed to restrain myself so as not to go dashing to unlock the door without waiting for the bell.

They came in, Nina first, then him, glancing at me indifferently the way he always does and saying: 'Good evening.' But even that didn't make me angry; it didn't dampen or darken my mood. As he took his coat off, he asked his usual question: 'Well, Nina, how's life?' and I replied cheerfully: 'The same as ever!' When I was left alone, I looked closely at my hands and thought with good-humoured irritation: They could have trembled more. Yes, and my heart could have beaten louder. Is it really fading? Idiot! What was it you were thinking two hours ago?

Zhenya and he started practising a waltz for four hands, and it was awkward for me to go in. I heard his laughter echoing happily and painfully inside me. 'Zhenya, play a waltz,' I heard Nina say, and I went in. I stood by the wall and looked at him with mixed feelings, giggling yet feeling annoyed with myself. Somehow, yesterday, he looked especially attractive, his jacket suited him particularly well, his eyes were glowing with a special merriment.

I was standing behind the lamp and couldn't see what was happening on the bed, but when I got up, I could hardly prevent myself from exclaiming out loud. He was lying with his head pressed against Nina's breasts, covering his face with his hand, and Zhenya was laughing as she ruffled his sleekly combed wavy hair. 'It suits you better like that,' she said.

When he got up, his face was thoughtful and, I think, sad. 'Right, Zhenya, let's do the composition,' he said.

Zhenya gave him some paper and began getting something else ready, but he stood there with the sheet of paper, gazing into mid-air, until Nina noticed him: 'What are you doing there? Sit down.' I was a bit surprised, but still at ease, and I listened to Lyalya [*who had just come in*] and Nina playing for a long time without suspecting anything, smiling and repeating over and over to myself: God, I love him!

I giggled. What sort of tragicomedy is this? Three sisters in love with the same pretty boy? The only thing we need now is to start causing a scene about him! No, I'll have to keep this completely to myself. I felt amused and ashamed (a stupid, false shame). And giggling only made everything seem funnier.

Nina soon left. I was sitting alone in my room when I heard someone go in to see Mum. Wanting to spend at least a moment with someone, I went in. Zhenya was lying on the bed, her face pressed into the pillow. 'What's wrong?'

'I fainted,' said Zhenya, frowning.

But I didn't believe her, and I looked at her closely.

'I didn't think I would ever faint.'

'Why not? Everybody faints. You're just anaemic.' But I wondered to myself what this meant.

'You go now, I'm going to sleep.'

That finally convinced me that something was going on. What was it? I didn't feel like laughing any more. Is it really true about Lyalya and Zhenya G.? He did know she was at the skating rink tonight, didn't he? But perhaps he was hoping . . .? I listened to what was happening on the other side of the wall, but there was absolute silence. For a moment it became depressingly quiet; there wasn't a single sound from the room.

The doubts began. Yes, this evening is probably going to end in tears, I thought. Soon, I could hear Zhenya getting up, and I began feeling less on edge. Then she came into my room. 'Let's go for a walk, Nina. I've got a headache.'

'For a walk?' I asked, and I felt nervous and out of sorts.

My doubts were soon over. We walked across the frosty, hard snow of the path on the boulevard under the dim light of the streetlamps. It was so fresh and bracing outside, but what was happening in my heart? Zhenya told me that she wasn't the one who had invited him over; it had been Lyalya. She'd noticed a long time ago that Lyalya liked Zhenya G., and now she'd deliberately left them alone to explain their feelings.

And I had to smile, ask questions and give answers as if I felt nothing, when there was a new ache tormenting my heart, and it was unbelievably painful and distressing. 'Lyalya's so lucky,' said Zhenya. 'Everybody falls in love with her.'

I felt so unhappy and lonely, because I knew that this heartache would last not just for a month or two, but my whole life.

Half an hour later, we went back home. I started copying out the study programme but, occasionally, when I couldn't stay sitting down any longer, I went over to the wall and listened. His voice was quiet and so different from the way it had been, strangely hopeless somehow, and slow. I went in to ask a question and glanced at him briefly. He was sitting leaning against the back of his chair with his arms folded, staring into the corner, and his face looked so haggard and sad. Lyalya was sitting beside him; she was serious, too.

I bit my lip and went out quickly. I felt like crying. I was beginning to feel annoyed with Lyalya. It's envy, I thought, and laughed. I was afraid to go in there and, after waiting so eagerly for him to come, now I prayed to God that he would go away. Twice more, I had to go in and look up some words I didn't understand, and both times I saw his face with that serious and hopelessly suffering look. Eventually, there was a bustling in the corridor, a coat being taken off the hook. Well, thank God for that, I thought with relief.

However, he went back into the room and was in there for so long that I decided I must be mistaken and slipped out into the corridor to look at the coat rack. His coat wasn't there. He can't bring himself to leave . . . I listened closely. Zhenya came out of the room. She's left them alone together, I thought painfully. He left very soon after that. I rushed in to the girls. They were standing there examining the composition.

Lyalya's face and voice were strangely calm and almost joyful. I sat down, thinking to myself: I won't go away. They can tell me off if they like. It doesn't matter. Perhaps they'll start talking while I'm here. But they didn't. When she was already in bed, Lyalya just asked Zhenya something in English.

'Yes,' she answered.

I stood up and went out. But, in my room, I quickly slipped off my shoes and went over to the wall. My sisters were talking about something in quiet voices. I got undressed and went to bed and, perhaps for the first time in my life, I felt I wouldn't be able to fall asleep; it was impossible to lie still. Everything was churning and bubbling inside me. I sat up, hugging my knees, and looked straight ahead with wide eyes at the bright little square in the door where the light from the kitchen came into the room.

They didn't say anything on the other side of the wall for a long time; there was just a ringing in my ears. Then Zhenya spoke in a loud, irritable voice: 'Do you hear me? Lyalya!' She answered very softly, and somehow I had the impression that she was crying. 'Well, tell him that,'

Zhenya said, more quietly this time, but remarkably clearly. I clutched my head in my hands, staggered across to the bed and fell on to it, and began sobbing silently, my face pressed against my bent knees.

I didn't understand what the feeling was inside me, but it was so distressing and painful, like something boiling up . . . and I clung on to my hair with my clenched fists, biting my lips and suppressing my convulsive sobs. Then, when I had calmed down a bit, I lay back on the pillow.

Love was over after that. I have to change everything now. I have to make myself stop loving him, I mustn't wait for him any more, mustn't ask Zhenya and Lyalya about him, and must never see him. And if I got a chance to go to the Polytechnic Institute? Don't . . . But I could tell I wasn't strong enough for that. I couldn't be here for the New Year either . . . My first impression wasn't wrong after all. Back there in the hostel, didn't I think he liked Lyalya?

And now I've just been thinking: I have to forget, I have to stop loving. I've gone too far. This morning, I lay with my eyes closed for a long time, trying not to wake up. Then I started thinking again and remembered that I have to study, feeling like this! **I thought about opium and death again.**

Evening

I'm writing my diary because I can't do anything else. My eyes ache and sting, my eyelids are puffy and it's hard to open them. I've just been sitting on the floor in the corner of my sisters' cramped room, crying. No, crying isn't a strong enough word, I was sobbing, writhing and sobbing, clutching fitfully at the slippery edge of the piano.

And it's only now that I've realized that I was still hoping right up to the final decisive moment, and that this is real love, not the same thing that I felt for Lyovka at all but more serious and stronger. It might perhaps have ended in a joke . . . if not for yesterday evening. Now, I'm not likely to forget it any time soon.

This afternoon, I was still holding on and controlling myself, and then, when Zhenya came and started playing the piano . . . I didn't say anything for a long time, trying to find an appropriate way to ask her about yesterday. But she was stubborn and didn't say anything, although she seemed quite cheerful, and there was something unkind in her silence.

'Well, then, Zhenya, did Lyalya and Zhenya G. have their intimate talk?' I finally asked cheerfully.

'Oh, no, it wasn't anything special. What kind of intimate talk could there possibly be?'

You're lying, I thought, but I didn't ask any more questions. Lyalya wasn't there; she was going to meet her group at Nina's today.

'Ah, I really shouldn't go, but I will anyway,' said Zhenya.

'Why shouldn't you?'

She didn't answer. That means that he'll be there, but it was no longer funny that we're both in love with him.

My sister was singing some old gypsy romantic song. I

stood beside the radiator with my head thrown back and listened. My heart was filled with dread, but I was still struggling to control myself. Then she started getting dressed to go out, and I started tapping out with one finger the little song that had been in my head all day: 'I shall end up under the dacha train, smiling out from under the wheels'. It was absurd, but also frightening and tragic, and that was why it moved me.

'Are you bored, Nina?'

'Yes.'

'Well, come with me then.'

'No.' But I could feel the tears welling up in my eyes and my lip trembling silently.

'Why not?'

I stuck my face into my hand and cried, feeling angry with myself and afraid that she would guess. 'It'll be boring there, too.' She tried to comfort me and suggested I walk her to the tram.

'Are you feeling low too?' I asked.

'Yes, it's sad to lose a friend.'

I guessed: 'But is he definitely in love with Lyalya?'

'Yes.'

'Has he told her how he feels?'

'Yes . . . I don't know . . . Lyalya didn't tell me the details.'

'Lyalya did tell you,' I said firmly, remembering my horrible night.

She gave in: 'Yes. Yes, he told her in a note, but Lyalya told him that she loves Zhorka.'

'She told him that? . .'

'He must be suffering very badly. This has been an

awful day. You know, he usually fools about and tells jokes, but in all the breaks at college, he pretended to be reading a book. And I can't stand it. The girls have even started to notice how low I am now. If I knew for certain that Zhenya's coming to Nina's place, I wouldn't go. But I can't just sit at home, with the misery gnawing away at me.'

Just think what kind of misery's gnawing away at me! I thought, and I suddenly wanted very much to tell her: Ah, Zhenya, you know I love him too.

But I stopped myself, thinking how stupid we both were to have fallen in love. As she got into the tram, she said: 'Some day I'll tell you all the details of how they quarrelled and why Zhenya G. was so smitten with her.'

I forgot all my caution and squeezed her hands in gratitude and looked back and waved to her for a long time after the tram started. Then I went home.

15 December 1934

This year Zhenya G. moved into the hostel. Four of them – Ozerov, Kolya N., Zhorka and he – all moved into room 208. They were young, jolly and friendly and, like all young men, they fell in love with girls and girls liked them. The girl students who often visited the hostel included Zhenya and Lyalya. Full of life, always at the forefront, always first in everything, they were keen on art and PE and stage design. And all of that meant contact with room 208.

They organized a drama club and would often meet for

rehearsals, calling in to see the boys. Last year, Lyalya already liked Zhorka a lot; now this feeling was becoming deeper and stronger. But they were just friends. I think that Lyalya's feeling for Zhenya G. was no more than friendly, and he was afraid to declare his own feelings and reasonably content with the situation.

At the very height of the rehearsals and preparations, Lyalya started to feel attracted to Zhenya G. He was the director of the play. He's one of those people that others can't help liking, women in particular. Remarkably kind and sensitive, with an enchanting smile and eyes, he was, as they say, the darling of the company.

And in this very open and friendly family of students, where it meant nothing to take someone by the arm and hug them, he turned many heads without even meaning to. But he was affectionate with everyone and the same with everyone, and it was hard to guess who he really liked. Even Lyalya couldn't guess that, and she loved him.

After the show, an attractive and wonderful girl called Dusya, with whom Kolya N. was in love, became drawn into their company. And it began to seem to many people that Zhenya G. liked her a lot. Lyalya was strong enough to call a halt to her own feelings and break off with him for a while. One day at the college, she wrote him a very insolent and insulting note. His reply was a question: 'What's wrong? What's happened?'

'I want to offend you. I have a good reason.'

He was stung and, perhaps, intrigued. 'Tell me the reason.'

Lyalya refused, and they quarrelled.

Three weeks went by, and Lyalya felt that her

infatuation had passed, that now she could look at his enchanting smile and blue eyes with indifference. He remained obstinately silent and didn't pay any attention to her. During this time, he became very close to her sister Zhenya. And, like everyone else, Zhenya fell in love with him.

She never said anything, perhaps she never even thought it, but she was happy that she often saw him, that he started coming to visit us. There was only one problem – his quarrel with Lyalya. And Lyalya decided to make up. One day in class, she went up to him and said: 'I hate the way we're treating each other. Let's make up.'

'I can't stand it either.'

Lyalya let him know the reason for their quarrel through Zhenya: she had felt fond of him at the time, but now it had passed.

'What has she done! I was in love with her!' he exclaimed. And the feeling, which was slumbering and might possibly have faded away without a trace, flared up in him with new strength. It had always been there inside him, but he had managed to conceal it so well that Lyalya had not even noticed it and actually confused it with something else. But now? What now? He was horrified. Was everything completely lost? How could he have let this happen?

And on one of those evenings when he was here with us, he decided to declare his feelings: 'Lyalya, is it really all over? Is there really nothing left inside you?'

'Nothing.'

'Well, then, I'm sorry, I won't torment you any more.' That evening, he wasn't able to work, and he sat there for a long time looking crushed, silent and strange. Happiness was so close, so possible! And now I can't bring it back. In his sadness, he began to neglect everything and everyone, and Zhenya suddenly realized what he had meant to her and what she had lost.

A painful, silent drama began. He didn't speak to Lyalya any more, he didn't approach her, but he was no longer the same boy who used to scamper around between the easels and say in a funny voice: 'I's in a-love with you, but you's not int'rested in hugginankissin.' In the group, the others began to notice that something had happened to him and to Zhenya, but they never thought of putting two and two together and adding Lyalya in as well. Her feelings are mixed now. Like any woman, she is flattered and delighted by her effect on him, but she pities him, and this pity makes her go up to him, talk to him and invite him to visit her. But why won't she make him stop loving her? What a mess.

Tomorrow is the *profotbor* at school. I'm going, but I'm horribly frightened. School again. It terrifies me to think about it . . . But I have to forget, I have to think of him and his love as no more than an interesting episode that has nothing at all to do with me. Damn!

> *I shall end up under the dacha train,*
> *Smiling out from under the wheels.*
> [From a classic Russian chanson, a little comic song
> that begins with the words: 'I shall put on my black hat
> and go to the town of Anapa . . .']

205

But love does not want to believe that there is no hope, that it is not possible to see that cute, laughing face and those glowing eyes again.

The profotbor *was a kind of vocational test to select students for training in particular trades or professions. The personal preference of the student was not considered as important as the quotas set for each profession.*

Evening

All day long I battled on really well. **I read a novella about our Russian terrorists right through without a break**, even when the painful, depressing thought of it all kept breaking through the cold words of the book. Only two days have gone by since that evening, and it's entirely natural that I'm still thinking about one thing and only one thing, but this ability to struggle with myself which I've developed today is a great success. I don't allow myself to think or remain idle and, so far, that is quite enough.

But the stifling, unanswerable, unformed question and the confusion still break through somewhere in the depths of my soul. And I only have to allow my imagination the tiniest scope, and the old familiar memories start stirring. Zhorka and Lyalya have just arrived, and they remind me so painfully of everything that I ought to forget. When Lyalya told me that he and Zhenya had gone over to Nina's place, there was a piercing pain in my heart, and tears sprang to my eyes.

17 December 1934

I went to the *profotbor* today. It was fun walking along the slippery pavement in the blue light of the streets before dawn. Wouldn't it be great to walk along every day with this unusual feeling of morning cheerfulness, on my way to my studies, not to school, but to the place that I dream about, where there are other interesting people, where I would be eager to go? Then I could say: 'See, a new life has begun for me. A new life!'

However, after a month away, I did find what was going on at school interesting. I was glad to notice that I'm not keen on any of the boys at all any more. Margosha was only an ugly, clumsy 'bear', and even mop-headed Lyovka didn't set any strings vibrating in my heart.

The girls told me about their adventures; Musya told me about Margosha and their friendship with great enthusiasm. I found it a bit strange and boring. And with horrifying clarity, I realized that there was not even the tiniest thread binding me to school any more. I'm by no means a clever or particularly intellectual girl, so why do the things that Ira, who is much cleverer than me, takes an interest in seem not only frivolous but banally stupid? Why?

Yesterday, Mum said that there's no point even thinking about the *rabfak*. They only take in people from the age of seventeen. But I can't stay in school, I simply can't. I hate it; I'm sick of it all. At the end of the day, I got bored, and I wondered how things would be in class in the weeks to come, if even on the first day I didn't feel involved.

18 December 1934

The skating rink. Bluish ice, covered with a white coating of snow. The rapid figures of skaters leaning forwards slightly. Wh-o-o-osh . . . Wh-o-o-osh . . . The ice crunches gently and scatters in little crumbs under the blade of the skate. It's dark. The running track is lost in the twilight. How pleasant it is, swaying smoothly in time to the music, sliding forward, turning and manoeuvring. A special feeling of lightness and speed.

In the circle, Lyalya is cutting the ice on the bends, lightly and confidently, and Yura T. with her. They are holding hands, describing quick semicircles together across the slippery ice. Yura is short, dressed in a blue ski jacket, and he skates excellently. He is very funny and attractive. They virtually carried me into the heated shelter, taking me by the arms on both sides. My legs were buckling, they felt so tired, and I kept losing my balance.

And again the thought of school was frightening and tormenting me. I talked to Mum about it at home.

'What is it in particular that makes you so fed up with school?' she asked.

'Everything.' I don't know exactly what it is, but I can't stay there any longer. Just imagine me walking around in the hall during break for a whole six months for no reason, listening to people's romantic adventures, stupidly shouting crude abuse after the school yobs.

'I just love sleeping,' I said to Mum. 'You forget everything, all the thoughts that drive you insane.'

'Don't be silly, Nina,' she said. 'What's this about going insane? You just need to study, and that's all.'

I laughed and regretted that, even just this once, I had tried to open up to her.

20 December 1934

Tomorrow, Zhenya G.'s coming to see us, and I'll be waiting, feeling that old heartache and longing for him again, just as I did back then. I still love him, I still think about him, although not with such a sharp and agonizing pain now. I dreamed about him today, smiling affectionately, sitting beside me and asking, 'How's life?'

But, tomorrow, Zhenya G. will come and, by a strange coincidence, it's our *profotbor* tomorrow, too, and that means I don't have any lessons. This would have made me so happy only a week ago. But now I can't go into my sisters' room and see him there, and I'll go crazy sitting in my own room. They'll be doing a composition, the way they did on all those other evenings, and, on one momentous occasion, Zhenya told me a lot of things, which aroused and inflamed my feelings again.

Two days after the dramatic bust-up, he came to her sobbing and imploring her to help him to get over it all. He told her: 'Everything could have been so different! Ah, Lyalya's to blame for everything! She should have told me.' He's lost weight and become haggard. He hasn't spoken to Lyalya since. He mopes around morosely and spends all his time with Zhenya. But, today, he suddenly cheered up. He laughed when he looked at my sisters, and he said to Zhenya: 'You know, it's passing. I went into the room today, and Lyalya and Zhorka were there. She was sitting on the bed with her legs pulled up, wrapped in her coat, and I felt almost OK as I looked at them. I only felt a little pain in my chest.'

27 December 1934

Zhenya G. was enchanting that evening, 21 December. His eyes shone so brightly, his face was so young and fresh, he talked and laughed in such a lively way. A few times he turned to talk to me, and I forgot about Lyalya and felt happy. I wasn't tormented by the thought that he was talking to me like a little child. I didn't want to think about anything, assume anything. And I passionately waited several days for him to come back, but he probably realized that love's not so easy to cope with and that his struggle's not over yet. He'll probably come for the New Year, or perhaps not. If I don't see him again for a month, then all my feelings will fade . . .

29 December 1934

It's wonderful outside today. This afternoon, there was light, soft snow falling and settling across the ground in a fluffy layer. And I could just barely feel the cold, gentle touch of the snowflakes on my face. The sky was covered with very high, very thin clouds, with the sky shining through them, and it was bright, almost sunny. And I looked out of the window at the fluffy, white, swirling blizzard with a poignant, melancholy pleasure, as if I were looking out of a prison cell.

Today, I've felt vaguely uneasy all day long. Thoughts come and go abruptly, and I can't make a single one of them out. I don't understand now what it is that I want, what I need, what's good in the world and what's bad. And whether I'll ever be satisfied with any life, and whether it's worth living at all. And my dreams of idiotic, hopeless happiness have got tangled up with what they call an idea, with something big, incomprehensible, strange, indefinite and fascinating. I don't know what to set my mind to, I don't know who I'm going to be . . . Everything somehow seems stupid, incomprehensible and dark.

30 December 1934

Many days have passed since Kirov was murdered in the Smolny Institute by Nikolaev, a member of an underground group of terrorists. There have been lots of leading articles in the newspapers screaming about the event, many speakers parroting bombast and Soviet time-servers waving their fists in the air and shouting histrionically over the heads of the workers: 'Finish off the viper!' 'Shoot the traitor whose cowardly shot has torn from our ranks . . .' and so on. And many so-called Soviet citizens, completely abandoning every last trace of human compassion and dignity, have raised their hands like sheep in support of the firing squad.

It's hard to believe that in the twentieth century there is a corner of Europe that has been occupied by medieval barbarians, where primitive, primeval ideas coexist so oddly with science, art and culture. Before the investigation even began, before anything was even known about any conspiracy, more than a hundred people, White Guards, were killed simply because they were unfortunate enough to find themselves on USSR territory.

Today, they shot another fourteen of the 'conspirators'. So that means more than a hundred lives for one Bolshevik life. I couldn't help recalling the nineteenth century, the reign of Alexander II and the action taken by 'The People's Will'. What an outcry there was, what indignation the public felt about the execution of the six killers. Why is nobody incensed now? Because now it's regarded as entirely in the order of things?

Why will nobody now say quite openly and frankly that they are all scoundrels?

And what right do these Bolsheviks have to deal with the country and the people in such a cruel, arbitrary manner, to proclaim outrageous laws so insolently in the name of the people, to lie as they do and hide behind big words that no longer have any meaning – 'socialism' and 'communism'?

How can they call him a coward, a man who went to his death openly and boldly, a man who was not afraid of dying for the sake of an idea, and who is better than all the so-called leaders of the working class put together? What are they thinking abroad now? Are they really going to say: 'That's the way it ought to be.' Oh, no! My God, when will all this change? When will it really be possible to say that all the power belongs to the people and that we have complete equality and freedom? This is the rule of the Inquisition, not socialism!

Nina is referring to a historical event: in December 1879, the Narodnaya Volya (People's Will), a radical revolutionary group, set off a bomb under the dining room of the Winter Palace. It was their second attempt at assassinating the Tsar. The floor was damaged, but the Tsar, who was late down to supper, escaped unharmed. The revolutionaries enjoyed popular support, and a massive row surrounded their execution.

1 January 1935

And now it's the New Year. I don't think I've ever seen it in so ... strangely, and it has certainly never started so painfully. Yesterday, I felt elated all day long; I waited impatiently for my sisters and I was happy to help Lyalya move the furniture around and tidy up. We took the bed and the table out of their room, and that made it spacious and comfortable. The first to arrive were Andrei B. and then Nina. Andrei kept paying Lyalya compliments, and she threw her head back and laughed as she teased him.

At nine o'clock, everyone arrived together, with the exception of Kolya N., Seryozha K. and Dusya. I couldn't help exclaiming out loud when nine people walked past me at once. I nodded to some of them as they walked by. Yurka T. gave me his hand. Zhenya G. was wearing a fluffy, light-brown jacket and nice grey trousers and, as I looked at him, I kept asking myself: Do I love him now or not?

For the first few moments of the dancing, I even forgot to think about Zhenya G. But then this new, unpleasant feeling took hold of me, and I caught myself following him closely with my eyes and quickly looked away when I realized what I was doing. He was dancing with everybody except Lyalya, but he wasn't as cheerful as he used to be. That evening, I felt very much alone and unwanted. I wanted someone to come up to me and say a couple of words to me or at least invite me to dance. But nobody there could care less about me, a stupid, crazy little girl.

At supper, I sat at the end of the table, with my sister Zhenya on one side of me and Zhenya G. just round the near corner. Oh, I was happy about that! Occasionally, I turned my head to glance at his cute profile. But, then, even this nearness turned out to be torture. From time to time, he would offer me a sandwich or some wine, and it was horrible to think that he was only doing it out of politeness. It was painful!

Before they left, they danced again. But something happened to Zhorka: he was sick, and Zhenya G. didn't come out of the kitchen for ages and, when he came back, he looked concerned. Zhorka wasn't able to go home; they laid him out on the trunk and left him there for the night. Yurka, half-drunk, Nikolai and Zhenya G. got ready to leave. The four of us stood there: me pressing myself against the wall, our Zhenya, Yurka and Zhenya G.

'I'm going to give up drinking now, on principle,' said Yurka T.

'And so you should,' I blurted out, looking straight ahead of me and feeling Zhenya G. glance at me. Then, unable to stand it any longer, I turned to him; he looked at me seriously and then smiled, and his eyes sparkled gently. And I stared into them for a long time, too, and smiled back at him.

He hadn't spoken much to Lyalya, but when he did, his attention was completely focused on her, his eyes became tender, glowing and deep. And then I felt upset and afraid. When the boys were saying goodbye, Lyalya suddenly said: 'Zhenechka, come here,' and called him aside.

I watched him and my sister closely and noticed out of the corner of my eye how tenderly he took hold of her hands. 'I's in a-love with you,' Lyalya said in a sly, affectionate voice.

'I's in a-love too,' Zhenya said in a quiet, restrained voice. 'Everyone got so drunk, you were the only one who stayed sober and good.'

'Well, now,' he drawled jokingly. He laughed and suddenly grabbed hold of her head between his hands and ran his fingers through her hair: 'Ah, you're my Olga.'

I couldn't bear this and turned away towards the table. 'All the best, Nina,' he said and held out his hand, and I actually felt glad to shake it. That was the last glimpse I had of the sweet, flushed face I love so much. Yura was very drunk; he kissed Zhenya and Lyalya's hands and almost wept as he begged forgiveness for buying the fourth bottle.

I went to bed at three, but even though it was so late and I'd drunk wine, I couldn't get to sleep, Zhenya! Zhenya! Oh, this New Year's Eve! I kept remembering different bits of the evening. Everywhere, no matter where

I go, no one wants me there, I'm a stranger, I feel stupid and even ridiculous.

4 January 1935

Musya and Tolka were at Ira's place . . . I quarrelled with Musya. I was sulky and angry, stoking up the pain and misery in my heart. We started talking about suicide. I told her about my attempt to poison myself, and everybody laughed at the comic ending. Then I kept asking Ira to give me some opium. I got home after ten, thinking: Will he still be here or not? and trying to make myself stop hoping that he would be.

Nina K. and Zhenya G. were already getting ready to leave and Nina was standing in the hallway with her coat on, but he had gone back into the room for some reason and, as soon as I heard his voice, I went through into my room. I wanted to come back out and say hello, but I wanted to keep the promise I'd made to myself, so I waited for them to leave.

But then I quickly put my coat on and went dashing down the stairs with Betka: At least I can look at him from a distance, I thought. Downstairs, I could still hear their voices, and then it sounded like they'd stopped. I picked up the dog and waited and, all at once, I heard steps coming upstairs. At first, I wanted to run back up and hide, but I controlled myself and calmly began walking down. When he caught sight of Betka, Zhenya G. halted in amazement on the gloomy staircase, and I caught a smile of surprise on his face. 'Aha, hello,' he said. We walked past each other.

'Nina, wait, I won't be long,' he called from above me. Involuntarily, I stopped for a moment.

'No problem,' I heard Nina K. call, and I set off again, trying to gloss over my mistake.

From the windows at Granny's place, I looked out for a long time at the dark corner of the building from behind which he and Nina K. would appear. My heart was full of such black despair, such dreary pain . . . All of a sudden, I remembered about the opium. It doesn't matter if it's mixed with other things, I'll drink it all. It should work. It's best to have done with everything. How good would that be. I've had enough.

As I was going to bed, I poured the dark drops into a cup; there were sixty in all. Granny will be so annoyed with me when she notices they're missing, I thought. She'll ask where I put them. But it doesn't matter, perhaps I'll die. I drank the drops and lay down. Quite soon, I began to feel a weakness in my hands, my head felt heavy and it ached, I felt sleepy. I soon fell into a very deep sleep. But now I feel awful, sick and nauseous.

The censors must have missed this reference to Nina's attempted suicide. Similar sections elsewhere in the diary are underlined. The attempt failed – the dose was not high enough to do anything but send her to sleep and make her feel sick.

7 January 1935

Yesterday, I asked Zhenya: 'What would you do if you liked someone who loved someone else?'

'You have to forget him,' she replied, giving me an understanding, knowing look.

Forget? Yes, forget. All right, I'll try it, I'll forget. After all, why shouldn't I forget? I thought. For a moment, I felt determined to do it.

Then Zhenya began talking about him: 'He has such tired, old grey eyes, circled with wrinkles.'

'That means that his love for Lyalya has affected him very strongly.'

'No, he says it's all passed off now and that it was a mistake.'

So he doesn't love her? My heart started beating faster. Maybe I should try again. Perhaps it is worth trying? And I shifted the conversation back again to the original topic. Zhenya asked me about the kind of boy I liked, what group he was in. It was amusing to lie to her, I enjoyed it. If only she knew who I'm really thinking about! . . .

I hesitated for a long time about what to do and finally told myself: I'm going to make the effort to forget him, if only because it's the hardest choice and I must never take the easy way out. After all, we can never have a normal relationship, and seeing him once a week and waiting and suffering every day is stupid, to say the least.

And now I am making the effort. I think about anything else and, the moment I remember him, I tell myself 'enough' and cut the thought short. I quickly think about something else and fantasize about that instead. But I only have to start slipping into a half-doze and I suddenly catch myself transported to a different setting, making lively conversation with Zhenya G., and I always do it so well, I'm never at a loss. And then, again, I have to shake off the cobweb of dreams that I'm entangled in, rebuke myself and think of something else.

9 January 1935

It's weird. For the last two days, I've been struggling doggedly against love, but it's having exactly the opposite effect. Not only have I not forgotten about him but I think about him all the time. Or rather, I don't think about him, I don't allow myself to think about him. But he's always on my mind, almost subconsciously. And I'm alone all day. Sometimes, I wish that school would start again soon . . .

Yesterday, Zhenya said that she was starting to love Zhenya G. again. She had got over him but now, studying together every evening, the old feelings have come back. Zhenya sat playing the piano for a long time, dreaming and enjoying the sweet torment of love. She asks me if my infatuation has faded or not, is it a good person that I love. I don't describe him to her at all, because . . . she might suddenly recognize that it's him.

17 January 1935

They've changed our day off. I just can't imagine it,

219

everybody being at home, my sisters and my mother, while I have to go to school. No, it's terrible! And so odd. We have classes tomorrow, but the spirit of revolt has permeated us too deeply and ineradicably. **All the injustices of the leadership absolutely infuriate us, they make us fight and attempt to defend our rights. We never accept things without a struggle. And we're struggling this time, too.**

Yesterday, as Ira and I were walking home from school, we decided to start a petition. We have nothing to lose in any case – but we might gain something. Composing it was a long, painful process. We don't even have any substantial arguments for claiming a common day off, but we've tried to create them out of nothing. Just as Ira was about to copy it out, a question suddenly came up: what if they pick on her as the ringleader? Wouldn't it be a good idea to have it typed? 'Let's go to Linde.'

'Yes, let's.'

We chuckled a bit as we put on our coats and set off. He wasn't at home. Just like the first time, his mother came to the door and told us, struggling to get the words out: 'Dima's at school.'

'But today's our day off, and there aren't any lessons.'

'Really? But where's Dima then?'

The incomprehension and surprise must have shown in our faces. 'We don't know.' Ira wrote him a note and left it with the draft of the petition.

This morning, we went round to see him again. We were afraid there might be some kind of misunderstanding.

'Is Dima home?' I asked when the woman opened the door.

And before she had time to answer, I heard a deep bass voice from behind the door: 'Aha, that's for me.' We went in. 'Come in, come in,' said Linde, belching out the words with his whole body, flailing his arms about in his usual way.

His room was untidy, and there was a typewriter standing on the table. 'Look, I've typed it,' he said and handed me a sheet of paper. 'I've changed a few things.'

'Aha, that's what we wanted you to do.' And while I stuck my face into the sheet of paper and pretended to be reading it, Ira asked what he'd been doing in school the day before.

'Ah? Me? M-mm. But it was our day off, I went to the cinema.'

'And are you going in today?'

'No, I can't today.'

'Then it's a good thing we called round.'

'Yes. I've still got to go for an X-ray.'

He stood there behind a chair, leaning against its back. He was taller than me and slim, and his figure looked good in his blue suit, but I couldn't make out his face at all. When we came out on to the stairs, I leaned against the banisters, literally sobbing and choking in silent laughter.

But, at school, there was a disappointment in store for us. The boys weren't very keen to take up the cause. They messed around and signed with such fancy signatures that we had to tear off that part of the sheet. They seemed so alien and unappealing that day. And, once again, I felt like going away somewhere. And that was on the very first day! **But, by the end of the day, we had managed to persuade everyone**, apart from two (Valya Leitin and Margosha) and Antipka, who turned obstinate for some reason.

Letters of complaint and petitions were generally accepted by the authorities. The Soviet people saw letter-writing as a democratic way of having their opinions and feedback heard; Stalin and the governing bodies received enormous amounts of this type of mail. On a more sinister level, these letters also allowed the authorities to 'know their enemy' and were used to identify troublemakers. Nina certainly shows herself to be a ringleader here.

20 January 1935

School . . . A feverish, stupefying haze . . . Someone's eyes, someone's smile . . . The hordes of laughing pupils . . . Moments when everything's so dismally run-of-the-mill. But, more often, the intoxication of mad pranks and banal rudenesses. Mocking Valya 'the crocodile' Leitin, who's so silly and repugnant, watching Lyovka and Margosha, who's so obnoxious yet very interesting. I've been trying for a long time to get a good look at his big, dark, black eyes and his beautifully arched brows. For the last few days, Lyovka's been coming in a suit with a white collar, and he looks so charming that I'm afraid I might start feeling something for him again.

30 January 1935

We're having fantastic winter weather now. It's warm, and the snow's falling. It falls with an infinite, steady slowness, light and silent. The white flakes swirl and eddy in the light of the streetlamps. The air is exceptionally pure and fresh, and my heart feels unusually calm and easy. The feeling of youth, energy and joy in life is intense.

Today was a crazy day. At the beginning of the second lesson, before the biology teacher had arrived, someone started throwing snowballs. I noticed when the game was already in full swing and Valya L. was standing on a bench, raking in armfuls of cold, crumbly snow through the open window and sprinkling it all over Mila Egorova, a little plump girl who was trying, in a feeble sort of way, to defend herself.

As she was chasing him round the classroom with the white fluffy flakes in her hair, the biology teacher came in: 'What's going on here? Snowballs? Egorova? Leitin? I'm going to get the head of studies. This is disgraceful!' And she went out.

'You fool, Crocodile,' Margosha blurted out angrily. But he'd been throwing snowballs and had been hit himself.

The head of studies soon arrived. 'Look what they've done,' the biology teacher said to her. 'The whole floor and the tables are covered in snow, Egorova's hair and shoulders were all covered in it.'

'I see!' said the head of studies, a small but all-powerful despot. And it was strange to see this little, ordinary woman with scornful blue eyes dealing with the boys so boldly and confidently. She seemed in control: 'Follow me, Ivyanskaya and Sharova.'

Surely I'm not going to be left behind, I thought in annoyance, and I was ready to ask her to take me as well when she said, 'Lugovskaya'. I smiled slightly. 'Come out!' she ordered, and we skipped cheerfully out of the classroom. I had such a bizarre, new feeling, almost pride, on this, my first ever trip to see the headmaster. But, even so, my heart was pounding in alarm: 'Girls, we have to agree on what to say. They must have called us out because of maths. Remember, they took our names down then.' And, taking advantage of the absence of the head of studies, we consulted on the stairs in an excited whisper. Then, Liza K., Raya, Ira and the boys came up.

We straggled across the hall in an untidy herd, chuckling and whispering, and our little tormentor said in a loud, angry voice: 'This is disgraceful! You don't want to study in a Soviet school! You do nothing but mess around! There's no place for you here!'

We stopped outside the headmaster's office. 'The boys will go in first.' When we were left on our own, we grew more elated, we found the unusual situation so deliciously funny.

By the end of the lesson, we were in such a crazy mood that we completely stopped feeling even the slightest bit worried and were laughing non-stop. During break, we dashed back through the hall to the classroom at a noisy gallop. Then we went for lunch. **The boys who were being interrogated soon got back. The school authorities had been trying to make them reveal some underground counter-revolutionary organization** and apparently abused them in really bad language.

What pitiful, despicable cowards and Bolsheviks! They're so afraid of everything that they can even turn innocent jokes like what the boys got up to into something serious. The boys had written some kind of spoof document with a decree from the Emperor Croc II. Naturally, the poor Soviet custodians of childhood have taken fright. Such a horrific, unheard-of reaction in the USSR!

Even schools, these little children's worlds, which you'd hardly think would be infiltrated by the oppressive influence of 'workers' power', haven't been left out of it. The Bolsheviks are partially right. They are cruel and barbarically crude in their cruelty but, from their own point of view, they're right. If they didn't intimidate children from an early age, they soon wouldn't have any power left. But they raise us as submissive slaves, ruthlessly exterminating any spirit of protest.

Any hint of a critical attitude, the slightest hint of free will and independence, is punished harshly. And the Bolsheviks are achieving their goal. Where the spirit of protest used to grumble faintly in the depths of people's hearts, they have finally killed it off, and where it was speaking out loudly and openly, they have driven it down so deep that it will never surface again.

But we could never have imagined that we, too, would be summoned on a matter of politics, and we giggled light-heartedly as we waited our turn. Finally, the boys came out. 'Klempert and Egorova!' the head of studies called, and the two girls left us.

'Lads,' we shouted to our boys. 'What else did they talk about?'

'Ah, they keep trying to find a secret party!'

The girls soon came out. 'Your turn.'

The three of us stepped up.

'Ivyanskaya first,' the head of studies said.

I was beginning to feel a bit uneasy and even afraid, standing outside the headmaster's hateful door. I could hear Musya's quiet, squeaky voice saying something. 'All right, don't forget what to say,' I whispered to Ira. They called us both in together.

The head of studies was standing there, and **the headmaster, small with broad shoulders and a terribly unpleasant expression on his face, was sitting at the desk. His face, with its sparse features, coarse and devoid of any inner beauty or even fellow-feeling, was the typical face of a worker, a man who has been around and been hardened by it, a repulsive man who owes his rise in the world to his party ticket, his mean character and his ability to carry out all orders from above diligently, without thinking. He looked as if he spent all his time in the vulgar company of thieves, or perhaps prostitutes, but certainly not in a school.**

When we went in, he nodded briefly and pointed to a spot by the wall. Ira was standing there with her hands clasped behind her back and her head lowered slightly. I leaned back with my elbows against the wall, perhaps too casually for a conversation with such a high-ranking and self-important individual, and looked around at the desk and the furniture. The head of studies fussed about, not looking at us and saying to the headmaster: 'The same

226

questions for these as for Ivyanskaya. It's the same case.'

She left, and he began our appalling and disgusting interrogation. 'Didn't you have some kind of discussion in connection with the death of Kirov and Kuibyshev [*Valerian Vladimirovich Kuibyshev (1888–1935), a member of the Central Committee and chairman of the USSR Gosplan or State Planning Committee*]?'

'There were only the public meetings,' I said, not completely understanding what he meant.

'No, among yourselves, the pupils?' His voice was very calm, almost gentle and ingratiating.

'No, we didn't have any discussions about that.'

'But didn't you say that a lot of people seemed to have died this year?'

'Ah-ah! We did talk about that,' said Ira. 'Kirov, Kuibyshev and Sobinov [*the tenor singer*] have died, and Ippolitov-Ivanov [*Mikhail Mikhailovich Ippolitov-Ivanov (1859–1935), a famous composer and conductor, a pupil of Rimsky-Korsakov*] just recently . . .'

'Well, and didn't you say anything else?'

'No, I don't remember anything.'

He paused expectantly, tapping his pen on the desk.

'But I don't think there's anything reprehensible about that, is there?' I blurted out, unable to contain myself.

He looked at me with his hideous, flat green eyes, like a cat's. 'Reprehensible? We've only called you in to explain a few things to you. We're simply asking a few questions, and you are obliged to answer.'

And then, immediately, as if he'd just remembered who he was, he added, in a voice that had become harsh and more severe: 'Stand up properly!' I altered my position and looked at him with a feeling of mounting irritation, fury and burning shame at his rebuke. 'You answer, and I draw conclusions: that's not up to you. I don't even allow the teachers to draw conclusions when they're talking to me.'

A fine dictator! It was the first time in my life that I'd come across so-called 'local-level power'.

'And who else did you talk about this with?'

'No one else. Just the two of us.'

'Then why do the others here know about it?' he asked, and pointed to the sheet of paper covered in writing lying in front of him.

'Perhaps the others spoke about it too?' Ira said.

Every question was followed by a pause, and every pause made me feel calmer. Eventually, apparently thinking things over, he said: 'All right, go.' The nurse showed us which class to go to. It was physics, but we couldn't even listen let alone answer questions, and we kept whispering to each other, alarmed and angry. Kolya K. came across to sit with us, a horrible, sneaky small boy with ginger hair and protruding ears. 'Well, what happened, Luga?'

'Nothing much. The same as with the boys. About Kirov and the others.'

'We've got informers in our group.'

'Yes, they're everywhere,' I replied, evasively and cautiously.

The summons to the director had set me thinking that the strangest and most suspicious person among us was Kolya K., and somehow I was certain that he was the one who had told on us. We couldn't wait for that lesson to end. During the break, the three of us got together – me,

Musya and Ira – on the little balcony and told each other about our talks with the headmaster. He had asked Musya: 'Don't you have a friend called Lyalya?' And she'd written down her name, school and class.

That's really going too far. What right do they have to interfere in personal friendships outside school? What appalling things are going on! They didn't do that even in the tsarist schools! The administration has never been so cowardly and petty and pitiful. Yes. We do have an informer in our group: someone must have told about the ill-fated letter from Lyalya K. [*a friend outside the school*] to Musya that the boys stole.

When we went into the classroom after the bell, the headmaster was already there. Everybody was standing. He was saying something in his obnoxious voice, not pronouncing the letter 's' and the sibilants properly, and that was really vile. Then we learned that, before we came in, he'd been talking about the petition about the day off, the one Ira and I had instigated and given to the head of studies ages ago. But wasn't it odd that we were the only three who had gone out into the hall, and everybody else was sitting in the classroom when the headmaster came in? He went over everything: that game of snowballs had reminded him of all our sins, real and imaginary.

Nina was lucky not to get into more serious trouble with the headmaster given her outspoken views on the system of informers that operated at school.

10 February 1935

I could go on reading Chekhov's stories and plays for ever. Oh, I just keep coming across myself in them over and over again! And that hopeless, despairing tone, that pessimism and helplessness are so familiar to me, so like me. How could I possibly not recognize myself in his Ivanov and Treplev! All of them are failures, dissatisfied with life. They're all tormented by social stagnation, a stifling, musty atmosphere. But what can I do? That's the way life is, life is like that, and it never has been and never will be any other way. What are energy, enthusiasm, joy and happiness? Just moments we experience only rarely in life. Writers love to add them all together and create an idealistic picture of life, but it's a lie, not life.

Yesterday, Ira had a date with Lyovka. They're already friends, they'll be happy, they'll have lengthy conversations on long, dark evenings, and I think I envy them. Envy! What a horrible feeling. It pursues me everywhere, poisoning my life. It's always asking the same question: Why aren't you like that? Why haven't you got that? Why can't you do that?

It's all right if Ira provokes only envy in me, but I'm afraid that it might turn into jealousy – after all, Lyovka does do something for me. I like watching him more than the others, his good looks excite me, his radiant blue eyes are bewitching! He looks tall and funny in his short jacket and, yesterday, he almost made me feel that I love him. Yes, and he was with Ira, he was talking to her, he loves her. I'm afraid! Could this really be jealousy?

He told Ira a lot about his life, about how he used to be a delinquent. Lyovka a delinquent . . . and now he's so charming. But you can still see that he knows all sorts of things, that he's been through a lot and seen a lot, and yet, despite that, he still looks like such a little boy. No, what rubbish I'm talking! Surely I'm not in love? What nonsense! But what is this? I want to think about him now as much as I want to think about Zhenya G., who still hasn't arrived back in Moscow, by the way. What's happened to him? I think Lyovka's overshadowing him . . .

The great Anton Chekhov (1860–1904), whose works Nina admired, was born in southern Russia. Ivanov and The Seagull were two of his most important plays and were first performed around the turn of the century. Treplev, a character in The Seagull, suffers from unrequited love, becomes depressed and commits suicide. Ivanov, a frustrated idealist, also suffers from serious depression and romantic turmoil. It is easy to see why Nina identified with them.

21 February 1935

Ira wasn't at school today. I passed on a note from her to Lyovka and started watching him. During the early lessons he was at least even-tempered, if not really cheerful. He talked with the boys occasionally and was told off several times. But after that! After that, he didn't smile once for the rest of the day, he didn't crack a single joke and sat there on his own with his face in a book. From time to time, he turned round, and then I could see him sitting there motionless, leaning on the desk and staring into space with his big, serious eyes. And his face looked so thoughtful, almost sad.

And, once again, I couldn't help watching him and asking myself if I was in love with him. He livened up a bit in the last lesson and teased Shunya a bit, and I caught his glance several times when it sparkled with laughter. His tousled hair was like a gold halo above his high, white forehead.

Yes, I'm infatuated with Lyovka again. Now what can I do? It's still not too late to resist, but what will happen next? I don't understand my feelings for him! They're not the same as they were in fifth class, and they're not what I feel for Zhenya G. I don't want attention from him, I don't want him to write me notes but, even so, I feel a strong pull towards him. It forces me to keep turning my head in his direction to look at him; I can't help myself. How can I resist this feeling that's engulfing and enveloping me?

24 February 1935

My sisters have completely broken off with Zhenya G. now, they have nothing to do with him at all. Our Zhenya has been trying to uproot her love for him, and I don't know if she has managed it, but neither she nor Lyalya says a word about him now. It's as if he simply doesn't exist for them. And even I have almost totally forgotten about him, although now and then I think of him and feel I'd like to see him, to resurrect his face in my memory.

And what about Lyovka? He called me Ninka today,

and I liked the way it felt. Ira said to me once: 'You know, he's very fond of you.' I didn't ask exactly what he'd said about me, but it seemed strange that Lyovka could still have any friendly feelings towards me. But, then, I can't look at him the way I look at myself and the girls.

Last night, there was a fire. I had almost fallen asleep when I heard Lyalya's voice calling: 'Mum! Come and see it spread!' I ran into her room. There was a broad, pinkish-crimson glow flickering behind the house and occasionally flaring up into a semicircle of flame. It looked like the sun rising. Just for a moment, I felt terrified, a sharp pang of fear shot through my heart and a lump rose stubbornly in my throat.

I sat on the table by the window for a long time, watching the red glow and thinking, trying to suppress a thrill of horror at the thought that life is such a terrible thing and I've seen only the rosy side, but the side that sometimes opens up and brings death was something unknown and terrible. And afterwards, when I was in bed, weird thoughts came into my head.

I felt frightened of the darkness: it seemed to be full of living creatures following me in malevolent silence, and this watchful silence was frightening. Why does darkness affect people like that? I'm sure there was nobody in the room, and there couldn't have been. What was there to be afraid of?

The thing people are most frightened of is the unknown. And darkness is the unknown. Or perhaps we really are surrounded by other beings, invisible and silent. Perhaps there is a life after death and people who have

233

died are here; we can't see them, they can't do any harm, but we feel their presence. This is an oppressive, scary feeling.

4 March 1935

How bizarre! It was spring, the snow had almost completely melted, the buds had swollen and were poised eagerly in anticipation of warm, fragrant days and, suddenly, we have frost again. Now, Irina and Lyovka have nowhere to meet. Her mother's at her place, and she might suspect something, and it's cold outside, so we decided to arrange for them to meet at my place sometimes. I'm in the strange position of helping to bring someone I like together with another girl.

But not only do I not feel jealous of Ira, I don't have any bad feelings at all towards her. I think that my liking for Lyovka is friendly, nothing more, and I'm beginning to feel OK about it all. Lyovka came at about nine o'clock, but Ira wasn't here yet. It was weird and exciting to see a male visitor here for me. It was the first time.

While Lyovka was taking his coat off, I stood there in the doorway of the room, laughing and wondering how to sort things out so as not to put him in an awkward situation – after all, he'd come to a strange house. Lyalya came out at the sound of a male voice; she probably thought it was someone to see her. I didn't turn my head and stood there, choking with laughter, imagining her surprise. She said hello, and Lyovka came through into my room.

With his tall, thin, well-proportioned body, he looked

gorgeous in his grey shirt with the sleeves turned up. We chatted for a while, just a few phrases, and then, sensing that silence was about to set in and that Lyovka was feeling very uncomfortable, I suggested a game of chess. But, just then, Ira arrived. I sat them both down and left them alone for a while.

Mum didn't ask any questions; she just said with a smile: 'That's the first time a blond lad has visited your home, Nina.'

'Aha.' I was grateful for the simple, tactful way she spoke to me.

'Whose admirer is he? Ira's, I think?'

'Why does he have to be an admirer, he just called round.' But I thought to myself that my sisters must have said something.

7 March 1935

A few days ago, Lyovka and Ira had their second meeting at my place. I sat them down in my room and went into the girls' room. There was no one else in the flat. Struggling to suppress the uneasy annoyance I felt with myself and a certain curiosity as well, I immersed myself in a book. The door into the corridor was open, and I heard someone come out of my room. Who's that? I wondered, and I listened closely, although I didn't show it and carried on reading.

Finally, I heard Ira's low, muffled voice calling me from outside. I was puzzled – Ira was standing there, tall and slim, her face turned to the wall, holding her head with that beautiful black hair in her hand. 'Ira, what's going on?'

'Nothing. You go in to him.'

'But tell me what's happened?'

'I told you, nothing.'

Lyovka was sitting there, leaning his elbows on the table, and he gave me a serious, indifferent look, and I thought he seemed a bit embarrassed. But he acted as if nothing had happened. 'What's wrong, Lyovka?'

'I don't know,' he said, curling up the corners of his mouth good-naturedly.

'But something must have happened?'

'She just got up and walked out,' he said with a grin.

'What were you talking about, at least?'

'Nothing at all. I was sitting here not saying anything, and she just walked out.'

'Oh, so she walked out because you didn't say anything?' We both fell silent again for a moment, and I racked my brains, trying to think of something else to say. 'Why don't you go and comfort her?'

'What an idea. Let her calm down a bit first. She's all right.' He laughed and started looking like the usual Lyovka again. I couldn't see his face from the other side of the lamp.

'Well, go on, call her,' I said as I went out. Ira was sitting on the bed in my sisters' room with her head thrown back, staring upwards with her big, sad black eyes.

I couldn't help listening to their voices, now lively and cheerful again. Lyovka laughed, and I suddenly wanted to see his large mouth laughing in that cheeky, impudent way. I closed the door, annoyed, and switched on the radio so that I wouldn't hear them. Soon Mum came back: 'What's this, are you arranging their dates for them?'

I thought for a moment and said: 'Aha.'

I didn't feel like lying, and it didn't seem necessary. Somehow, I wanted to be more open with her, I thought she'd understand. We spent the whole evening talking. Mum forbade any more visits of this kind except on special occasions. And, as I should have expected, she said very harsh, negative things about love. I defended Ira because, at the same time, I was defending myself. Mum said: 'Love is nothing but nonsense. And if it comes, you have to fight it. It's a load of rubbish!' And that caught me off balance.

After all, I had enough respect for Mum's opinion not to simply ignore what she said, and now she had gone and shaken the very foundations of my whole way of thinking. Love was nothing but nonsense? That was a twist! Without even pausing to think, Mum had called the one thing that brings me to life, gives me happiness and energy, gives the whole of life meaning, nonsense. Incredible!

I thought of dozens of novels and couldn't remember an opinion like that in a single one of them. Everything that I wanted to live for, that seemed so fine, important and serious, it was all nothing but a stupid whim. Mum's opinion on this matter is very simple (it must have been formed over the years or else she has changed): love means marriage, children, and so forth. So is the thing that seems so extraordinary and beautiful to me a mirage?

11 March 1935

Yesterday, there was a party at Musya's place; I was there, and Musya, Ira, Lyovka and Tolka. It was a boring party, full of pointless conversation, as always. I just can't break free of Lyovka's charm, and things are starting to get ridiculous. Looking into his eyes, listening to the wonderful squeaky way he giggles – it all gives me immense pleasure. And yet, as a person, I find him almost repulsive.

I came home in a foul mood. Was my emotional balance really going to be disturbed again? My sisters told me two sensational pieces of news that had been in the newspapers just recently. On Sadovaya-Triumfalnaya Square, four boys had started pestering two girls and then wanted to see them home. In a secluded back-street, they started trying to put their arms round them. One broke free and ran off, but the other suddenly dropped dead on the spot. She'd been stabbed in the chest with a knife.

The other news was that, a few days ago, Tonya P., **a girl from my sisters' group, was walking back home from the theatre with her boyfriend. Four boys came up to them and suddenly started punching her boyfriend in the face. Tonya naïvely tried to stand up for him, and the four of them immediately set about her as well. The boyfriend seized his chance and leapt over a fence and stood there in safety, watching to see what would happen next. The hooligans beat up the girl for a while and then left, and her boyfriend went back to her and managed to get her home. 'That's socialism, that's Soviet culture!' I said, fuming with rage.**

An argument started, and I went back to my room,

barely able to stand. My fury was choking me, it was rising up like a heavy, burning lump in my throat. **I think I'd shoot all of them for their bragging, for the lies, for all the lives that this much-vaunted socialism is built on.** And I'm a woman. What can I do about it? This eternal dependence on men, this helplessness and stupidity are driving me insane. And there's no way out. Damn it! I can't take a single step on my own. It's awful!

Will men ever be decent and, if they are, will it make me happy to have them treat me respectfully as an act of charity? Mum has a lot to answer for. Why has she been poisoning our thoughts ever since we were little: don't go out alone, something bad might happen to you. Hooligans aren't enough for her! Her fear that we might be raped is an appalling threat hanging over our entire lives.

14 March 1935

My schoolmates don't by any means consider it cool or clever to sit mulling over your homework assignments for days on end, to study hard and seriously; they refer to people like that disdainfully as 'model students' and 'swots'. But just you try getting 'unsat.' Then those pupils snort and think: Stupid lazy fool. Now, just you try balancing between these two stools without falling off to one side or the other.

Does it mean pretending in order to fit in with the way other people think? Yes, of course. But other people's opinions always play an important part in the way people behave, whether they're right or not. You have to be excessively intelligent and independent and stand a whole head taller than the people around you in order not to attach any importance to the opinions of others. You also have to have no respect for people, but there are many people that I do respect, and so I can't help taking what they think into account.

And it always seems strange, somehow, that in school, an institution established for studying, people actually despise this studying, put it last in their lives; it's seen as almost reprehensible to study really hard, to play by the rules and be considered a good student. What's behind this weird, centuries-old struggle between the school administration and the pupils? Do we really have to try to provoke our teacher, to play dirty tricks on him? Why can't we be on friendly terms, helping each other . . . ?

Something has to be broken down, some sort of barrier that separates the pupils from the teachers; things have to be approached differently. After all, the teacher is always forbidding the pupil to do something, causing unpleasantness, making critical comments, and that makes us furious. The conditions just don't exist for developing the good sides of your character – after all, bad instincts are always dominant, and they don't allow for any sense of satisfaction in the spiritual sense. Isn't it odd that the world is built on hostility, or is that a law of nature?

This Thursday, I was a little bit lazier than I should have been. I got so many 'goods' that I felt a bit ashamed to face Ira and the others who had got 'excellent'. And it was especially embarrassing and hurtful for me to realize that I have no ability, that I'm more stupid than the others. I'm two years older than many of them, and I'm not ahead of them but probably behind.

Here's a question: why is my pessimism passing and starting to be replaced by a more normal attitude? Either it's a morbid condition with no foundation in reality that is often found in young girls during adolescence or it's the result of oppressively serious thoughts. Perhaps the first explanation was partly true, but the second was definitely more important.

After all, there was a time when an hour couldn't go by without me thinking about my unfortunate appearance. It was bad enough if I remembered it myself, but when someone else reminded me of it . . . Living with terrible thoughts that never leave you, the knowledge of your own ugliness and a concealed envy of everyone else that borders on hatred . . . How could you not come to hate life?

Now, it's coming to an end. The operation has played a part: even if it didn't correct my eye, it has affected my feelings about it. They've begun to fade away. There've been times when life has been so great that it has smothered them completely. But I do still remember my stigma sometimes and feel the sharp sting of the old pain. I find it strange that no one ever mentions it to me now. Why? Can people really be as generous as that? Or has my defect really become so unnoticeable?

15 March 1935

Sensational news! Lyovka keeps a diary! Hey! How d'you like that?

18 March 1935

In my sisters' college, the students' cultural activities are really well organized: they've set up a drama club and a choir. The drama club has been going for ages. They've hired a professional director and prepared a production called *Personal Life*. Zhenya got incredibly involved, and all the other members of the club are always very lively and jolly. On 16 March, they had the dress rehearsal, and Zhenya suddenly became terribly hoarse. She had to sing.

'I can't go on stage,' she told the director.

'You have to go on. You can't let the others down. On you go.'

She strained her voice terribly, and it kept breaking, but she went on, although she couldn't sing and, in the final act, she could hardly even speak. And the performance was set for 18 March! The college is demanding a performance, and the director is forcing Zhenya to perform. For some reason, everybody was quite, quite certain that she and Nina P. would get over their hoarseness. Nina did, but even though Zhenya was feeling better today . . . she didn't want to fail completely and make a laughing stock of herself in front of an audience.

Nina came this afternoon, and they spent the whole day eating eggs whisked up with sugar and drinking hot milk and, to train their voices a bit, they sang and recited a few parts of the play. Zhenya didn't know what to do; there was a massive scandal brewing. The posters had been put up, the invitations given out, everything was ready.

At five o'clock, Yura T. turned up, sat in the room for a while in deep thought and started trying to persuade Zhenya to go, sitting beside her on the bed and taking hold of her elbows.

'I can't, Yura,' my sister said, almost whispering. 'Tell them all I can't. Take Nina with you and try to make them understand.'

'It's that troublemaker Nina who's made you drop out,' Yura remarked angrily.

Nina flew into a terrible fury and began shouting: 'I'm not a troublemaker! And why would I want to make her drop out? I've got my voice back.'

'Well, if someone's ill and has a sore throat, how can she go on?' I said.

They left, and Zhenya seemed to calm down a little. I went over to Ira's place and sat there until nine o'clock. While I was going upstairs at home, I suddenly had a persistent, worrying thought: What if they've gone out? I opened the door quietly and glanced at the coat hooks. Only one coat there; Zhenya must have used the others to cover herself up. I went into the room, feeling almost relieved. Lyalya and Zhorka were standing by the window, but Zhenya wasn't there. Lyalya said: 'The concert's going ahead. The director and Yurka came and took her away. Are you going?'

Go there to see Zhenya suffering, sit there in torment, anxious and afraid for every word she says? Suffering and blushing with her for every burst of laughter from the audience? No, thank you! And, worst of all, not to be able to help her, to be a passive spectator. 'I won't go,' I said to Lyalya, and started taking my coat off. She's already on now, she must be feeling terribly nervous.

It's strange, but when the director came, she didn't even try to object and just obediently put her coat on – she must have been in shock. Mum said: 'She almost started crying.' No, that's awful – to go on stage and act, knowing that you're going to fail, to wait in horror for every hoarse note in your voice and every laugh from the audience, to strain your voice until it hurts, until your eyes start to water. After that, you'd probably swear to give up acting altogether.

22 March 1935

Quite recently, I re-read Tolstoy's *Childhood, Boyhood and Youth*, and I think I've only just realized now what a great artist Tolstoy is. Only Tolstoy can reproduce an age that he left behind long ago so truthfully and accurately. I don't think anyone else has ever attempted such a huge task – describing three major stages of life – and no one could have depicted them as masterfully. In relatively few pages, he manages to show more than anyone else could in several books.

The thorough craftsmanship of the work is blindingly obvious from the very first lines. No single event is unnecessary, each one helps to define the characters and show them from different angles. There's none of that exhausting clutter you often find in other writers. In Tolstoy, everything is so apt, so harmonious and wonderful.

It's amazing how many things I find in this book that resemble my own experiences. It just goes to show yet again that Tolstoy was able to pick out and depict things that are common to everybody at that age, everybody knows them and recognizes them and therefore they are particularly moving. Someone might object: why write about familiar things? They're boring to read about. But that's wrong, they're even more interesting and they can be a wake-up call to the reader.

Here's an interesting comment, very subtly observed: 'The suffering of shy people is caused by not knowing what people think; as soon as that opinion is clearly stated, no matter what it might be, the suffering stops.' Shyness is probably closely connected to pride.

Tolstoy was ugly, and that caused him a lot of suffering: 'I was bashful by nature, but this bashfulness of mine was increased by being convinced of my own ugliness. And I am convinced that nothing has such a striking influence on a person's development as his appearance does, and not even so much the appearance itself as the certainty that it is attractive or unattractive.'

There's a lot in common between Tolstoy's adolescence and mine: in both, there are a lot of joyless experiences – with the single difference that my adolescence is even more joyless. About his habit of withdrawing to dream and think during this period of his life, Tolstoy writes: 'From out of all this serious moral effort I took nothing at all except a resourceful wit that weakened the power of will in me, and **a habit of constant moral analysis that destroyed my freshness of feeling and clarity of judgement**.'

28 March 1935

Every day is the same: in the morning I get up at nine o'clock or half past eight, with a feeling of regret that the happy, calm state of oblivion has ended, that once again I have to start on the dreary, boring round of the same old things, the same old desires. My first thought is: Can't I just go on dozing for another half-hour or at least five minutes?

But I do have to get up, and so I start getting dressed mechanically, with difficulty and, as usual, the thoughts start whirling round in my head. Everything is calculated down to the tiniest details. After pulling on my coarse boy's shoes and tightening my belt, I take a comb and a little mirror and, with a habitual glance out of the window at the thermometer, I start combing my hair.

There's snow outside ... I won't open the small window, it's too cold. Or perhaps I should? Oh, that dad of mine! He's broken the plant, what was he doing in here?! But I shouldn't really be so angry with him ... The branches are unfolding, it's a lime tree, and this isn't lilac, it's an elder. Then I make the bed and get washed, and all the time I keep thinking about how to spend the day more rationally. I put the kettle on and sit down in my sisters' room to read.

Then I go to Granny's place for the bread, taking Betka with me. I drink tea on my own, or sometimes with Mum, and then we sit there without talking, chewing intently on our bread. I restrain the imp of boredom that comes creeping up and starts whispering to me. All day long, I think of nothing but how to get so many things done. Sometimes, I sit down at the piano and tinkle a tune clumsily without enjoying it at all.

Or else I start thinking that, some time soon, I'll play or draw really well. I read again. The boredom gets stronger. If Dad comes, we start quarrelling. He bursts into the room and says in a voice that is measured but insistent: 'What's that you're reading, Nina?'

'Tolstoy,' I reply, thinking to myself: Answer politely, control yourself.

'What exactly?'

'I've already told you more than once.'

'Well, tell me again anyway.'

I say nothing and strain every nerve to stifle my mounting anger as I try to get on with my reading.

'What are you going to bring me from Granny's today?'

'I don't know.'

'Never say "I don't know",' he tells me for the hundredth time. 'You have to know everything.'

'Well, how could I know?' I suddenly shout. 'Whatever she gives me, that's what I'll bring.'

'Why are you getting so annoyed?'

I don't say anything.

'You know, Nina, this plant here needs splitting and potting on.'

I don't even look round.

'Look how many shoots there are.'

'I'm not going to do it.'

'Why not? Do it at once!'

'I don't want to!' I say, raising my voice. 'Pot them yourself.'

'Anyway, you've planted rubbish. Nothing you do ever turns out right,' he says imperturbably, almost gently. 'These stocks are no good for anything.'

Where did he get the idea they're stocks? I didn't even plant them, I think, clenching my fists, but I don't say anything and read the same phrase over and over again. 'Dad, stop bothering me, will you? Go away.'

If I'm lucky, he'll go into the kitchen and start pottering about and grumbling in there. And I listen against my will, seething with fury. 'And where's the cloth?' he says to himself. 'Not a thing, you can't find a thing. What a bunch. Three daughters and they can't even tidy things up. Anarchists.' I used to object to what he said and argue back, but now I say nothing and the simmering, silent, unexpended fury, occasionally spilling over into hatred, drives me insane.

29 March 1935

Recently, Sergei Keller, Aunt Sonya's husband, arrived from Kashira. He works there, and he comes to Moscow for his days off. Sergei sent me to get some vodka and then, suddenly, with a good-natured laugh, he offered me a drink. 'All right,' I answered and laughed.

'Attagirl!' He poured a glass for me and I poured it

down my throat, gung ho. The vodka was slightly bitter, and it scorched my throat in a hot stream, getting warmer and warmer as it ran down into my gullet.

I felt a remarkably pleasant blow to my head that filled it with a heavy heat. But I was entirely sober ... After several glasses, Sergei's mood grew mellow, his face flushed and, although he is usually reserved, he began talking a lot. For some reason, the wrinkles on his flabby face stood out especially clearly and I felt I'd only just noticed how old he was.

He told me about his work, and I realized what a good man he is, an excellent, valuable worker, and that I hadn't really known him before. He is the top-grade kind of engineer that everyone loves, the kind who knows his job, a hero just right for a short story. Looking into his bright-blue eyes and searching for responses to the things he told me, I dissected every word that I said and thought what a hindrance analysis is to natural, simple relationships between people, and how it makes them prejudiced.

6 April 1935

What is this condition called? When you feel as if you want something, as if you haven't eaten for a long time and are hungry, but not with a physical hunger, with a moral one, and you don't have what you need to understand this elusive and vague feeling. Then this vagueness dissolves, and you feel as if at any moment you'll catch and comprehend the feeling that is stirring in your soul. It's your blood 'fermenting'.

I want love, I want to immerse myself completely in this feeling, dissolve myself in it, forget about myself, stop analysing, in order to feel nothing but love and a peaceful happiness. But I can't. This feeling, this sense of unease, aggravates me – at times, it gets so strong that, somewhere inside, in my heart's blood, in what we call the soul, there's something stirring persistently, something cold and quivering, enveloping me in a strangely pleasant cob-web. And I want to get rid of this feeling and at the same time keep listening closely to it over and over again.

Not long ago, I heard from Ksyushka that Zina has a 'fancy man', and that Vera L., who looks so serious and so unlike 'our girls', also has relations with boys. So do lots and lots of girls. But I don't! I'm the exception, and therefore abnormal, and all abnormalities produce illnesses and peculiarities. What is already familiar to Ira at the age of fourteen is still unknown and incomprehensible to me. I'm becoming sadly convinced of the terrible consequences that flow from ugliness and deformity in childhood. It's enough to say that, apart from my early childhood, I have never had a single boy as a friend.

I remember that, already in the fifth class, the boys were just boys to me, and it's not hard to understand why – after all, I was fourteen years old at the time, the same age Ira is now. And, at our age, two years makes a huge difference. My interests and those of the people around me were so different that we couldn't possibly understand each other. And something that would have passed off without any problems if it had been given an outlet sooner went on developing because it was suppressed and retarded; it expanded and began to torment me.

Sometimes I want to swear a passionate oath that I'll never abandon my children to the mercy of their wild fancies, that I'll create a strictly correct, calm and happy atmosphere for them and watch over them, watch over them non-stop. I'll follow all the experiences my child goes through with keen interest. To be able to understand him and guide him on to the right road without any coercion or suffering is a great art. And it's a mother's sacred duty to devote her life to her child, so that no peculiar monsters like me are produced.

THE THIRD NOTEBOOK

7 April 1935

It's only the beginning of April, but spring is completely here already. There's no snow left and today Ksyusha and I walked to school without our hats and in our autumn coats. It's so good to feel that sharp chill of a spring morning, to unbutton your coat, face into the fresh April wind and feel it embrace your body and neck in a cold wave, tossing back your hair and buffeting your face in an impetuous, irregular rhythm.

Sometimes, boys call your name or shout out some joke and you forget to be angry and laugh in reply because everything's so jolly and cheerful. Ksyusha and I stood for a long time at the entrance to the student hostel, laughing at the wind and staring curiously at the students. Most of them are no longer young, and they are all pale and thin, with intense, miserable faces and foreheads covered in wrinkles. We felt sorry for all of them, but it didn't mar our happiness.

'Well, see you. Come tomorrow, my friend,' I said.

'I'm not your friend. Crocodile's your best friend, then Ira and Musya, and then me,' Ksyusha replied with surprising seriousness.

'What kind of nonsense is that, Ksenya?' I took her by the hand and tried to explain the way I feel and justify myself as I walked along the pavement beside her. 'In the first place, you can forget Crocodile. That's absolute rubbish. Who could have made that up? And, as for the rest, you, Ira and Musya all mean the same to me, I love the different things that I like about each one of you. Basically, I love you all the same.'

'Oh, yes, and what about Musya?'

'What about Musya? I don't love Musya any more than I love you.'

I'm very very vain, so vain it's quite disgusting, and so I was really pleased to suddenly realize that Musya, Ksyusha and Ira were all fond of me. The most frank and naïve of them turned out to be Musya – she started telling me ages ago that she loved me, and she's always so tender and affectionate. I love her, too, but for her external appearance, her elegant little figure, her pretty, delicate face, her rosy cheeks and fresh, soft little mouth. I love to look into her eyes with those long black lashes when she's talking; she screws them up and they sparkle with laughter. I enjoy hugging her, stroking her shoulders, feeling her soft, beautifully formed breasts against me.

But there are no spiritual ties between us, and I don't respect her as a person – in fact, I suppose, I don't really like her. She's such a frivolous, unthinking little scatterbrain.

Every evening when we meet, she says hello and tells me with a happy smile: 'I've got so many things I have to tell you. Such news!' And then the endless stories begin, about the same old things: what time they got to Lyalya's place, who sat where, what they talked about. Sometimes her chatter irritates me, it's so empty, meaningless and uninteresting.

Now for Ksyusha. She's silly, stupid, frivolous and coarse, yet our friendship is very strong. I need her and look out for her sometimes. After all, Musya could never be of any use to me in any practical matter. Everybody knows that even affection is measured according to how useful a person is. The bonds that tie me and

Ksyusha together are weird – one is a passionate desire to fool about and play jolly pranks; another a love of PE. Sometimes I long for a bit of variety, something to stop me thinking, and I just love all of that for that reason.

We're both reckless, bold and crude; we often curse the authorities and pick on people in the street. I've got the more highly developed sense of self-control, and I sometimes put a stop to her escapades when they're just too brazen and vulgar, but most of the time I join in everything with her. To my shame, I fall under her influence against my will, although reason forces me to be more cautious and restrained.

We both have a stupid, hopeless longing to be boys, and we envy everything they do: she envies their physical superiority and, as well as that, I envy their intellectual superiority too. We often have different views about things, and we argue, but I have a lot in common with her: if I feel like going to the skating rink, I go with Ksyusha; if I want to do something rotten to a teacher or skip a lesson, the only person who'll go with me and support me is Ksyusha. In this respect, we're soul sisters. I've never thought before about what motivates her or, if I have, then it's always seemed to me that she loves me less and less. So it was strange to hear her tell me that she loves me but that she thinks I like the others more.

15 April 1935

Lyovka has become seriously infatuated with Irina. In

class, he often turns his head and stares intently at her for a long time, his eyes probing her impudently, searching for something. He can never hold her gaze and turns away, laughing and turning down the corner of his mouth in that handsome way of his. He's not the old Lyovka so much now, the foul-mouthed lout and arrogant squabbler, as insolent as a hooligan. Often, now, he sits there looking serious, resting his elbows on his knees or biting his lips and frowning. He's become more respectable, and we no longer hear the obscenities that made even the boys blush.

Today, Lyovka wrote Ira a note in which he asked her to stop writing notes to Antipa and threatened to break up with her. I don't know exactly what answer she gave him, but it was something very sharp, and she started chattering not only with Antipa, but with Margosha as well – I know she did it deliberately. Before the last lesson, Lyovka got drunk: the boys said that he drank three glasses of beer.

It was a history class. Lyovka was sitting turned halfway towards us, occasionally talking to Margosha, who was also drunk and kept booming in his deep bass and laughing stupidly so that the entire class could hear him. There was something odd about Lyovka from the very beginning of the lesson, and then he suddenly stretched out across the desk, his face stuck in his hands.

'What did you get drunk for?' Margosha asked him.

'Go to hell!' Lyovka replied, raising his tousled head, and his eyes were wet and angry.

He spent a bit of time ripping pages out of a book, folding them up and tearing them into little pieces. There was a wild, rebellious glint to the strange, cunning gleam in his darkened eyes. His face was blazing dark crimson-red, with bulging veins on his forehead and neck. And now he was talking to Margosha at the top of his voice, turning towards him and laughing.

Then Lyovka tore up several tram tickets and, with a sullen grin from under his brow, blew them off the desk, then he scattered money across the desk and told Margosha that he was going to the militia station. His laughter was sneering and humourless and, instead of despising him, I felt a sort of maternal tenderness towards him and a desire to comfort him, make him change his mind. After the bell, we put our coats on quickly and dashed out after him. He jumped on to a moving tram that was going to Zubovskaya Square.

Ira suddenly spotted him walking along the road, swinging his satchel, and she began following him: 'Look, now he's jumped on a bus . . . he's jumped off . . . What's he doing? He's got into a tram coming this way, he'll probably get a fine.' A tram came up; Ira turned away: 'I'm not going to watch him.' Lyovka was standing on the platform, leaning against the wall with his flushed face thrown back, without his hat, so his golden mane was clearly visible. We got on the next tram and saw him walking along the pavement.

'He'll probably turn up at your place.'

'I don't think so,' said Ira.

18 April 1935

Lyovka showed Irina his diary. How I'd love to read it! It's not simple curiosity, it's a deep interest in him, in his feelings. I don't want to think that he's bad, that he can do anything nasty, but the diary would tell me everything. No, Lyovka is good but unhappy. We're just used to seeing him happy and carefree, and it doesn't seem possible for him to have any serious feelings.

But he was a street hooligan, after all: his mother got divorced and married for a second time, and that has a very bad effect on children. Then his stepfather died, and Lyovka was left alone, unbalanced and searching. And now he has Irina, but why does she put him through so much? And it's because of her that he drinks like that. Ah, what a lousy life! If two people love each other, why do they have to torment each other? Why can't they be happy? Just forget everything and love, love ... Lyovka writes in his diary: 'How sick I am of everything, what bastards they all are. Some day I might just put an end to it all ...'

30 April 1935

Yesterday, Irina had a party. The only two of the boys to come were Valya L. and Zelenin junior – Volodya. For some reason or other, possibly because they felt awkward surrounded by so many girls, they were both in a pretty bad mood, especially Volodya. He barely said a word over tea, sitting between Tamara and V., his stubborn little blue eyes glinting now and again from under his brows. There was something about his face that was both attractive and repulsive, and his large, protruding ears and wide-set eyes gave his face a strange expression.

Leitin, all red and disgusting, either raised an eyebrow and looked around on all sides or laughed stupidly and screwed his eyes up in a horrible way. He has such disgusting sheep's eyes, which look at you so sweetly and submissively, in a timid, pleading, sensual sort of way. I realized yesterday that I can't have any ordinary kind of relationship with him. I find him repellent and he hardly interests me at all any more, but his indifference is beginning to annoy me: it provokes a persistent, morbid desire to know if he likes me or not. Why do I need to know? It's part of the female character, I guess . . .

When we hit on a line of conversation, Volodya said that Valya had a blonde girlfriend, and I was glad to hear that, but when we started playing blind man's buff and Valya was 'it', he grabbed hold of my skirt and wouldn't let go for a long time, clinging on tight with his big, strong fingers. I laughed at first but then got angry and indignant as I pulled his hand away, and the only feeling I had then was that he was a man with bad intentions. And my revulsion grew so strong that, all at once, I couldn't bring myself to blindfold him and had to ask someone else to do it.

1 May 1935

Jolly May, wonderful May! The best month, the month of youth, love and desires, warm evenings, full of the languorous scent of lilac and bird cherry, with flirtatious, damp-smelling winds. Yet the month has never brought me anything except the troubled dream of an impossible May love and a bitter yearning. But I still feel drawn into the fragrant evening gloom, to hear the rustle of buds bursting open under the dark sky. And the longing to get caught up in the whirl of life, to surrender to a dream and fairy tale, scratches deliciously at my heart.

My entire world is filled with thinking about boys and, compared with them, everything seems dull and unimportant. When I'm reading and when I'm doing my homework assignments, there's always a thought about a boy in my head. In bed, I only think about one thing; I often dream, building up some stupid fantasy or other, and, as I live through it, I can actually feel my heart melt.

8 May 1935

What, exams already? So unexpected and so soon. After this, I'll never lug a bag full of my books about again. I've thought so little about the exams that they seem like some kind of scary new thing, something quite unanticipated. This whole year seems like a vague dream, painful, monotonous and full of misery! It has all gone clean out of my head, as if I wasn't even alive before. I'm never interested in the past, it doesn't exist for me: I live only in the present and the future.

The first test is the day after tomorrow – the written literature exam, and I just can't make myself think about it. The fact that it's so close makes me feel frightened and happy at once – after all, then comes the end, then comes the summer. Not that I'm expecting anything from the summer any more, not the way I used to; I don't dream any more. Life has become less up and down, with no prospects. But the old thoughts and the old nightmares do come back sometimes.

In the evening, when I arrived at Ira's place to study maths, Lyovka was already there. I sat down facing the mirror and glanced at myself, not by chance but out of habit, hoping to see myself looking at least tolerable. I was in a happy, springtime, satisfied sort of mood. Ira and Lyovka were there with me, both friends I cherished and loved.

But the creature staring out at me from the rectangle of glass was so appallingly ugly that I felt agonizingly ashamed for myself, for my hideous and ridiculous face, for my tangled hair sticking out above my ears, for being so plain altogether. I turned away, ready to burst into tears, and it took me a long time to recover from the painful feeling of an appalling, undeserved insult.

19 May 1935

The huge eight-engined aeroplane *Maxim Gorky* crashed yesterday. Not only was it the pride and joy of our USSR, it was the biggest in the world. But I don't actually know that for certain, and you can't trust what our newspapers say. The *Maxim Gorky* took off escorted by two biplanes, and one of them started performing stunts, looping the loop too close to it.

The blue depths of the sky, which seem so gentle and

not at all forbidding, were invaded by a terrible accident. The biplane crashed on to the *Maxim Gorky*'s wing and damaged it. The 65-metre-long hulk somersaulted and went hurtling downwards, slicing through the sunny expanse that it had always floated across so freely and easily, shedding parts as it went. The biplane crashed to earth together with the *Maxim Gorky*.

All that was left of the beautiful giant was a grey and red heap of metal debris and forty-seven mutilated corpses, which only a minute before had been living, thinking, feeling people soaring high above Moscow, their hearts flooded with joy. And these people, the crew and the passengers, men and women, were suddenly transformed into a hideous bloody mass, warm and sticky, the brains and bones showing white, what people call a bloody pancake.

What a terrible, irreparable tragedy! Forty-seven people have died because a pilot made an awful blunder. **And what a great plane the *Maxim Gorky* was, too, to fall to pieces when it was only hit by such a tiny one. It wasn't built to be flown – it couldn't be used either for public transport or for military purposes – it was built just so that our Soviet Union would hold a world record, so that we could say: 'See how wonderful our aviation technology is! See what giants we build!' We have so much of this showing-off that has no basis in common sense, so much bragging and boasting. And it's this bragging that causes us so much suffering.**

The Maxim Gorky *was indeed billed as 'the biggest aeroplane in the world', and it crashed over Moscow. Only one model was ever built. Aeronautical engineers, along with pilots, were heroes of the*

Stalinist regime, and much investment was made in aviation technology. The celebrated Maxim Gorky (1868–1936), after whom the plane was named, was a writer who, having left Russia for political reasons, returned to live there and was much celebrated.

22 May 1935

Yesterday, Irina was at Yulia's place, to see her, not Lyovka. They had a long talk, and she spent the entire evening there. Yulia is terribly kind to her, always so considerate. If this had happened a year ago, I would have been really upset, but now I'm just annoyed and envious. How come she can talk so well, why is she so clever and beautiful? What a fool I am!

Irina has phoned Leitin. What they talked about isn't important but, several times as I listened to them, I felt uneasy (to put it mildly) because I had the impression that he likes her.

26 May 1935

> *The bird cherry sprinkles down snow,*
> *Leaves drowning in blossom and dew . . .*
> [a poem by Sergei Esenin, written in 1910]

Bird cherry . . . It's standing here on my table. A wonderful, magnificent bouquet of white flakes. The transparent, snowy-white clumps hang down delicately, and the smell they give off is so full of spring, so intoxicating. Ira's garden is covered with dark, gleaming foliage, and I sit there for a long time, looking at the leaves and the grass. Unless I've forgotten, I've never enjoyed spring so much as I do now.

First thing in the morning, I lean on the windowsill to see the dark shadows creep across the road as the sunlight becomes brighter and harsher, and I lie here for a long time, sticking my head out of the window with my eyes closed, or turning over on my back and looking up at the misty, faint, blue sky. The morning wind is a seducer. I love it the way I love people, and its burning caresses give me a thrill and make me smile. Its fresh, abrupt gusts are affectionate and gentle. At times I feel I want to give it a name and a face.

27 May 1935

I've finished school, finished for ever, and I don't have a clue what the coming year holds for me. I feel like a helpless little girl who doesn't know anything outside of school cast out into the immense world. Maybe that shows that I do love school? But I don't think so. It's just as cosy and familiar to me now as an old room I've lived in for dozens of years, which I feel sorry to leave because it has so many associations, both good and bad.

A few days ago, Irina, Lyovka and I called round to see Linde. He wasn't at home, but his mother and grandmother were delighted to see us and insisted that we come in and wait for 'Dimochka'. We could see that they both adore him. We agreed to write him a note and went in, and this time the familiar room seemed bigger and brighter, the desk standing opposite the door, the wide armchairs upholstered in brown leather against the walls looking very comfortable and soft, and there were masses of books.

While Irina was writing the note, Linde's mother, small, grey-haired and very pleasant, talked to us, looking at us through her round horn-rimmed glasses with eyes that were gentle, kind and almost loving, as if we were loved because we were Dima's classmates. I don't remember how the conversation about school started, but she said: 'Dimochka's taking exams today.'

One of us asked: 'Taking exams?'

'Yes, yes,' the grandmother replied simply, surprised at our surprise.

Lyovka and I exchanged rapid glances. His eyes glinted cunningly, and he asked: 'How's he getting on?'

'Surely you know that?'

'We're in a different class. We take ours separately.'

'Yes, he's doing well. Only, in geography, he got difficult questions, the teacher was trying to fail him. He doesn't find geography easy at all.'

And while she was speaking, stammering slightly, I watched her closely, agreeing with what she said, and my lips involuntarily twitched and curved upwards. But I should have cried, not laughed, because now it was clear to us that all year Linde had been deceiving his family, all year he had been going somewhere else instead of school and lying about it.

Today, after the exams, Lyovka picked up Antipka and Uklon, and they went to Linde's place. Ira and I decided to intercept him, and we got on the tram and found Linde was on it. He turned out to have grown no taller than me. He was well built and not bad-looking, with white teeth and absolutely black eyes. Out in the street, we met the boys, and all of us, including Linde, went to Ira's place.

Linde gave the impression of being a perfectly normal and well-developed individual; he was easy and natural with us. We played volleyball for a long time. Linde kept running round the court, often falling over, and he even managed to invite Ira to his place, supposedly for some books. I wonder if she does fancy him? That would be a serious victory!

8 June 1935

Yesterday, there was a party at Ira's place, and I really wanted it to be a success, not like all the other parties with the 'riff-raff' and dreary obscenities. I wanted it to leave me with a good impression of the boys and of school life. These free days have been strange; we've all been feeling anxious and talked a lot about the party, collecting money and crashing down from the dizzying heights of lively enthusiasm into the dark depths of hopeless despair.

An hour before the party, our excitement evaporated. Everything was suddenly boring and uninteresting, and we felt sure the party would be a flop. But it was impossible to be depressed for long – the rooms were so bright and comfortable; the white bedspreads, clean table-cloths and gently swaying net curtains looked so lovely. The girls were all dressed in white. They were happy, exceptionally lively, airy and light: they suited the decor down to the ground.

The boys arrived in their light-coloured suits and, straight away, there was a chill in the atmosphere. Irina kept a feeble conversation going for a few minutes.

'Let's go and play volleyball,' Margosha suggested. Out in the garden, everybody immediately became more lively and cheerful, fighting over the ball and trying to take it from each other. Volodya, short and sturdy, played well: he flew into a passion, got his hair in a mess and went red in the face as he jumped after the ball with surprising skill. Margosha was as clumsy and rough as a bear, and there's nothing to be said about Yura, except that he played very badly.

Our idea was to have a real party, with wine and flirting, and so we wanted to seat the boys and the girls alternately, but the question was how. It would have been stupid to sit Musya with Linde and me with Volodya. In order to avoid arguments, we called Boris M. in to consult. 'I don't know,' he boomed, flapping one hand as he waddled off. 'I'd better get "Professor" Zelenin.'

'Well, go and get him then.'

Volodya arrived: 'What's up?' Musya explained our seating problem to him. 'All right,' he said. Then he sat down on the couch, wrote the names on narrow slips of paper and began arranging the seating. We settled on Irina sitting between the two Zelenins, with Lyalya and Dima on one side of them and Raya and Boris on the other, Musya and I facing them.

The boys had brought four bottles of wine with them, and the snacks were pretty good, too. But everyone sat there at the table without starting. It was absurd, and very awkward, and Musya turned to me and whispered: 'How awful!' She was used to a different kind of company, and the boys' gaucheness seemed barbarous to her.

'Boys, the usual thing is for you to begin,' I said, but they only laughed and talked uncomfortably among themselves, and no one would make the first move and start eating.

'Nina, you're in a man's place too,' said Irina.

'Yes, that's true.' I smiled, picked up a bottle and started pouring wine for myself and my neighbours. Yura drank a lot at first, but he didn't get drunk and didn't talk at all. Boris quickly got tipsy and began laughing. He started talking in a loud voice, carried on drinking and poured for Raya – soon that couple were merrier than everyone else.

Volodya didn't drink much, and Lyalya and Dima hardly drank anything at all. Dima sat there with a long face, trying to make toasts, then Volodya started adding his own commentary. I took small sips of the thick, transparent orange liquid in my glass and ate without saying anything. After two glasses, I challenged Musya to a drinking contest, although her glass was only half the size of mine. We tried two sorts of alcohol, and after that I paid no attention to anyone, I just drank glass after glass, observing the way the wine affected me, but my head didn't start to spin and I didn't black out. I went on calmly analysing my thoughts, and they were crystal clear. All at once, I felt completely free and easy, everyone seemed very precious and close to me, and my shyness totally disappeared.

I kept shouting, offering Margosha more to drink,

making him laugh and laughing with him. The two of us would probably have drunk too much if Ira's mum hadn't intervened and forbidden me to drink any more. Altogether, I drank ten or eleven glasses, but I ate a lot, too, so I was only just a little bit merry. Nevertheless, I felt very hot, so hot it brought tears to my eyes, my face was burning, and sometimes the blood rushed to my head, which felt too narrow, as if it was being squeezed with equal pressure on both sides. Perhaps this is what 'it went to my head' means, but there was nothing spinning in front of my eyes, and I was quite prepared to assure everybody that I wasn't drunk.

The girls laughed and said that my eyes looked drunk, shiny and shifty. I got up from the table and went to the mirror, I was feeling very happy and wanted to go on playing the fool . . . Gradually everyone began leaving the table, and someone suggested going into the garden. I laughed and, in my own mind, I was sure I wasn't drunk, except that I felt so comfortable with everything and so talkative, not like me at all, and I completely forgot about the present and the future.

'Margosha, get me a drink.' He chuckled, looked at me with blank eyes and shook his head. I grabbed hold of his hand: 'Come on now. What a coward! Let's have a drink!'

He goggled at me and said: 'I'm a coward? They won't let us drink any more.'

'Don't be silly, of course they will.' I dragged him over to the table and picked up his glass and my own. Yura dashed across to take the wine away from us, and Ira's mum got angry and categorically forbade me to get Margosha drunk. She told me to 'go for a walk'.

It was absolutely dark outside, and the black shadows covering the square were bearing down on us. Ahead in the distance, we could see the bright, well-built figures of Ira and Volodya, who had gone out before us and were walking along the path. There was a sweet, moist smell in the air; the chill of night was creeping through the branches. I stood on the volleyball court and looked around. First, Ira and Volodya walked by, talking excitedly about the theatre, then Margosha and Raya, holding each other tight. The other girls had gone off somewhere, and I was left alone with Yurka. What else could I do except promenade with him like the others were doing? I walked slowly, laughing in the darkness, and talked with him as freely and easily as if he wasn't Yurka, a person who had nothing at all to do with me.

Now, it feels weird and shameful to remember this, but there was a horrible, unpleasant feeling in my heart, a certain resentment that I had ended up with Yurka, that I was talking to him and laughing at him at the same time. From time to time, I began spouting nonsense, and then I would go running to the girls or into the house but, when I came out, I always ran into him again. The poor boy was so ugly that everybody ran away from him and he had to make do with me.

I had nowhere else to go either, and I tried to suppress my boredom and carried on walking, sometimes swaying a little so that my shoulder touched his arm. My usual self felt humiliated in the eyes of the other girls: it was seething with envy and offended pride, mocking itself for the stupid situation it was in. My other, drunken self just wanted to have fun, to forget everything, let everything sort itself out. That was why I had to have wine; without it, I would have been in a complete state.

This terrible memory of Yurka and the fact that I could talk to him so frankly has been haunting me and upsetting me all day long today, lodged under my heart in a cold, hard lump, as if there were something gnawing on me there.

18 June 1935

My feelings as a woman are talking to me so loudly that they drown out all the others, and I keep thinking about the boys all the time: about the Zelenins and the others. I've been meeting up with them quite frequently just recently and, a few days ago, we went out into the country. My overall impression of the trip was a very pleasant one, a memory of a day spent quite differently from a day in Moscow, but at times it was boring too. In Bolshevo, we took two boats out. The little river, some tributary of the river Moscow, is very picturesque, slow moving and deep, with dark creeks overgrown with water-lilies, and lots of rapids and meandering bends overhung by spreading willow trees.

After five hours, we took the boats in and went into the forest, and then I began to feel very miserable. Margosha was with Musya and Lyalya, Ira was being unbearably capricious and sulky, Volodya walked either with Shunya or with the girls. I couldn't walk with Yurka, because I began really not liking him at all and, in any case, he never said anything to me and, even though I understood why, I was still angry.

It was a northern forest but, even so, I had cheered up a little until Volodya said something extremely nasty to me. We had sat down to rest and eat our picnic, and we started talking about the fight, and Volodya said to me: 'Why don't you have a fight with me?'

'Come on then,' I replied defiantly.

'No, I won't fight you, I refuse.'

'Why not? Do you think I'm too strong for you?'

'I should think so, you'll be nineteen soon.'

I felt so hurt and offended, I blushed and said in a serious voice, trying to sound as if I didn't care: 'No, I'm nowhere near nineteen yet.' Whether on purpose or by accident, he had touched on my most painful spot; in the crudest possible manner he had taken the thing that I've always tried so hard to ward off, tried not to think about, and flung it in my face as an irrefutable and terrible accusation.

I felt so angry and insulted I could have cried, and I stood up quickly, trembling inside: 'Let's go, shall we, Ira?' This incident destroyed the benign, peaceful mood I had been in lately. It was a long time before I could forget his mocking and insulting tone of voice when he said: 'You'll be nineteen soon.' Why do they insult me at every turn? Am I really so very repugnant and old that I don't even arouse their pity? What depths have I sunk to? Begging for pity. For a while, I felt that I hated this short boy with the broad shoulders and small, intense eyes.

2 July 1935
Kashira

Three hours have carried me a whole world away from Moscow into the small, lively settlement of a future town. It's clean and spacious and, in an odd sort of way, even poetic. New little white houses and light stone pavements, and all around the forest – tall, slim birch trees. The forest is very big, deserted and absolutely derelict. Dry earth scattered with pine needles and leaves, everywhere dense, scrubby bushes and trees – oaks and maples that claw at you.

I'm feeling strangely unhappy. I'm always surprised and frightened by the speed at which trains move, covering huge distances in such a short time. I don't think much about the present and the future, but I keep thinking about Moscow, the boys, our meetings and outings. I feel very warm and tender towards them and the girls, and I feel a little sad, as if we're never going to see each other again. Why have I become so fond of them that I long to see them so badly and at times even feel something like regret that I left today and won't see them for a while?

We rode from the station in a home-made bus fashioned out of a truck, and that was where I first made the acquaintance of Sergei's work colleagues. There were four of them: one was an old Russian in dirty clothes, and the others were clean, well-groomed Jews. I particularly noticed two of them: one a little older, already filling out a bit, with a rather mocking smile and equally mocking blue eyes, and one a very young man with an intelligent, open face and very dark brown eyes. As we were walking towards the house, those two fell behind and I heard their indiscreetly loud conversation.

'Is that the same one?' the young man asked.

'No, it's a different one.'

'This one looks a bit more serious.' Then they laughed and said something else that was carried away by the wind.

Now I have learned how stupid, and even ridiculous, it feels to be an unwanted outsider. Sergei and I went to have lunch in the canteen, a small room with three little tables, each with four places. He knows everyone, he said hello and made conversation, but I sat in the corner, not knowing what to do with my hands or where to look.

Kashira is a small town located outside the 100-kilometre Moscow exclusion zone. Nina was visiting her uncle Sergei there.

3 July 1935
Kashira

My mood is a bit sad, but pleasant and full of memories. It's an absurd confession, but I've become attached to our group in Moscow; it's the first one in my life and it will have to be the last. This year is the first time I've had such close, good male friends, and I won't forget them for a long time. It sometimes seems to me that this is the first vivid and vital experience in my life. Now, all my thoughts are filled with them, and every step I take brings back a swarm of memories. I'm alone here, and I fill my loneliness with images from the past.

Yesterday evening, a fine rain fell and it was unusually quiet and warm. All around, the bright green forest was wet and fragrant. Sergei and I were picking flowers, and I had a pleasant ache in my chest. And I wished so much that instead of him there was someone young, interesting and exciting there with me.

Today, I went to pick berries. There's no one in the forest; it's wild and in places so thick that it's almost impossible to get through. I was having fun, because I wasn't on my own – there was a little fox-terrier with me. Who does he belong to? I have no idea. He's very sweet, jolly and sociable. We clambered through bushes and then lay in the grass and picked berries. I very soon lost any idea of where I was and wandered wherever my feet took me, sometimes coming out on to narrow, shady pathways and wide, straight cuttings cluttered with brushwood, sometimes making my way deep into a dark, damp thicket where it was quiet and the wind rustled the branches overhead. The light fell in pale, uncertain patches, and I enjoyed the wildness and the solitude.

Late yesterday evening, I set off to walk round the settlement. The darkness was advancing slowly and gently. Some people were playing volleyball on some wasteground, and I went up shyly and watched, then, afterwards, I went to the big rope swing. Several girls were there, laughing as they went soaring high up into the air.

I'm bored. Sergei promised to take me to the river Oka, but he's got held up somewhere – perhaps he has a meeting, although he did promise to come back early. I didn't buy any milk, and now the two of us have nothing to eat, so I'm feeling a bit uneasy. My feet hurt, and I don't feel like going for a walk. I'm bored. The forest is unusually welcoming some of the time, and then it suddenly starts to scare you because it's so deserted. You can walk through this 'forest wilderness' for a whole day and not meet a single living soul.

25 August 1935

The summer has passed, just as everything in the world passes, and now, once again, the winter life, as cold and severe as winter itself, stretches out ahead. But what sort of life will it be? I'm not at school any more, and I don't think I've got into the *rabfak* either. So where am I, then? I took my last entrance exam the day before yesterday, and already I'm bored with the monotony of my free time, because now I have no goal. But only a few days ago, my life was filled with a thousand different feelings and sensations. New surroundings, new people . . . I was happy to be entering into a new life and, at the same time, there was still a sad feeling about school somewhere in my heart, almost a regret.

The Moscow Polygraphic Institute is a wretched, squalid little institution. Narrow, steep stairs, corridors with low ceilings and miserably spartan and uncomfortable lecture halls. At the written exams, I had no contact with the others except for the three girls sitting beside me, and I imagined them to be better than they really were. But on the twenty-third we had the oral exam. The corridors were crammed with people sitting exams, and everything about the way they spoke and laughed was so vulgar, it grated on my ears and sounded so stupid. The boys (like factory workers) leered suggestively, and the girls huddled against the far wall to get away from them.

For the first few minutes, I felt terribly lonely, and I began giving way to loneliness and shyness. Nobody paid any attention to me, and it made me fume. But then a girl I know came in, young but already bearing the special stamp, if not of looseness, then of undue familiarity, her ugly little eyes screwed up. The moment I saw her I thought: There's a Soviet girl for you.

You can recognize the type everywhere: they always wear a bright, flat beret; a tightly curled quiff of hair, very often dyed, fluffed up and pulled over to one side and out from behind a naked ear, small and white as porcelain; a dress in the latest fashion, always very inelegant and in vulgar taste, and always in loud colours; and an expression that's an open invitation to men, slightly brazen and never embarrassed.

And so, my small acquaintance was not particularly nice but, in the end, everyone has some good features, and so did she. She was cheerful and chatty, and I didn't feel awkward with her. In circumstances like that, people are generally friendlier and kinder than normal, because the bad side comes from idleness. I answered the Russian exam questions quickly and ran downstairs into a different hall, where they were taking maths.

At the Moscow Polygraphic Institute (MPI) students studied drawing, printing, publishing and graphic arts. The artist

Aleksandr Deineka (1899–1969), known for his Social Realist paintings, was teaching there at the time. The lithographic process was particularly popular in the 1930s, and new forms of communist art such as (propaganda) posters depicting industrial scenes were devised with strong emphasis on typography and simple design. The exams Nina was sitting were for the rabfak *– evening classes at the institute.*

26 August 1935

It's stupid. So unbelievably stupid! I'm going back to school. Who was it who only two weeks ago was talking about her no-going-back decision? Who thought that she was finished with school? But is it really my fault? They're moving the MPI to Lefortovo, and it would be crazy to make the journey all the way there. And so I'm going back to school again. Only they might not take me back. The headmaster very nearly refused me. He seemed to be a bit confused and started saying that there were no places left and that it would be better for me to go to school number 42. Tomorrow I'm going to see Yulia and then to school again and then, if they accept me, I'll take the good news home.

The Zelenin brothers got back not long ago. I saw them for the first time at Ira's place. Yura's still exactly the same, uncommunicative and odd but not nasty at all; Volodya's grown a bit, he's incredibly lively, full of witty chit-chat, with a hint of elegant, subtle unruliness. For some reason, I feel I'd really like to see Yura right now . . . and take him away from Irina, because I get the feeling that now he is just as fond of me as he is of her.

When they find out that I've gone back to school, lots of people will think that I couldn't stick it out, that I surrendered. No, I will never surrender, I only retreat. Now, when I'm with my friends, I feel so backward, such an idiot, and it torments me constantly. What is this strange delusion that everyone has about my abilities? Everyone thinks that I'm very clever, and that way they cause me even more pain.

30 August 1935

Here's some news! Mum told me today that she had been looking through my diary because she was afraid of finding something counter-revolutionary in it. Wouldn't it be nice if she came across the entries about the Zelenin brothers and the others? **I'm not exactly pleased about it, although I didn't get angry. I know she was only doing it with my best interests at heart.**

I'm not going to the MPI *rabfak*. I suddenly decided that they won't give me enough general education there, and to turn out only half-educated would mean betraying myself and my goals. I've decided to go back to school, but only on condition that in January I'll transfer to the Moscow University *rabfak*. I've decided now that's where I want to go. And that is mostly the reason I've broken off with the MPI completely. Sometimes I give myself a hard time for doing it, but there's nothing to be done now. Now, I have to focus on something else.

They haven't accepted me at school number 35. I can say that for certain, even though the headmaster (the sly snake) is encouraging my hopes. I don't believe him, and now I'm going to find a place at school number 45, here, close to our flat. Why should it be any worse than the others? After all, number 35 was new too when I started there, and number 2 on Usachovka Street was new once, and now it's a model school.

So, now I'm going to number 45 – that's not so bad – and I have to register as soon as I can, so as not to be tempted by the sight of Musya, Irina and the others. My new school is a big one, so there'll be a lot of people there and an awful lot that's new. But I'm going to leave in January anyway. A few days ago, I called into school number 35. Yulia was there, and she started trying to persuade me to join a foundation course for teacher training college. **Oh, teachers! They just can't resist propagandizing. There are not enough teachers at the moment, and she was trying to exploit my desperate situation. Oh, no, not on your life! I don't want to shackle myself to teaching – God has given me enough chances to learn about that eminent profession just recently.**

Mum is doing admission tests for the new seven-year school that's being organized this year. The poor thing simply can't cope without some help, and she's called on me and Irina. It felt a bit funny at first, to be giving instructions and explanations to grown-ups and old people. But then we got used to it and felt perfectly comfortable with it. These strange, hostile workers became just like little children when they found themselves in school. Many, especially the old men and the women, had trembling hands. They blushed,

stammered and spoke to us in a friendly, deferential way.

The names of schools in the USSR were changed to numbers when the education system was reformed; this was to reflect a supposed new equality. Enrolment was dependent on class numbers and on the social background of the student. Nina had evidently forfeited her place at her old school by giving notice that she was leaving.

Nina's mother was a teacher and worked in adult education; often the applicants could not yet read or write. Nina has taken the fact that her mother read her diary surprisingly calmly considering her earlier concerns.

31 August 1935

I'm not displeased that I had so much to worry about this summer. I've grown up somehow, and stopped being so afraid. Only I've started getting this triple crease in my forehead and look as if I'm concentrating on some unanswerable question. I'm left with nowhere to go now, and I regret withdrawing my application to the *rabfak* at the Polygraphic Institute. If only I could find a place somewhere, and then I'd stop feeling sorry about it! I've been round all the schools; there are no places anywhere.

I went into school number 35. Yulia made a final attempt to persuade the headmaster to take me. The awful man laughed a little and curtly assured her that there was nothing that could be done now. Yulia's so sweet. She appealed to him on my behalf with such tenderness, insisting that they couldn't leave a capable pupil like me out in the cold, suggesting that they throw Linde out for not taking the exams. Her pleading smile and agile body language, everything about her, begged so eloquently, but he callously cut her arguments down. And I felt disgusted and ashamed that she was asking for my sake and being turned down because of me. Her lips are so delicate, and the smooth skin on her sculpted nostrils so young-looking.

I left the school with a bad taste in my mouth and dropped into school number 6, where Volodya Zelenin is studying now and where I once studied too. I don't have any choice now about whether to study with Volodya on the second shift – all I want is to be accepted somewhere. But the head of teaching was at a meeting and there was no one to talk to, so I came away having achieved nothing.

This year, things have got serious and so all the stupid thoughts about boys, about my appearance, about our relationships have automatically retreated into the background and the split in my personality is no longer so great. I don't think very much now about the right way to go through life. All these years I've been floundering about in a vicious circle, caught between serious life, study, learning, female dreams and desires, and boys.

3 September 1935

What's happening to me? Something nasty and disturbing at any rate. A feeling that something terrible is bound to happen soon, something I know nothing about and have no power to change. I move about and study with a constant sinking sensation of dread in my heart. I'm going to school number 2 on Usachovka Street. But why am I so unhappy about it? The eighth class is a good group, all capable and very advanced. But I feel so limited and un-intelligent, and I'm afraid of studying with them and, though I'm ashamed to admit it, I really want to go back to school number 35.

Yesterday, Irina told me that the headmaster had con-descended to take me back into the school. And now I find myself in a total mess. Where should I go? I can't remember ever feeling so tormented by such awful doubts. If it were impossible to switch school, I would calm down, but Mum said: 'It's up to you. Perhaps you could switch?' I suddenly feel as if I've lost all my in-dependence and resolution and turned into a real helpless little girl again.

For the last few days, I've been missing Musya and Irina and everyone. My new school comrades are strangers, I don't understand them. At school, I'm always on the alert and unsettled, as if I were in the enemy camp – all those doubts, all those questions! The old life affected me so deeply and now I realize how much I loved it.

All my boastful words about studying and being serious have turned out to be hollow: I'm the same empty-headed, stupid girl who thinks about her studies with revulsion and is searching at the same time for some vague ideals – a vain dreamer. I often think I'm an Oblomov.

Nina is rebuking herself for her laziness and is reminded of the indolence and apathy of Oblomov, the eponymous hero of the famous nineteenth-century novel by I. A. Goncharov

*(1812–91). 'Oblomovism' came to be seen as an unfortunate
Russian national characteristic.*

6 September 1935

Today is the first day off school in this academic year. I'm
in a good mood and feeling at ease with myself because
I'm back in my old school. The doubts and agonizing are
over and, after wandering 'rudderless and without sails',
I've docked at a quiet mooring. It's amazing how good
everything feels, how naturally I acted yesterday; that
nasty, tense feeling I had in school number 2 has gone.
Now, there's only the most frightening part left – fetching
my documents back from school number 2. What if they
won't give them to me? That would be all right, as long as
they don't complain about me to school number 35.

I can't believe that, so far, I've got away with these
extravagant pranks. Dad's very displeased with me. He
abuses me and calls me a coward, but I don't care. I don't
think that last year's horror of school is going to come
back; I think I'll study well right through this year. Of
course, I'm beginning to accept my own limited ability
and lack of talent without getting upset about it, but I
can't abandon the desire to study – that would mean
abandoning my final goal. It's very possible that through
stubborn effort I will manage to stand out from the
crowd, but I'll never be more than a well-primed
simpleton; I don't have the flair that they call talent.

23 September 1935

My room is being painted now, and somehow they managed to soak my diary. It's really annoying – it's so filthy and illegible now that I had to go over some parts again. Well, never mind.

The days are flying past like clouds ahead of a storm, with such incredible power that I don't have time to gather my thoughts. Perhaps that's why I'm not feeling depressed. My thoughts and my aspirations are focused on only one thing: studying, studying, studying. Making myself clever. And this is so hard (to put it mildly). I've learnt to regard my shortcomings even-temperedly – that means I've learnt to resign myself to them, because flying into a rage won't get me anywhere.

It's become a nightmare. To become clever! When I listen to explanations in class, the same thought keeps nagging away inside the brain that I have carefully primed to absorb information: You have to know this really well, you have to go through this in depth. At home, I go to bed and wake up with one thing on my mind: Today I'm going to read Pokrovsky [*Bolshevik historian and Marxist, author of the five-volume* Russian History from Ancient Times]; today I'm going to start learning German. It's bad that these remain only thoughts. Am I to blame for that? I don't know. I just don't have enough time.

During these three years at school, I must get on so that, when I finish ten-year school, I'll be able to tell myself with satisfaction: Yes, now you can consider yourself clever and advanced. It's a real burden. And there's no way I can change it! It hurts that no one believes how tough I find it – I'm sure lots of people think I'm just fishing for compliments. I just hope it does change, that my memory gets better, that I won't forget a single thing.

I keep thinking about how to sort out my life so as to combine fun things with the necessary ones and to avoid falling back into last year's moods. I've decided to study with Musya (and with Irina). True, it will take a little more time, but then I feel so much better afterwards. I have to learn to express myself, and you can't do that on your own, so that's a direct benefit. I'm going to spend all the rest of my time on an expanded programme of serious study. Sad that I still can't get away from that pathetic phrase 'going to' – I've been intending to do it for a month now . . . Oblomov . . .

I've clearly learnt how to philosophize, and 'to philosophize means to learn how to die,' as someone once said. But I see things differently: for me, to philosophize means to learn how to live. I have no time now to think about boys, about how I look, about conquests – that will all come later, when I've become clever. In school, I try to read even during the breaks, but I'm afraid of wearing myself out.

I don't fancy anyone now, I don't even find anyone particularly interesting, and the woman in me stays quiet. Of course, she does still show herself sometimes, but she doesn't torment me any more and she doesn't interfere with my studying. In lessons, I often turn round and look over at the other end of the classroom, at the so-called 'Kamchatka'. Lyovka and Zyrik sit over there and – of course I could easily be wrong, but perhaps I'm not – Zyrik seems to glance at me quite often. And I find it so funny when I suddenly meet his big, wide-open brown eyes.

I'll laugh and turn away, and then, slyly, as if by chance, I'll run my eyes across the furthest desk and feel angry if the long, funny face is not turned in my direction. There, behind the head with black hair, is another head, often thrown back towards the dark-green wall, that I like to look at – with light, slightly curly, marvellously soft golden hair that looks as if it's been crimped at the temples and with a tangle of curls at the back. The only person I can fancy now and who I feel a warm liking for is Lev. He has grown even taller and thinner, but he still has that dashing, good-natured air about him and the same beautiful, shining eyes. The girls say that he's lost his good looks, but I don't think so – he's still as gorgeous as ever.

The Kamchatka was the gang of unruly boys who were banished to the back row of desks in the classroom. In school slang, this was dubbed 'Kamchatka' after the easternmost peninsula of Siberia, a place of exile.

3 October 1935

Well . . . Musya was at my place today, and we couldn't study all day long, so we sat and chatted. She's quite a clever girl and very capable, but I've got so stupid I'm thinking of going to the doctor. I'm always anxious and can't relax at all.

On 29 September there was a party at Irina's place. The fact that I'm only mentioning it four days later shows how little I thought of it. I was bored, I felt really out of place and ridiculous. I was afraid of the boys; I skulked in the corners and kept expecting some pathetic trick from them. For some reason, Dimka asked me to dance, I agreed and, as always, I dragged him off very clumsily and a little naïvely into the other room.

I felt at my most natural and relaxed with him, although I knew Dima to be a dangerous person. He is the same height as I am and, as I danced, I could feel his face at the same level as mine, and sometimes his stubbly cheek. He is very well built and strong, and I could feel the muscles rippling in his arm and shoulder under his thin shirt. Dima is very interesting, but I don't like him at all as a person. I wonder which way the scales will tip? What rubbish! I'll never be one of his large crowd of admirers. No way!

Well, then. That was the only time I danced the whole evening; the rest of the time I sat in the rocking chair and looked around, as angry as hell. Dima and Musya were 'talking', sitting on Irina's bed with the light turned off, Kolya and Nina were kissing, Irina and Yura Zuy were dancing. I've turned down an invitation to a second party. No, I definitely can't go on like this, it's an insult to my dignity.

It's interesting to analyse how I feel about Dima. He's handsome, he's a Pechorin, but I've never met such a flippant and shallow person. His sole interests in life are love affairs, girls and parties. He didn't even seem clever to me, and I am profoundly glad that I don't like him.

Pechorin is the existential hero of another popular Russian nineteenth-century novel, Lermontov's A Hero of Our Time. *He is young and intelligent but suffers from a sense of frustration with his life, and he is romantically unreliable.*

16 October 1935

There's a war in Abyssinia. A war! How awful. I read about the victims, about the attacks, about shrapnel bursting and bombs being dropped, and I just can't comprehend that there, infinitely far away, in the stifling heat of Africa, bloody slaughter has broken out. I know very well what war is like from books – I don't know how many times I've shuddered as I read about bellies ripped open and human stumps with no arms or legs – but as I read the dry reports I just can't imagine that now legs are being torn off and people are dying in the real world.

It's an insult that all around me everything calmly carries on as if nothing is happening. People keep on studying and working in the same way, they keep on seething with their own petty little passions even in the face of unrelenting death.

Nina is referring to the Italian invasion of Abyssinia (now Ethiopia). The following year, Emperor Haile Selassie would lose power as a result of Italian dictator Benito Mussolini's military campaign in East Africa.

23 October 1935

I'm changing my way of life. I don't want to study so hard

any more, because it's quite enough to get 'good' in all my subjects – I'll have time to crank up to 'excellent' in the final, tenth class. In school, they teach a lot of unnecessary details that are quickly forgotten and you can only absorb by swotting. That's a waste of time. My God! How quickly the days fly by, and I don't have time to get anything done!

I've distanced myself a bit from Musya and Irina because of the boys. I was always an outsider in that group, and now more than ever, because Dima is very angry with me. What a snake! Without even noticing it, day by day, I'm turning against him more and more. His conceit, his egotism and selfishness drive me up the wall. As far as he's concerned, everybody else was created to pander to his whims, to serve his purposes.

On 29 September, at the party at Irina's place, Dima proposed a toast to his success and clinked glasses with everyone. I knew a bit about these successes of his and refused to toast him. I remember him saying in a measured tone: 'You don't want to drink to my success? As you wish.' But he whispered in Musya's ear: 'I'll never forgive Nina for that.' Weird. A quiet, timid girl who is afraid of everyone and has avoided him has suddenly provoked Dima's intense dislike. I reckon he thinks I'm cleverer and more dangerous than I actually am.

At times, I can feel hate building up for that handsome pink face with the classical profile and, without bothering to think whether it's a good thing or not, I start looking for opportunities to offend him. My desire to make him angry is strangely tangled up with a desire to make up with him. I deliberately leave the courtyard to Dima as soon as he starts to play; during breaks, I briefly glance his way now and again and, sometimes, when I catch his wide, unfriendly eyes perhaps not quite on me but somewhere very close, I think: How does he feel about me and what does he think about me, this bizarre individual?

But, even so, this bizarre individual is devilishly handsome. I don't know how all this will end – after all, Dima is one of those people who never forget anything. Musya once told me: 'If Dima got the chance, he'd do anything to spite you.' It's odd to think that I've made a serious enemy, I, who have always been, if not on friendly terms, then at least on diplomatic terms with everyone.

3 November 1935

Musya and Ira's groups have a bad influence on me. Without them, I would still have had the chance to turn over a new leaf, but they tug and pull at me and, with my lack of will power, I just can't break free of their influence. Who would have thought it? All day long we talk about nothing but boys. We're always mentioning Dima, Kolya, Ira. How many times is what they've said repeated, their actions discussed. I have to admit that Dima comes first in these conversations: what he did, what for, how he stood, how he looked at someone, how he laughed as he did it. My God! So much precious and irreplaceable time has been wasted on these conversations.

Well, now it's clear why women are so much stupider than men: they share one distinctive weakness – spending their time idly and using it irrationally. I often listen to conversations in the street: the boys talk excitedly and argue breathlessly, about the war, cars, about how a tram is put together, about films; the girls either say nothing or spout some kind of nonsense ... about boys. And not once, *not once* have I heard men or boys talking about us. It's quite amazing!

But how can I change any of this? I try talking about Abyssinia with Musya, but she doesn't read the newspapers. I don't know how to bring it up and, anyway, she'd just tell me where I could put my Abyssinia. And the boys despise us so much they'll never agree to talk about serious things with us.

4 November 1935

The last year of my life and the year before it have been nothing but a protracted, strange and stubborn fit of hysteria. I've got over it, but I've paid for it with the loss of my abilities. It's clear to me that I used to be far from stupid, and I had an excellent memory but, now, I've lost it completely – yes, completely. I sometimes feel so bitter: if only I could remember everything that I read, my God, how much I'd know already, how many different interesting ideas and facts.

I've just read the newspaper and tried to reconstruct what I read in my mind – but I'd already forgotten half of it. Irina has an excellent memory: she remembers so many little things, sometimes I'm really astonished at how so much can fit inside that narrow little forehead of hers. It's

such a pity she's not a boy – she could have made something of herself.

What is this urge that's come over me? I feel like writing,
but I've got nothing to write about. But, then, I'm talking
nonsense: anybody else in my place would find so much to
write about, but not even my imagination is working.

8 November 1935

The holiday is over, the great revolutionary holiday, but
my heart is filled with a kind of dull fury and
dissatisfaction, and there's no celebration in it. I'm a
little bored, a little sad, and I don't feel like studying at
all. It's incredible! I enjoy reading serious scholarly
books, I take an interest in glancing through the
newspapers, but anything that has even the slightest
whiff of school or drilling or compulsion about it just
turns me off, no matter how interesting it might
actually be.

A few days ago, there was a scandal at school. The
whole eighth class bunked off the written literature test.
Liza K. was the only one left, and she went to the headmaster and told him everything, and we boycotted her
for that. The next day, they gave us a really bad telling-
off, decided that it was counter-revolution and looked
for the ringleaders. Poor Lev was called to see the headmaster twice, and he came back with his eyes all red.
Things have almost got to the point of him being expelled
from school, and I suddenly decided that was what I
wanted, because . . . Where will he go? Probably they'd try

to get him a place in the *rabfak*, and then I could go to keep him company. But that's all pie in the sky, no more than one chance in a hundred.

I really long for more life, more movement, and I haven't even got anywhere to go in the evening. But I still happen to have plenty of things to do today and, apart from that, my lessons! Lessons! Whichever way you look, that's what everything comes down to. It looks as if I'm going to drop out of the 'excellent' grades for the whole of the second term. I have to admit that it's all due to my stupid moods; my resentment and dilly-dallying lie at the root of my dissatisfaction. What I should do is fall in love with someone, but there isn't anyone in school. I can't love Dima, can I? The only interesting boy in the school, and he's a creep.

8 November was a public holiday to celebrate the October Revolution (November in the Western calendar) that had led to the Bolsheviks seizing power in 1917.

17 November 1935

As I was taking my coat off and handing it in, I was thinking of how to walk through so that I could take a quick glance at myself in the mirror and see whether I truly am so very unfeminine or if I'm not too bad really. My poor figure and, as ever, my plain face are always on my mind; I've even begun to walk in a cramped sort of way, holding my arms half-bent across my stomach, like some unsophisticated little girl. I'm afraid to make a single unnecessary movement in case I look ridiculous. I took my number and walked on further into the spacious, bright foyer.

The clinic was beautiful, gleaming clean, the broad white staircase led upwards with two symmetrical branches running off it and circling round above to lead on to the second floor. I walked past it and went up the other, more modest 'back' staircase. On the third floor, I was deafened by a hubbub of deep voices, and I felt frightened and stopped on the stairs, raised my eyes and looked up at the landing.

A tall, strong-looking young man looked over the banisters and watched me from above. I suddenly felt embarrassed and afraid and I nearly ran away, but I had to go up there no matter what, otherwise my memory would never be cured. But to go through the *profotbor* . . . I really didn't want to do that. It seemed to me that there were only boys up there, and I felt really scared. So I didn't go up after all, and walked around the clinic for a while, thinking. Then I went home.

But, at home, we had a big row. Mum just can't understand us, and neither can any of the other grown-ups. They insist that we must help at home, tidy, clean up and cook. It's easy for them to talk, when they don't have anything to do apart from cooking. What difference does it make to Mum whether she goes to work or stays at home to keep house – she's wasting her time in both places anyway.

But what about me? Every minute's precious for me. All I look for all day long is something new and useful. At school, at home, I only have one thought – to learn. But then I have to peel the potatoes and wash the dishes. That means I have to waste a whole hour or two, furious, repeating to myself over and over: The time's passing, it's passing, you're wasting it, this precious golden time.

Questions often pass through my mind: is it right or is it wrong? Should I give up all housework and devote myself totally to studying, stop taking any notice of Mum's reproaches that there she is, tired and getting old, and I'm just sitting there reading. Or just the opposite – should I help her with everything, be a diligent daughter but then remain a stupid mediocrity for ever? No, not for anything!

I must prove that a woman isn't any more stupid than a man, that she is also a human being, that she can work and be creative. I know how men think, how highly they think of themselves and how they're always insulted if a woman beats them at anything. And I want so badly to prove to them that we can succeed, that our heads are not just full of clothes and boys. Ah, if only I could get into some other group, in different surroundings, with serious people.

28 November 1935

I sat down to wait for the neuropathologist. A nice, cosy little room, almost empty, dark walls relaxing to the eyes, comfortable wicker armchairs. I sat down beside the table, leaning back in my chair and crossing one leg over the other, and all at once a pleasant feeling of calm came over me, as if this were not a strange waiting-room but a room that I had known and loved for a long time. I didn't like getting up when my turn came. I walked timidly into the office.

Sitting at the desk was a huge, black-haired doctor, and the simple fact that he was a man and so frightening and bull-like made me instantly dislike and distrust him and feel embarrassed. He looked at me closely, with his big bull's eyes. I suddenly decided there and then that he didn't know anything and that I wouldn't believe a word he said. The whole time he was asking me questions and carrying out his examination, I was just waiting for the end of the consultation.

He stood me up, took hold of my head and looked into my eyes: 'Has your eye been like that since you were born?'

'Yes,' I replied dismissively. Naturally, just as I thought, he didn't say anything that was any help, and I left feeling frustrated, angry and depressed. So he noticed my eyes straight away ... So they're that obvious, then? Yes, of course they are. Where did you get the idea that it had gone away? So I'm a monster again? Yes, again. And so I sit here in front of the mirror, looking at myself ... and crying. And I haven't cried for a long time. Somehow I just couldn't squeeze the tears out before; there was just the old, familiar, terrible stifling feeling inside.

I've never given in to anything before – after all, I was always able to find a way out: when I didn't get into the *rabfak*, I didn't despair; when my memory started to fail, I still hoped to get it back, but now it's beyond repair. That means more whole days of torment, fear and isolation. I was in a state of happy ignorance before. But now I just feel ashamed of myself.

Ugliness is the most terrible thing in life – but on your face and in your eyes! Damn, damn! Sobbing in helpless fury, pulling your hair out and knowing that you'll never be able to change anything. To be branded for no reason with a stigma that never heals for the rest of your life can drive you insane. And it's nobody's fault, no one's to blame, and you start feeling furious with yourself. Feeling hatred, contempt and anger. Tomorrow, I won't be able to look anyone in the eye – I'll feel so ashamed. And so, now, no more illusions, no more dreams? No, I can't live like that! My God, I think I'm going to go mad. What can I do now? What can I do?

I'd only just started to change, just started to calm down, and now . . . I suffered two blows today. I'm a fool and a monster! Why was I given these things they call pride and self-respect? I want to be brilliant, famous, I want love and happiness, but I've been given shame, hatred and despair. Despair! What a lovely-sounding word, and what a terrible one. Despair means death. It means there's *no way out*. There, now I can feel that repulsive, heavy viper coiled tight round my heart again, sitting there and gnawing away at me. It's the fury of powerlessness, it's the hatred of a monster.

My God, how stupid I am. If you read my last entries and the very first ones, you can't find any difference between them – not only the style but the expressions are exactly the same. In three years, I haven't advanced at all, and the doctor says: 'It'll pass.' No, it will never pass.

28 November 1935

Really early yesterday, Mum and I went to the Butyrka. It was just beginning to get light: the blue night seemed to be completely saturated with the subtle, barely tangible breath of morning. The air was somehow especially fresh and pure, or it seemed like that because I had only just got up and I was feeling bright and cheerful. Snow was falling in finely scattered flakes; people were hurrying on their way.

I reached the prison frozen and furious. There were a lot of people there. There were women sitting on benches, half asleep, with little bundles, big bundles, bags and whole sacks. Almost all women and all very different: old and young, cheerful and numb with misery, simple and cultured, a lot of workers. And they all had expressions of apathy and a sort of resigned grief.

As far as the politicals are concerned, there seems to have been a change: the Butyrka has become their prison; they don't exile them any more without trial or investigation, like they did five years ago. And they explain things to the relatives more politely.

Although Nina does not mention it in her diary, her father had been rearrested that autumn and taken to the Butyrka prison for political prisoners, where he was held for several months before being exiled to Kazakhstan.

My God! I can't bear the idea of going to school to-morrow. There'll be technical drawing, and I don't have a single drawing; it takes a whole evening to do one, and I have to go to Musya's place for the sketches. Will Mum let me stay at home? What if she won't? Then I'll be done for. But I'm sure she will, I really am a bit unwell.

I want to leave school again. A few days ago, I was talking with Yulia, and we left school together: 'Yulia, I'd like to have a talk with you.'

'Come on then, my girl,' she said gently, speaking in the way that only Yulia can, and took me by the arm.

'Yulia, I'm already such a little gypsy, but I want to leave school again. What do you think, will the *rabfak* be taking in students in January?'

'No, Nina, no. There are never any free places in good *rabfaks* in winter.'

'Never?'

'No, but I suppose I could have a word with Klavdia Ivanovna – there's a chance there'll be a place, but it's a long shot. Wouldn't it be better for you to stay in school? Or, perhaps the financial situation is bad at home? Of course, you'll tell me why you don't want to study at school, won't you?'

So, naturally, I told her: 'Yulia, you see, I'm already sixteen, and I'm surrounded by fourteen-year-olds, little children.'

'But that's nothing. It used to show when you were younger, but now the age difference will even out more and more with every year. And you haven't got many fourteen-year-olds in your group, most of them are fifteen, and they'll be sixteen soon, so they'll be the same age as you.'

I didn't tell her that I'll be seventeen in a month.

My God! Seventeen already, and I still feel like a little girl.

How ridiculous. I haven't lived yet. I have absolutely no memories to keep from those seventeen years. I don't mean just feelings, but you have to admit that feelings do play an important part in life, as a stimulus for work, for study, for life itself. I haven't had any real friends yet, or any happiness.

24 December 1935

I don't know how to cry, I just hate spitefully, drily. I hate everything, myself and the entire world. I want something that I can't get and I'm profoundly dissatisfied with myself all the time. I feel like crying, but I don't know how. I'm so bored, depressed and ashamed for being such a failure in life. But I'm not the one to blame for that, God knows I'm not. Where can I get more intelligence and ability from? Oh, if only I were clever. I can feel such strength in myself for work, if only I had some confidence in myself. That means I should give up everything: school, and books – what do I need all that for now? I became convinced a long time ago that I'm not clever, but I can't get used to the idea. It really hurts. Now, I can give way to debauchery, because I passionately want some kind of powerful, unusual feelings. What if Mum were to read this? Ha-ha! Why, it's all just a load of nonsense.

29 December 1935

For two days I haven't been able to make myself write about what happened on the twenty-seventh. It made me frightened and embarrassed to remember it, but all the same I kept thinking about it every moment. I flunked literature and chemistry. It's so disgraceful and shaming. My God, how ashamed I felt. I couldn't look anyone in the eye! I felt they were all laughing at me. And the really awful thing is not that I didn't get 'excellent' for my answers, the awful thing is that this is the death blow to all my hopes. Not to get a little thing like that. What a disgrace! It means I'm a complete fool. At home, I sat and cried angry tears, then I went to the exam board, but I didn't get any sense out of them. By evening, I was totally hoarse.

Yura and Valya came to see Zhenya and Lyalya, and they decided to make fun of me. That made me so furious that I ran away and refused to talk to them. I was so hurt and upset, so upset I could have cried. Strange how all these horrible things happened on the same day – I simply lost heart. Yesterday and today, I didn't go to school, and I just tried to sleep all day long, I didn't attempt to do anything, but there was one thought weighing down my heart like a heavy stone: What's the point of studying and learning now? It made me want to give up school and everything. I was almost at the point of thinking about suicide.

Although Nina considered that she had failed, she actually got a 'good' in both subjects but not the 'excellent' she had been counting on.

4 January 1936

On New Year's Eve and the next morning, I could feel the movement of time. There it was, crawling along, slowly and inexorably, immense and implacable. Another year had rolled by and disappeared. I'm not thinking about it any longer. I keep striving forwards, still dreaming and wanting something, and there's not a single good memory to mark the past year. Life was colourless and grey.

I feel terribly ashamed that I'm seventeen now. I've reached the stage of lying and saying that I'm sixteen. It's the first time I've ever lied about my age in my life, and I think I'm beginning to regret that I left the *rabfak* in autumn, but nothing can be done about that now. I'd be happy now to study night and day for another month or two in order to be able to leave school. It's absolute torture to be aware of your own powerlessness. Now I've gone and spoiled my mood, when I'd been keeping my head above water until now.

Now I know how to do it, and I've changed. Now I'm not afraid of my sisters' friends: I don't sit there never saying anything and, most important of all, I can be bright and cheerful, laugh and joke. And I know why. Nobody used to pay any attention to me before, because I was little – that really hurt me; I used to turn shy and timid and instantly become stupid.

Zhenya G. came before anyone else was there. I went to open the door, absolutely certain that it was Mum, and, when I saw the familiar face I hadn't seen for so long right there in front of me, my heart skipped a beat the way it used to and started pounding away really hard, but then I behaved with him just the same as with all the others. Zhenya arranged some unusual lighting by covering the lamps with coloured paper, and it made everything look so beautiful and festive. The mood at the table was lively and amusing; Nina P. started kissing everybody, to general hooting and laughter.

She drank a lot, flirted with Andrei and was looking really good. Andrei was odd somehow and a little bit off-putting: he never says anything, just sniffs with his long nose and laughs unpleasantly. In the group, he got in everybody's way and was a real pain in the neck. He kept running off with Nina into the next room, for a kiss maybe, or he was trying to get his arms round her. What a toad! Always trying to touch everyone, get his hands on you or stoop down over you. Only his eyes are any good, large and really blue, exceptionally bright.

10 January 1936

Tomorrow I have to go to school, but since I never picked up a single textbook during the holidays and didn't think about school at all, I feel as if I've finished with school for ever. I don't feel the urge to see anybody, not even Musya and Ira: they are complete strangers to me – I hardly even know them. Either I'm very hard-hearted and insensitive by nature, if I can forget my friends so quickly, or there wasn't any real thread that bound me to them and we didn't have any common interests, apart from boys. And I was only interested in how the boys looked, and because the other girls were interested in them.

A few days ago, I went to the doctor about my nerves, and he examined me attentively for a long time (because he gets paid a fee) and, after not finding anything (of course), he prescribed me two medicines and sponge baths. I'm taking the medicine, but I don't expect it to make any real difference.

I went to the Textile Institute today to register at the *rabfak*; I'm doing it all in great secrecy. I've learnt from bitter experience not to tell anyone about my attempt until the very last moment. Yesterday, I pinched my sister's student ticket from her on the quiet and hid it. This afternoon, I approached the institute building with a sinking heart, afraid that I would meet one of their friends, and trying to think what to do about it if I did.

In the institute, there were students going in both directions: some had only just arrived and were taking their coats off, others were on their way home. At one point, I thought I saw Yura approaching – I didn't know what to do with myself, my mind started racing. Then, I went into the study section and asked some office minion how I could find the *rabfak* office. 'There isn't any *rabfak* here, it's in the other building.'

'Can you tell me the address?'

'It's just over there, across the road, 51 Donskaya Street.'

My heart started beating faster: number 51, so that meant the same place as Zhenya and Lyalya? That really was lucky. I went home feeling absolutely certain that they'd accept me there, because they told me to come back in a few days' time and, in the other *rabfaks*, they'd rejected me outright. Now, I'm not even afraid of school any more: on 13 January, I'll go to the *rabfak* and, meanwhile, I'll be living in hope.

11 January 1936

Dad's been in prison for several months now. It's strange that none of us worry about it any more, we're not horrified by it, and we talk about it quite calmly like something perfectly ordinary. His trial ended recently, and Mum went to apply for a visit. She was given an appointment for today. She put in an application last month for herself and me. Today, we went to the Lubyanka to get the order, and I didn't go to school. I hesitated for a long time, not knowing where to go, to school or to see Dad. Later, I was unpleasantly surprised to realize that my desire to see Dad was mixed with an appalling feeling of vanity. Several times, I thought that, if I didn't go, Dad would call me self-centred and, if I did, he'd be very pleased with his loving daughter and perhaps wouldn't be able to help thinking: But the older ones didn't come! That was exactly what I wanted (to be singled out), and what I was thinking about most was not the pleasure I'd bring Dad, but the pleasure I'd get from satisfying my vanity.

They gave us the visiting order, but only for Mum. It made me feel so upset I could have cried, and I had to walk along with my teeth clenched in order not to burst into tears. Did I really want to see Dad that much? It's quite possible. Only, even at that moment, I couldn't stop myself thinking about making some dramatic gesture or saying something to impress people and make them take notice of me and think: What a good daughter.

I immediately told myself off for having such a thought and went home feeling as angry as hell. The anger sometimes filled my eyes with tears, and I even felt like shouting out or doing something outrageous. I felt a frenzied desire to tear up the order or throw it back in their faces. The bastards! But I didn't do any such thing: I didn't throw a fit of hysterics and I didn't even start crying, I just carried on calmly walking beside Mum and thinking that I wasn't thinking about Dad at all, or about not seeing him, all I was thinking about was that we mean absolutely nothing at all to these villains who hold the power.

My pride was suffering, my self-respect had been injured . . . and that was all. But all that anger and bitterness! It seemed to be flooding everything, drowning me. I hated positively everybody. And I took stock of all the people I passed, with a furious and gloomy glare, frowning and thinking about how people felt when I looked at them and that everyone was thinking about me.

The Lubyanka, where Nina collected the visiting order, was one of the most infamous NKVD prisons in the USSR, and later the headquarters of the KGB.

13 January 1936

There have been all sorts of incredible, sudden changes in my mood, but never one like this before. The third term. The first day at school, and I'm in a terrible mood, as if I've been studying for two months without a break. As if I hadn't got any rest at all. Before, I used to feel fresh after the holidays, and I would go to school with a certain feeling of hope, with desires, but now . . . just anguish.

Today in school, I joked and fooled about, because I know that I am a fool. But at home, I feel so bad I could cry. In the evening, I went to the *rabfak*, but the director wasn't in and, while I was waiting for him, doubts started creeping up on me. All sorts of nasty little questions came into my head, and I couldn't tell which was the lesser evil.

I kept asking myself: Will you feel comfortable studying in the evening? You'll be all alone, surrounded by horrible people; they'll laugh at you and mock you. And they'll be all around you, these repulsive faces, and you're sitting there in the corner, glowering at them suspiciously and looking around in fright, feeling the hostility and mockery building up in all these strange hearts. My God, there's no limit to what my obliging imagination is capable of sketching, the castles it can build in the air or cast down into a black pit.

I waited for an hour. But the director didn't come, and I went home with my torment unresolved and, all the way back, the dark shadow of these doubts lay in my heart. And at home . . . I knocked and heard a man's footsteps inside the door. Zhenya G. opened the door for me, then took several soft steps away from me with that unusual

walk of his and asked: 'Where have you come from? Ah
. . . yes, from the girls' place.' I was a bit embarrassed,
having been taken by surprise, and, for the rest of the
evening, I acted a bit crazy. Not because of him, of course,
but out of loneliness . . . No, I won't, to spite them all, I'm
not going to suffer any more. Damn them! I won't!
I'm going to throw it in all their faces that I'm happy.

15 January 1936

I don't want to study, I don't. Our home help, Manya, has
fallen seriously ill, and I stayed at home with her. She has a
temperature of about 40 degrees, and she can't be left on her
own. I'm here, reading a book. The weather outside is hazy
sunshine and a slight frost, with sometimes a few flakes of
snow. The sky is exceptionally blue and brilliant.

I'm seriously angry with Zhenya G. because he talks to
me with such casual familiarity and tends to ignore me.
It's odd: he's sensitive enough to be able to understand me
and polite and kind enough to be nice to me. But he
doesn't do either of these things, although I'm not really
asking for special treatment, am I? He doesn't treat me
like Yura, Zhora or even Andrei do. They talk to me in a
natural way because they like me or they're curious about
me, but the way Zhenya talks to me is different. I feel that
every word he says to me is insincere, that he's forcing
himself to do it, in order to look kind and be kind. But he
does all this with his mind (and so it's all a pretence), not
with his feelings.

17 January 1936

It looks as though the *rabfak* is a lost cause. They told me to come in on the twenty-fifth and, although I'm stoking up my hopes, in my heart, I can tell that it will come to nothing. I try to reassure myself and say: Never mind, Ninok, just another five days in school and then you'll be able to go to the *rabfak*. And, immediately, the evil thought starts creeping up on me from a distance: Yes, just wait and see how they accept you. When they say, 'Call in after a few days, but I can't promise anything,' that means there's no chance. But still I keep on hoping, and I'm not going to school.

It's odd, but Mum doesn't try to stop me, as if she understands the state I'm in and completely agrees with me, although that can't be true. Or is she so busy that she's given up on me? No, that's not it. Probably, she knows that I have a good reason and she simply doesn't ask me about it because she trusts me completely. My God! **Poor Mum. I feel so sorry for her, and I hate everyone who's to blame for making her have such a hard life. Sometimes, I want to help her so much.**

It seems as if something unexpected will happen at any moment, and everything will change. But nothing does happen. And she's become old, sick and apathetic. Towards everything, even towards Dad. She's like an overworked carthorse who somehow keeps going in her uncomfortable harness all day long, pulling heavy loads by sheer inertia. Putting up with the beatings submissively and calmly out of habit.

Mum knows her duty. She'll carry on fulfilling that

duty until she has absolutely no strength left, until she dies; her own self and all other concerns come second to that. If she has the time to deal with them, she does, but if not, she tries to forget them, without any fuss and self-sacrificingly. Mum is the ideal of a mother. I've never met any other mothers like her, apart from Granny.

She has devoted her entire life to us. For her, having children was the most important thing in her life, because having children means losing yourself, renouncing yourself and living only for them. She takes no interest in her own health any more and talks calmly about death as a release, but she doesn't try to improve her life, because every hour of rest robs us of a badly needed kopeck.

But Dad's in the Butyrka prison. In prison, with his wild and helpless hate, with his energy and ability and sick eyes. I went to the Political Red Cross today and handed in a petition. It's a curious kind of institution that makes a lot of noise about itself and does absolutely nothing.

I heard from the other people that they've been going there for several years without getting anywhere at all. There are a lot of people there, and the room is disgusting, like a cattle pen. They don't say much at all in answer to the visitors' questions, only 'We'll try, but it's not likely anything will come of it.' What kind of reply is that?

I'm doing absolutely no studying at all but, tomorrow, I'll have to start, because on the nineteenth I'm going back to school. I don't want to be clever and serious any more, I don't want to do anything; I'm just going to dance, fool about, have fun and live for the moment. I've realized that you're only young once, and if I don't make the most of it, then these opportunities to live a little will never come back again. I want to live!

It's suddenly hit me that I'm *seventeen years old*, and this is the best time of my life (that's what people usually think), and I'm walking around in some strange kind of half-sleep, as if I was thirty years old, and all the joys of life are passing me by. I won't have a single memory left of my life, not a single, exciting, happy picture, and a life without a single moment of happiness is no life at all.

I want to fall in love, to make mistakes, but to love. After all, old age without love is a nightmare. I'm horrified now when I notice that I'm just dragging out a pitiful existence, and I immediately think: Don't worry about it, there's still time to set everything right. But in ten years' time, I'll be horrified and curse myself for not having found something to live for, and then there'll be nothing left to hope for.

The Political Red Cross, where Nina went to enquire about her father, was set up in 1917 to give assistance to prisoners. They presented petitions for improvements in the conditions in which prisoners were held, provided lawyers and supplied prisoners with food, medicines, clothes, periodicals and books. They also visited prisons and concentration camps and accepted petitions from prisoners. Perhaps the most important function of the organization for relatives was that, in the early days, it could obtain information about where prisoners were being held and the state of the investigations into their cases.

30 January 1936

Damn! I didn't want to write about my failures, because it makes me feel ashamed even to think about them. I kept on waiting for my applications to succeed, but now . . . I've been refused everywhere: for the architecture *rabfak*, for the Moscow Textile Institute and the foundation courses – as if they'd all conspired against me. And here I am in school again. Boredom . . . and anguish! When I think that I'm already seventeen years old, and my life is so colourless and grey, I start to feel afraid. After all, I know I'm going to regret these years that have crawled by so drearily so much that it will drive me into a frenzy.

It's crowded and stuffy at school, I get so very furious about my own shallowness and my friends' frivolity. Recently, they all offended me really badly. I hadn't been to school for the past six days – at first I was ill and then, I have to admit, I just skipped school – and not one of them came to see me. Not one!

I really can't wait for spring – I don't think that I've ever wanted it to come so badly. I know that I'll be so happy when I see the greenery again, when I feel that indescribable breath of spring that I know so well. Why do I love and want it so much now?

31 January 1936

Living like Oblomov! Today, Mum woke me up at half past six and, before I could even understand that I had to get up and go to school and that I really didn't want to get up at all, she said: 'It's terribly cold, Nina, 25 degrees below freezing. I don't even know if you ought to go or not.'

I didn't say anything but, now, I'm beginning to wonder whether I should go or not. And the more I thought about it, the more I wanted to sleep, and my laziness reared its head. 'I don't know, Mum,' I said, trying not to think about it. Why am I so listless all the time!

As she left the room, Mum turned back to me and said: 'Well, shall I turn off the light or not?'

I thought for a few moments, waved my hand and turned over on to my other side: 'Yes, do.' But I couldn't get back to sleep, and I kept thinking: Ah, you Oblomov, you ought to be ashamed of yourself. But still I went on lying there, remembering the quiet village of Oblomovka and the boy Iliusha, whose Mum used to keep him at home on the slightest excuse so that he would sleep longer and not get cold by going outside to go anywhere.

Yes, but Iliusha didn't think about the harm his mother was doing him, and so he wasn't to blame for the fact that he never made anything of himself. But I'm a seventeen-year-old girl, and I understand perfectly well how bad it is. Yet I still carry on doing it to myself. The idle life and lack of will power of Oblomov. And why doesn't Mum realize that she's turning me into a 'limp rag'. She's nothing at all like Oblomov, but I've already tucked myself up tight in the blanket and started dreaming up an idyllic picture of my future life.

I'm not asleep, but I get so carried away that, at times, it feels as if I'm having a beautiful dream. Some beautiful dacha and a large, merry group of young people, and everybody's feeling incredibly jolly and happy, and I'm there, too – cheerful, lively and also happy. Sometimes, I imagine such unbelievable, stupid things that an hour later I'm embarrassed even to remember them, but while I'm making them up, they seem so real and interesting.

So, I lay there like that until nine o'clock. It started getting light, and the reflections of the lights on my wall started getting paler. The back of my head hurt from lying down so long, and I wanted to sleep, but I didn't want to let go of my dream. I did fall asleep at last and, when I woke up at eleven o'clock, I carried on daydreaming until three in the afternoon. Now that's really bad!

5 February 1936

My sisters have arrived. After waiting for them so impatiently, now I don't really want to see them at all. My empty life continues, the same way it's been going for a while now. Not that you can call it a life, since life means some sort of activity and events taking place, and all I have is contemplation of my sisters' lives. In the evenings, Zhenya has Yura and Lyalya has Zhorka, and I have my anguish and spite.

11 February 1936

I'm feeling very angry – probably there's anger mixed up with almost every feeling I have – and I'm writing angrily, with hate in my heart.

I haven't been writing about the *rabfak*, but that doesn't mean that I haven't been thinking about it. But, then, probably, it's not going to happen and, because of that, I'll be complaining again, and not about myself, of course. Didn't I stubbornly go round all the *rabfaks* and evening classes? I travelled to the MTI six whole times, and they refused me there, and the same thing at the Architectural Institute, too, and all the evening classes. What else is there left?

For some reason, the idea of the Agricultural Institute has just come into my head – in all likelihood, that's my real calling. But it's way off in the sticks, or in Petrovsky Park (which is the same thing anyway), and the journey to get there . . . wouldn't that be fun! But I made up my mind to try even that. Today, after a few moments of total despair, I decided to have a word with Mum so we could finish this whole business on the thirteenth. I'll ask Mum to go to the *rabfak* at the Architectural Institute, and I'll dash across to the Agricultural Institute.

To be perfectly honest, the reason I don't want to go to school on the thirteenth is because they're going to ask questions in geography, and I don't know a single thing about it, and I can tell that I still won't, no matter how long I carry on sitting here, and that means I'll flunk it again. That'd be so humiliating! I'll try to fix things up with Mum for the thirteenth. I really do want to believe that everything will work out, only the moment I think about it seriously – all my hopes start to crumble. I get a painful, anxious feeling deep in my heart, and the kind of panic that comes in moments of absolute hopelessness, when you realize that there was a way out but you didn't find it, and now it's too late. Of course it's too late.

The second half of the school year's already started. I'd have known everything ages ago if it wasn't for Zhenya. The rotten bitch! I gave her my certificate and asked her to find out at the *rabfak* whether they'd take me there or not. I'd thought she'd be able to fix things up but, due to her being so casual about it, she failed to catch the director to have a word with him (the moment I even think about it, I start hating her). And then, today, when I had a word with her about not caring, she suddenly turned angry (as if she was being insulted) and called me a mean brute.

Zhenya and Lyalya are strange people – I've never met anyone so shallow and superficial (not to mention their lack of culture). I can't understand why they don't feel guilty about not doing what they promised, how they could be so incredibly hurtful. It's definitely thoughtlessness – not stupidity but frivolity that prevents them from thinking about life. Life has always protected them and been kind to them, they've always succeeded at everything. They flit about this way and that like little moths, not thinking about a thing. Let them flit about: some day soon they'll get their wings burned.

16 March 1936

My dear friend! It's so long since I talked with you and shared my sorrows. Do you think it's because I'm happy and I don't want to get bored with you? Oh, no. I'm just as unhappy as ever, and I still don't have anybody of my own. Do you understand? Nobody that I can talk to, nobody but you. Yes, yes, I know, you're surprised, you ask me why, in that case, I haven't turned to you, if you are my only friend. It's hard to find an answer to that. There have been lots of reasons, but I don't know if you'll consider them entirely serious enough. Well, anyhow, I'm used to telling you everything.

You remember the last time we talked about the *rabfak*? I was full of going there then, it inspired me and seemed to promise such incredible things, but it caused me a lot of anxiety too. But, even so, it was a hope, which made it worthwhile to live and work, and now it's gone for ever. Does it really matter how that hope was destroyed and how long I agonized about it when, now, here I am again at the very bottom of an appalling dark pit . . .

I won't stay unhappy for long. I'm sick of being a failure, and so I didn't say anything, even to you. I'm sick of complaining to you and, even in your company, I sometimes feel ashamed of my life, which has been filled with nothing but failure. I kept waiting for the time to come when something would happen out of the blue and I would suddenly come to life and be able to laugh and joke like everybody else, but . . .

You remember that at one time I hardly ever went to school. When the *rabfak* idea fell through, I told myself: Well, now, Nina, apply yourself to your studies, you've been lazy for long enough this year. It's time to do a bit of work. And I did start to work – after all, you know how hard I can work, especially when there's something to work for. I had a goal again. A drowning man clutches at a straw – and I also clutched at one. I decided (I feel embarrassed even to write it down) to apply for the *rabfak* again this summer. You can't fault me on persistence although, in myself, I'm just a laughing stock. I need good marks, and I'm going to try to get them.

We recently had a visit with Dad. He's grown a beard, and now he looks like a bishop. He's leaving soon for Alma-Ata. I love him now. Prison, the prisoners, a kind of wide yard, narrow passages, a little window and Dad's face, someone sobbing, cries, hysterics – it's all like a dream. It evaporated, like a scene in the cinema, and was gone.

I intend to go to Alma-Ata myself. I dream about it in the same way that I dream about the *rabfak*. I'll go away into that Asiatic backwoods, I'll walk across the mountains, eat apples and, perhaps, for a while at least, I'll escape from myself.

Alma-Ata ('Father of Apples' in Kazakh), the capital of Kazakhstan, was a frequent place of exile for former political prisoners in the 1930s, before the Great Terror had begun in earnest. Nina's father had been sentenced to three years' exile in Kazakhstan, for anti-communist political activities.

23 March 1936

The holidays have started. Only five days but, even so, it's a break. And I'm tired. For the first time in my life, I feel that I'm genuinely tired. My head aches, I want to sleep all the time and, all in all, I have quite a few symptoms of chronic fatigue. But I only have five days to rest. There will be a lot of studying to do during the fourth term. I have to store up my endurance. I still have another two and a half months to study. That's an awful lot. Exams . . . This studying is such a punishment!

It's spring outside, my seventeenth spring. And I have these seventeen years behind me now. My God! I've been through so much and lived so little in seventeen years. I reminisce a lot now, and reminiscences are a sign of old age. Damn! I've taken so little that is any use from these seventeen years. By now, I could have become really cultured and clever, but how have I turned out? A real dunce. It's incredible, but for some time now I've stopped developing. I'm just standing still on the same spot or, perhaps, now, I'm even moving backwards.

There are no letters from Dad. That's odd. I wait for them every day. What could have happened to him? No, no, it can't be anything terrible. Why do I get such stupid ideas into my head . . .

11 April 1936

There's no denying that people can get used to anything in the world; it's the only fair thing nature's given us. I've got used to everything, and that is a good thing although, occasionally, I still feel up in arms. Perhaps the ability to come to terms with things and accept them is only normal for mediocrities, but it's a fortunate state of affairs nonetheless.

Today, I made a sally out into the world and went round to Irina's place, where there was one boy, Mitya, from the ninth class. Like the rest, he was vulgar and superficial, and Musya was there, looking pretty and dissolute to the point of depravity. And, today, I decided that being utterly alone is better than being in that sort of company. No, there is no way I can make myself sink so low, no matter how good it might feel afterwards.

I understand a lot of things now; there are no question marks hanging over them. I'm an absolute mediocrity, so I can't go to any Moscow State University – that would be stupid. I could try my luck in the fine arts, where patience might still produce some kind of result. I'm nothing special, and I accept the fact soberly, as I should.

21 May 1936

Another fit of insanity. It came on several hours ago, and it's fluttering away like mad. It burst out so unexpectedly; all this time, nothing like it had happened, because I was studying a lot, an awful lot. This month has passed like they all have: there's nothing to say about them except perhaps that my relations with the girls have been more or less mended. Musya has even started talking to me about our friendship, and that's a good sign.

I promised myself not to write about the bad things going on in my diary, because I just find everything awful, but if I don't write anything, that means everything is carrying on as before. Exams from the twenty-fifth! My God! Give me the strength to survive until the seventeenth, somehow to pass them and be rid of them, and then rest, rest for ever and ever.

23 May 1936

God, it's fantastic to feel that soon I'll be free, that the summer is mine and I can do whatever comes into my head. Only I mustn't think about it now, I mustn't think about summer, not notice anything around me, not notice nature, because I only have to notice how fabulous it is for my peace to be shattered.

But I've stopped loving nature. It doesn't affect me like it used to, its beauty doesn't get to me; I've stopped feeling it at all, I've grown cold somehow, something in my soul has died. But, no, it's bound to come alive again as soon as I see the forests and fields, escape on my own into the dappled, dense shade of a birch grove or walk under the gloomy vaults of a pine forest; then the enchantment of nature will return. The fields of grain must look wonderful now, and the grass, and the flowers!

May, May! It is the best month. The air is fragrant with every open leaf, every blossoming twig, the sky is clear and fresh; the greenery everywhere; the nights, warm and quiet. I want to go away to the dacha as soon as possible; I'll get away for at least three days in early June. Surely I don't have to rot here in this pit Moscow? Oh, I've got to make better use of this summer than ever before. I feel such a thirst now for life, for pleasure . . . But these are crazy, empty words. I don't think I really want to leave Moscow as much as I'm pretending. It's all the same to me; at the moment, I'm feeling good.

1 June 1936

There you go. I got 'average' for algebra, and it made me ill for two days. I wept with fury at myself, and with indignation. It was in the evening that I really felt like killing myself, but now that's all over, although I still have absolutely no idea what to do with myself and my life. The weather's great, and I feel like going to the dacha. I can't bear to think that I've still got another seventeen days of school.

4 June 1936

Beauty is a powerful thing. Beauty in general and human beauty in particular. I believe I'm a serious person, I have no illusions and I know perfectly well how often a beautiful face conceals a very ugly soul. And, even knowing that, I still become infatuated with someone beautiful. An ugly person only arouses disgust in me or, in the best case, pity. This is not a good attitude, I give myself a hard time over it, but it happens against my will. A kind of instinctive attraction to beauty.

15 June 1936

The day after tomorrow is the last German exam, and then I'm free for the summer. I'm longing for a rest so much that I even forget about the *rabfak*. To get away from Moscow – that's my only plan, but what's going to happen in the autumn? I won't go to school, and that's a fact (can

I be trusted, though?). The *rabfaks* are almost all closed by now, and I won't be able to study all summer, not because it would be too much for me, but because of my pitiful mental condition. In the autumn, I'll go to a foundation course for some college, even if it's at the Pedagogical Institute.

27 June 1936
Gavrilov Yam

This diary gives a good insight into my character – the pettiness of my soul stands out; nothing can disguise it. To understand me, you only have to look at what I usually think about. Today, I read some of the entries and, I must confess, I felt ashamed: pessimism and boys, boys and pessimism. I can see that this is a bad thing, but this bad thing is the way I am, which is why I dislike myself so much. That's the first contradiction, and there are many more of them.

Pechorin says somewhere that every physical defect has some kind of effect on a person's soul, as if the corresponding part of it dies off. He's so right. I'll begin with my external appearance. You won't find a more incongruous, out-of-proportion figure anywhere: taller than average; powerfully built, mostly due to broad, heavy bones; well-developed shoulders, so broad they're a match for any gallant male's; a low waist; ugly arms and legs.

And so there's not a single positive feature, either in my appearance or in my character. The only beautiful thing about me is a small detail – long eyelashes, but . . . they're so fair they're absolutely invisible. I myself have no idea when the abnormalities in my character began to develop. I remember almost nothing about my childhood, and I haven't been told very much about it either.

When I was still very young, we used to live in Siberia, our family and the Ds, who also had a little boy. He was often punished and every time I used to go to his father to ask him to spare my friend his punishment. He often did, because everyone knows how difficult it is to refuse children.

After that, of course, I get the sequence of events confused. I can remember myself in Moscow already, living with Granny and Dad in our huge, beautiful flat, and Mum and my sisters in the children's home. I'm alone, I don't think I had any companions, because I don't remember them, but I'm playing with a big bright-coloured mouse in a large, almost empty room – for some reason, the sensation of surrounding emptiness and solitude remains clear. At about that time there was a fire during the night, and Dad woke me up and led me out into the street. I didn't feel afraid at all, just curious. No doubt about it, suddenly remembering your childhood is a sign of old age.

The family were vacationing in a dacha in Gavrilov Yam, a large village in the Yaroslavl region, a four-hour journey north-east from Moscow.

327

29 June 1936
Gavrilov Yam

It's raining, and I'm bored. On 1 July, we might go back to Moscow. Really, I don't have anything against the idea. It doesn't take much to make me happy – just one person, someone I can go roaming through the forest with, fishing, boating and generally indulging in all those fun summer things.

But I don't have anyone like that, and so I'm bored. Even though I'm here with Lyalya, I feel as if I'm absolutely alone, especially when she's with Zhorka. There's nothing more awkward than being the third person, feeling unwanted. You can put up with it once or twice but, when it goes on for years, it just gets loathsome. Why isn't a single one of the girls like me? And why is Ksyusha the only one I feel comfortable with? I can be completely at ease with her. Ah, if only I were a bit cleverer.

14 July 1936
Gavrilov Yam

This is the very thing I was afraid of – I'm beginning to get bored. The day passes by so lazily and without any excitement: I get up, have tea, wash, then lunch, sleep and another wash, and so on until the end of the day. And, even though there's so much time, I keep getting the feeling that there's not enough because, for some reason or other, everybody's waiting for each other and wandering around aimlessly with nothing to do. There's an atmosphere of such painful monotony building up that it's enough to make you go and hang yourself. Another reason it's boring is that there aren't many people here – in fact, there aren't any at all (that I know, of course).

I'm spending the summer here as if I were forty years old, that is, like my Mum. But is that really normal? The total physical idleness is making me feel ill; I feel feeble, my arms and legs are turning flabby. If only I could do a bit of rowing to vary the inactivity and tedium. My fantasies in particular have started running wild, and Lyalya says that I have a perverted imagination. I don't know about that, although I suppose it might be true.

7 August 1936
Lebedyan

I travelled from the north to the south, from Gavrilov Yam, abandoned among the pine forests and the gloomy nature of the semi-north, to the jolly, green fruit orchards of Lebedyan, laid out in the midst of the steppes and far more welcoming and attractive than Gavrilov Yam.

Gavrilov Yam is an ugly small town with tiny houses glued tightly to each other: not a single little bush or tree. The whole place simply reeks of unbearable provincial boredom; it's a factory town, and almost all the people who live in it are workers, although there are some bourgeois as well. The factory has altered the face of the town: the streets are full of busy working people, and you don't often come across a quiet side street that's fallen into slumber because it's so humdrum.

The people there are amazingly unattractive, and Lyalya and I used to call them the 'Toads of Yam'. Exhausted, angry, long women's faces would stare brazenly from the windows as we walked along the street: behind our backs, we could feel the cobweb of insinuation and rumour being silently woven. **By the time we left, we hated all the people there, and especially the coarse, stupid and limited workers, in the worst possible meaning of the word.**

It's a curious thing that the dogs were as good as the people were bad (although in Lebedyan it's the other way round). Instead of the constantly lauded solidarity of the workers, Yam was dominated by an absolute antagonism between the local workers and those from outside; name-calling and fighting were nothing out of the ordinary there. For me, all the horrors of provincial towns have come together in my idea of Yam, and we were happy to escape from it.

The thing I enjoy most of all is changing places and moving from one area to another, which I've told Lyalya more than once. I can't live in one place for a long time without starting to get bored, and then I start finding everything that's the slightest little bit familiar hateful and can only enjoy it very rarely.

Lebedyan is an old fortified town in the mineral-rich Lipetsk region, famous for its fertile black earth.

5 October 1936

I'd like to write poetry, only I can't come up with the rhymes. I've just entered a period of reconciliation and inner calm – after all, I'm staking everything on this year. That's what I've decided and, so far, I'm waiting to see what comes of it. This year, I have to harness all my strength, summon up all my energy, will and abilities in order to get as much done as possible. And, in spring, I'll carry out a review and look at what I've done to see if it's worth carrying on working and if there's any hope that I might have some ability. And, then, I'll either give up the struggle or be confident of victory.

My diary is a curious kind of chronicle. Last year, I wrote that I wanted to study, that I had loads of energy and that I was giving myself three years. But I only had enough energy to last a month before I started moaning and feeling unhappy. I really wonder how long I'll last this year. For the time being, I tell myself that I mustn't show any weakness of will and I must study, study, study for the whole year.

The way the girls in school treat me will be very important. At the moment, I'm on good terms with them. Musya says that she really loves me (but with her character, everything could change tomorrow), and Tanya and Ira like me because she does. However, it's a very unstable situation, and if I'm left on my own like I was last year, then school will be hard work for me. The boys who divided us last year are all gone, and that's good news.

13 October 1936

Come on now, jolly wind, and sing a song,
My jolly wind, my jolly wind . . .

He who is jolly always laughs,
Who truly wants will always win
Who truly seeks will always find.
[a popular song from the film *Captain Grant's Children* (1936)]

It would be good if these last lines were to become my motto. How fantastic always to laugh, always to win, but a certain something is required for that . . . Why can't I have that 'something'? I'll get what I want as well, but what it is I want I don't know as yet, because I want an awful lot, I want it all.

I have to fight like a soldier all this year – that's what I'm counting on. That's why I don't allow myself to despair – let all the doubts and all the disappointments come in summer, when I finish ninth class and can look back calmly at the entire year and see what I've achieved. But now – strong faith, resolute strength directed to the struggle, and hopes of victory. Hoorah!

15 October 1936

Here I am, taking it easy. The weather is absolutely marvellous, and the sun is shining in brightly through the window. The room is light, gleaming and beautiful, the bright green patches of the plants on the windowsills are beautiful. It's so great! So great to sing songs when you know that no one will hear them and, at the same time, to dream of singing them to other people, all of whom will enjoy them. It's so good to be alone, because no one forces me to be the usual Nina. I can be beautiful and clever. I can think about pleasant, stupid things and smile at the sun, the sky and my own reflection in the mirror.

22 October 1936

Why is it that I suddenly feel more settled? And it seems that it's going to last for a year: either I got a good rest this summer and restored my nervous system or the firm task set for this year is making me better, or I have simply grown more stupid and deteriorated even further. I feel almost satisfied with my life. I've got used to good and average marks and now I'm hardly unhappy at all. The moment a negative feeling starts to rise, I crush it.

At home, my day is so ordered, so strictly organized, that even if you wanted to you couldn't find fault with it. All my energy and my thoughts are focused on studying, reading and so on, there's not a single wasted minute, no useless conversations. In that, I've achieved my ideal.

At school, things still aren't exactly as I would like: firstly, I don't always hear the teacher (it's such a pleasure to sit comfortably and relax physically and mentally to the monotonous sound of his voice that I forget to listen); secondly, I get distracted by stuff I have to do outside school. Then, the teacher gets angry and tells me off, or I'm interrupted by Musya, saying that she's bored and wants to talk to me. And that's no joke – it's Musya!

I see school as a place of rest, since I have to get my rest for the whole day somewhere. There, I'm distracted from serious thoughts, I act normally, play the fool like a little girl: there, I allow myself to talk nonsense, laugh until my sides ache and exchange knowing glances with Lyovka. But, at home, I immediately become several years older. Here either I quarrel with my sisters, which is extremely nasty but can be put right, or I study, which always calms me down. But what I don't have and I do need for my own development is a circle of intelligent, cultured and serious friends to talk about serious and interesting things with.

Today, Linde gave a report on the events in Spain. Yes, he's a very bright boy, even though, I suppose, I didn't listen to him very attentively and just looked at him, studying his face and figure – it's a lot of fun to let myself do this kind of thing now and again. He has a face that reminds me of some little animal, possibly because it narrows all the way down and towards the nose. He has a huge, intelligent forehead, black hair, a swarthy complexion and little, dark-brown eyes, very sharp, with a way of glancing quickly from under his brows. A very clever face and an attractive, distinctive profile. It drives me crazy that he's so intelligent: he reminds me every moment of my own stupidity.

He is my ideal, the only person I want to be like. I wonder what he thinks about and what his inner world is like? I expect it's incomprehensibly complicated. I think he has a high opinion of himself, which is perfectly justified – you can see it in him: everything about him is permeated with the belief in his own perfection, although it's concealed to some degree by natural tact. Linde will certainly make something of himself in the future.

The Spanish Civil War, which began in July 1936, received widespread coverage in the Soviet press and was much debated, with workers volunteering to join up to fight on the Republican side with the International Brigades.

28 October 1936

Those who fail to adapt die. I had the choice and I chose to adapt, and, with every year that passes, I'm able to adapt more and more. I used to be tormented by my ugliness – now, that has almost passed; I used to be ashamed I was so old, and the awareness of it poisoned my time in school – now, it doesn't upset me and, most of the time, I don't even think about it, it's just occasionally that some casually dropped comment will get to me.

Last year, the awareness that I was stupid and untalented used to drive me to fury and despair but, now, I already feel philosophical about the fact that not everyone can be brilliant and that simple mortals can also be useful to society. I haven't quite got the hang of it yet – after all, philosophy (as abstract, objective reasoning about things) isn't easy when you're young and full of passion and vanity.

But, when all's said and done, it makes sense to believe

that it's impossible for everybody to be equally intelligent; everyone works and struggles according to the abilities they have. In principle, that suits me, and I know that after a while I'll come to terms with it, but I still have failings I'd like to change but can't – I don't know how. It hurts to think that the circle I move in is so empty-headed and shallow. But it's true. I don't want to condemn Irina, Musya and Tanya or set them below me – unfortunately, I'm on the same level as them (superficially at least), and our interests are equally shallow. Stupid and tedious conversations every day . . . Why do things turn out like that?

Women are so one-sided and limited but men, even the most mediocre ones, are really good at taking an interest in everything. No doubt this is partly due to the terrible legacy left to us by the previous generation. Or perhaps women are just more stupid? It's a difficult one. I won't get anything for nothing; I have to achieve equality with men. But are we women really doing our best to achieve it?

We sit in our filthy pit, dug out over tens of centuries, and shout slogans that men have 'invented' for us: 'Long live equality', 'Make way for women' – and not one of us even bothers to think about the fact that these are no more than empty phrases. Some of us are reassured by what our female vanity tells us, and the rest (the majority) are not even offended by their situation.

What can I do to break this vicious circle? My girlfriends are not interested in anything apart from boys (and then they have such spoiled and debauched ideas about boys, they actually think Lyovka's friend is

their ideal man and set him above Linde). All their conversations centre around boys or dirty jokes, and I'm no better than they are, I say dreadful and bawdy things myself. I'm disgusted with myself, but I talk that way because I can't just say nothing all the time, and they won't talk about anything else, and I'll get it all wrong anyway.

Oh, I really understand why the boys think the way they do! In their place, I would despise girls, I wouldn't talk to them. My former school friends were a bit more serious than we are, but they give off a smell of wasting flesh and school rote-learning from three miles away. They can make lively conversation about their lessons, but they're really limited; they wait eagerly through every break for the next lesson and tremble during a test. I don't want to put up with these textbook vultures, so I throw myself into the embraces of stupidity, hooliganism and frivolity.

6 November 1936

In my opinion, a diary is an unnecessary and superfluous thing that provides no benefits, and is therefore harmful. A diary cannot develop your style. It won't be any use to posterity, so what is it for? But I enjoy too much writing down everything that I have in my heart, confiding in someone.

I'm very strange – I've never met anyone else like me. I've got the desire to be liked, to flirt, to have fun, to be feminine and attractive, to laugh wholeheartedly and to joke, sometimes even to talk nonsense; the desire to fill my life with bright, cheerful moments. And, alongside this, I also have the urge to study. I have strict and stubborn thoughts about my future, about my goals in life; my mind is sharp and sound. I want to find something serious and worthwhile in life, a desire to devote myself to learning.

I'm tormented most of all by the company I keep, the people I associate with. Strange as it might seem, I actually despise them at times. But that's terribly unfair to them: I regard them as my friends but, in my heart, I smile condescendingly at the things they say. Sometimes, I envy them and their merriment; sometimes, I try to get away from them. I'm not open and honest with them, because I know they wouldn't understand me. I sometimes get bored when I have to listen to their idle chatter, and I feel ashamed if someone else happens to overhear our conversations. I can't get away from it. In the corridor, in the cloakroom, in the classroom, during the lesson, chatter, chatter and more chatter about nothing but boys. I used to think: Oh, Lord, what should I talk about? About Spain? But they don't read the newspapers. About books? We don't read many of the same things – they read light, amusing but really vapid novels that I won't even pick up.

Of course, they've read the classics, too, but I can't talk about a subject I've prepared in advance for the sake of turning the conversation to more intelligent things. I find that gross, hypocritical. I just can't do it! That's why, in order to have something to do, I start messing about, and then I beat myself up for doing it. I quite consciously allow myself to play the fool.

It's interesting: Ira – and probably the others as well – assume that my infatuation with Zhenya G. affected me so badly that I lost some of my mental capacity, and that I've become less intelligent as a result. It's amazing, the way everything comes back to love for them. Ah, women, women! How biased and shallow you are!

A lot of things have changed. I've grown older: in two months, I'll be eighteen. It's not pleasant, but I tell myself it's not shameful, that even at eighteen it's still all right to go to school, even if you're not little any more. Yes, it is annoying but, most of the time, I force myself not to think about it – so what, there's only two years' difference and, after I've left school, I won't be ashamed of how old I am any more.

My appearance no longer torments me the way it used to – after all, no one reminds me about it. I've become a pretty feeble student, and perhaps that's why I feel so free and relaxed in the lessons now – there's no one to be afraid of. I struggled with myself for a long time, but now I've done it and escaped for ever from the detestable 'bog of the excellent', as my father put it.

There are some things at school that quite excite me. Not long ago, Margosha told Musya in a frank conversation that Schechtman likes me. He's one of those self-assured types who are never at a loss, always maintaining a calm air of dignity and thinking that they're extremely clever.

At first, we all used to dislike Schechtman and called him an upstart, which he was. Now, I don't find him disagreeable any more, and I'm on good, although distant, terms with him. He's very ugly, with irregular and banal facial features, nothing outstanding or distinctive, and the head of a strong, young bull. He's a capable boy, he's read a lot, he knows quite a bit about history, he writes poems and, the strangest thing of all, he always gives them to me and Musya to read. We enjoy that, since his poems do have some wit and humour in them. That's all that I've noticed, and I must say that the girls were in raptures over this news and teased me mercilessly at first, so much so that I could have got totally fed up with Schechtman.

In her assessment of herself, Nina doesn't mention her frequent feelings of deep despair. Perhaps she did not see them as part of her character, but only as a reaction to her frustrations. It is likely, though, that at times she was severely depressed.

20 November 1936

When I have to study a lot, I'm always in a foul mood, because one voice tells me not to swot, and another reminds me how embarrassing it is to get mediocre marks and to stand there saying nothing and knowing nothing. Anyway, of course I study appallingly little and I'm very pleased that I do. As Dad told me: 'Don't wander into the "bog of the excellent".'

There are moments when I'm overcome by depression, when I think about my lack of ability or about Linde. Most of the time, these thoughts are all mixed up together: I only have to think of Linde to remember my own stupidity and vice versa. Perhaps in another year, or maybe two, I'll finally stop tormenting myself about it. Is that good or bad?

Oh, I'm so spiteful and envious! And it's all to do with Linde. He's the only person I admire without any reservation, because he's the only person with talent in all the people around me. He's my ideal person. But it's so stupid: striving for an ideal and not being able to reach it. It's true, ideals are unattainable and, then again, it's quite possible that, in my usual way, I idealize him too much. No, I don't fancy him, I just envy him.

23 November 1936

The evening before a day off is an evening of idleness and relaxation, and sometimes of doubts, thoughts and painful conclusions. When you have free time, you can't help giving in to reflection and, for me, there's nothing worse. On this, the only free evening that I have, I really don't feel like studying. So let's assume I can allow myself this little rest and fill in the pleasantly boring time by writing my diary.

Yesterday, I could feel my liking for Linde particularly strongly: I wanted to watch him, to give all my attention to him. Spending a lesson together already meant something to me. In military training, I went with several girls and boys, including Linde, to a new place to practise shooting there. I didn't shoot because of my stupid cowardice, but I watched Linde with a thrill in my heart.

It's curious that, when girls are in the minority, they always feel a little bit embarrassed and awkward, they always expect some kind of nastiness from the boys, nobody knows what to do . . . I started joking about and kept chasing the boys, because Linde was laughing and, instinctively, I like that. How he's standing and where he's standing, far away from me or not – all this is taking on such a special meaning, it all seems to reveal aspects of him I didn't understand before.

'The first touch decides everything,' Pechorin once said. It's unbelievable: how can a touch be so thrilling? It was Linde's turn to begin shooting and, as he was arranging himself on the floor, he touched my legs, and I really liked it. I've noticed that he is naturally shy, sensitive and extremely modest. Yesterday, I kept bumping into him all day long. I was standing in the doorway and looking into the corridor, when Linde came up from behind me, so I didn't notice him straight away and only heard his low voice, saying something nice, and I suddenly felt the fleeting touch of his warm jacket on my back. No electric shock ran through me, I wasn't scorched and I didn't suddenly turn cold, but the keen warmth of the moment was hugely enjoyable.

Yes, he stood behind me, just touching my back, and there was a gentle warmth in his touch. But, today, I hardly even thought about him at all, I didn't notice him very often, and I thought I'd cooled off towards him, because I spotted him acting like a hooligan. My love must be an ideal: I know it doesn't exist, but I still say it.

Today, something that had been going on between me and Musya came to an end. We'd had a bet: I tried to tell her that Schechtman doesn't like me, and she said the opposite. She won, and when Musya read me his note, 'I say yes', I blushed and felt as embarrassed as a little girl. But, even now, I can't believe that it's true; I don't understand how it's possible to be infatuated with anyone just like that. But, then, if they asked me if I liked Lyovka, wouldn't I say yes? It must be the same thing for Schechtman.

But I'm infinitely grateful to him for not showing that he likes me in the way that boys like to do. He treats me exactly like all the others, and sometimes pays less attention to me than to Musya and, without my even being aware of it, that makes me angry. Today, I felt a bit embarrassed and ridiculous, but I didn't feel any awkwardness with him. Schechtman is obviously interested, because he wrote to ask Musya what was going to happen.

Musya wrote to him about our bet and advised him to ask me himself – that way the whole business is set on the right footing – but I think that if he's smart, he'll never ask. The day after tomorrow, he's going to tell me everything. It's amusing and distracts me from thinking about Linde – I got angry with him today and went around all day loudly saying that there's someone who likes me. I feel embarrassed now and I think that everyone must be laughing at me but now, when the girls say stupid things about me, I really like it.

Recently, as I was leafing through a little book about Sophia Kovalevskaya, a remarkable personality, a woman with an extensive intellect and unwomanish mind, I became more and more convinced that I myself am stupid, hopelessly stupid, and that I'll never rise above those millions of people that they call the masses, the crowd.

Sophia Kovalevskaya (1850–91) was born in Moscow. A mathematician, she discovered a partial differential equation, studied the rings of Saturn and was also a talented novelist. She lived most of her adult life outside Russia, in Germany and Sweden, amongst other places.

26 November 1936

Today, there was a group meeting on the question of poor discipline. The usual stuff! A class is a strange thing. Separately, I understand each of them very well – I like many of them – but the moment we find ourselves together, all hell breaks loose. **What a rotten attitude we have to the teachers; we're secretive and spiteful, there isn't any new, good spirit at all, no 'Soviet' spirit, as they say now.**

We just want to provoke them, be really nasty to them and then, afterwards, keep silent like martyrs to the cause and not rat on our friends (that's what we think admirable). To be quite honest, when I looked at this class today, through the eyes of an outsider, I felt disgusted by these stupid and stubborn creatures, and it was very difficult to restrain myself and maintain solidarity with them. Well, just suppose I had spoken out, what would I have achieved?

28 November 1936

Will there ever be a time when I don't have to feel afraid and ashamed of my age? I don't know.

Lyalya says that it's not good to fight and act the little child the way I do. She's partly right – after all, I am eighteen years old – but I'm surrounded by a crowd of children. At school, I have to be in a state of passion all the time, cranked up in a constant state of false excitement, in order not to feel bored and not be driven into a fury by obsessive thoughts about my age and abilities.

Irina once said that this pretence is very noticeable in me, that I laugh and act happy when I don't really think things are funny at all. But, at school, I can't have even a moment's peace and quiet; I'm always looking for a chance to have a laugh, for someone to pick a fight with, to share a joke or have a chat with. I want to escape from myself and I don't even care if what I do is good or bad or what impression it makes on the people around me.

Linde has nothing to do with me, never pays the slightest attention to me; he's never said a single word to me. Not once! Why? But, anyway, it's all a load of nonsense. Nobody ever talks to me first; I'm always the one that starts talking, and I'm not ashamed of that any more. What of it? If I want to do something with the boys, then I will. Ah, how I hate the girls, I have nothing in common with them, nothing. And how I'd love to occupy a position of authority among the boys. But, of course, that's a tired old refrain.

Today, at the reading of Stalin's report, we got talking with one of the boys, Moskal, who I and Musya are

345

friendly with at the moment. Musya laughed and asked: 'Is it true that Schechtman fancies Nina?' 'Musya, shut up, please,' I screeched, and I got so embarrassed that they burst out laughing. I blushed, hid my head under my coat and turned away. Was he joking when he said that, or did he mean it?

Now, here I am at home, and everything works differently here. I'm the same old Nina who's already eighteen, who's always thinking about books, about studying, about my own development, who's afraid to waste a single moment in shallow talk.

Stalin's report on Soviet progress was presented at the 8th All-Union Congress of Soviets on 25 November 1936 and was evidently read out at school. The congress was dedicated to the adoption of the new constitution of the USSR planned for 5 December that year.

22 December 1936

Love is an interesting feeling: it brings so many new and unusual things with it that it forces you to notice every little detail, to admire every movement and word. A person you have never noticed before suddenly becomes precious and close and excites you the way the smell of delicious food excites a hungry man.

A few words about Linde. Yesterday was a day when I felt that he was particularly close to me. He was moved to the desk in front of me, and I spent the whole lesson looking at the back of his head and his body and thinking about him. It's odd, the way I feel about him: I don't feel any excitement at the sight of him, my heart doesn't beat any faster, the blood doesn't rush to my face and I don't catch my breath, but I do think about him all the time. I look at his tatty blue jacket, which I think is so appealing, at his inclined head and smooth black hair that ends in a dark, curly line on his neck.

He didn't sit still. He was fidgeting all the time and probably feeling agitated. He laughed several times and, almost subconsciously, I tried to laugh, too, so that he'd hear me. He turned his head round several times (there was a perfectly good reason), and before I could even think what I was doing, I also turned, so I couldn't see his face.

I promised myself not to turn round and, then, the very next moment, I made the same stupid mistake again. It was like instinctively holding your hands out when you start falling. It's almost impossible to fall without making some effort to stop yourself. It's strange, but this turning round of his brought a number of thoughts into my mind, or the shadows of thoughts.

It was like a light breeze creeping through the leaves without even stirring them, slipping across the mirror-smooth surface of the water without raising a ripple but still making the imperceptible breath of its presence felt. I wanted to know why he had turned round. Had he really needed to? I suddenly remembered how often I use the same trick in order to get a glimpse of him, at least out of the corner of my eye. So why did he? It meant that he wanted to look at someone, but who? I wouldn't let myself think a single thought beyond that, although my heart was telling me something, but you can't set down on paper what the heart says, and I'll say no more.

In any case, I'm only describing all this in order to point out that sometimes people act illogically when it comes to feelings. I think that no reason is capable of restraining these superfluous, dreamlike thoughts. Only an hour earlier, I found a telephone number which (I'm almost certain) is Linde's. Why should I have any more doubts after that? And yet, perhaps, the longed-for dream finds the facts to justify itself and cunningly hands them to you.

2 January 1937

Another year has gone flying out of my life, another small, unnoticed one that I don't need any longer: I don't want to remember it or think about it. What would be the point? I look forwards and only forwards. All my past failures oblige me to try to set myself to rights, but not to torment myself; after all, people learn from their mistakes. This is what you might call the prelude to the New Year: it has to be celebrated at least that much.

29 December was the last day of lessons and, in the evening, the school had a New Year party. I was still full of thoughts about boys and school stuff, and the lessons passed by happily – they were fun. Musya and I were on song; we sat at the very last desk behind Linde, and that alone put me in a lively, happy mood. It really was nice to see him there so close, to listen to his voice, to watch him. Although, not being in love, I managed to do other things,

too. We took a pine-tree branch and painted it and then gave everybody sweets and fooled about for all we were worth.

3 January 1937

Nina and her elder sister Lyalya saw in the New Year with a group of students at the Institute hostel.

A few words about the New Year. The party was quite lively and jolly, although it could have been better. But, then, some people were in better spirits than others and, after all, I was a stranger there, but I was quite pleased with myself. Either I've changed, or I look more grown up now, but everybody talked to me as an equal and I didn't feel awkward. I wasn't on my own. Like me, Lyalya didn't know the group very well, and so we were together. I soon started getting on all right with two or three young men and felt perfectly at ease with them.

One of them was Yura M., a completely grown-up man, married (his wife, a small, lovely woman, was there too), who had obviously been through hell and high water. I always get on really well with people like that, because they're always open and they know how to make you trust them. Timid people like open, self-confident characters, and I behaved naturally with him precisely because there couldn't possibly be any flirting between us.

I really liked another young man, Boris, who was average in height, sturdy and well built, with a handsome, attractive face. There are some men's faces in which every feature expresses the firmness, manliness and strength that women like so much. His face was just like that: a straight, noble nose, small, firm lips, always with a gentle smile, but with a certain irony to it.

His whole face was given a distinctive appearance by a slightly protruding lower jaw and the firm, straight folds of his mouth (by the way, our Nikolai's smile and the expression of his lips are similar to Boris's). He has large, black eyes with long eyelashes. Boris was alone (without a girl) and, initially, he was a bit bored, so during the first half of the evening he often talked to me and Lyalya.

The wine made him and us more cheerful and sociable, made us laugh and warm to everybody there. And the whole night (I don't count the morning) left me with a vague memory of something tender and pleasant, full of friendship and closeness. Certain hints at tender feelings, the warm touch of hands, an affectionate smile, a close, smiling glance – all those things that lose their meaning once you try to put them into words.

When I drink a few glasses of wine, the first sensation is one of companionship with the people around me; all the barriers come down. I feel close to people. Who hasn't felt that pleasant, dizzy excitement from shaking a man's firm hand or suddenly felt someone take you gently by the shoulders, or stood alone with someone in the room and said something, gazing into a handsome, exciting face? Perhaps it is drunken excitement, but it is beautiful and innocent.

This is the final entry in the diary. The following day, 4 January, a search was carried out at the Lugovskys' flat, in the course of which all correspondence concerning Nina's father, Socialist Revolutionary literature and the diaries of Nina and Olga (Lyalya) Lugovskaya were confiscated. Nina's mother was summoned for interrogation by the NKVD. Poor Nina must have been terrified. According to the secret police report, the girls shouted from the window, 'Goodbye, Mummy! Be brave!', while their mother called back, 'Goodbye, my darlings! Goodbye, for ever!' She was released, but more than two months later, on 16 March, Nina, her sisters and her mother were all arrested and interrogated by the secret police. The NKVD had gone through Nina's diaries with a fine-tooth comb, as the passages in darker print demonstrate. The psychological pressure and torture they subjected Nina to during the interrogation was too much for her, and she confessed to many crimes, including a clearly fabricated plot to assassinate Stalin at the Kremlin gates, inspired by her schoolgirl fantasies of hatred and revenge. By contrast, Nina's mother denied she had committed any crime, except that she had sent food and money to her husband and other exiles.

With her father still in prison himself, Nina and the rest of her family were sentenced to five years' hard labour in Kolyma prison camp at the furthest north-eastern tip of the Soviet Union, far from Moscow. They made up just four of the quota of 30,000 exiles Stalin had ordered his secret police to find in their home city. (In 1937 Stalin's government had decided on a quota of the population to be repressed – 72,950 were to be executed and 177,500 exiled. In Moscow the target was 5,000 to be executed and 30,000 exiled.)

In Kolyma, conditions were unbearable: Nina and her sisters had to contend with bitter cold, the temperatures falling to around minus 40 degrees Celsius. As political prisoners (enemies of the people), they would have been singled out for the harshest treatment and would have had to work either on state farms or in the goldmines, often ill and always exhausted. It was difficult to get supplies to the camp, and food rations were scarce. They must have seen hundreds of their fellow prisoners die. A year after their incarceration, a new series of purges made conditions in the camp even worse, as thousands of new prisoners were brought in and rations were made to stretch even further.

Quite remarkably, Nina, her mother and sisters all survived Kolyma and were released in 1942, although the photos after their release show them dangerously thin and pale. Nina was exiled to Magadan for five years, where she married a fellow campmate and political prisoner, Viktor Templin. Nothing is known of their union, but it is to be hoped that after all Nina's frustrated, adolescent yearnings, Viktor fulfilled some of her romantic ideals, as well as being an intellectual and artistic equal. They later settled in a provincial town, Vladimir. Perhaps because of what happened to her family as a result of her incriminating diaries, in spite of her literary aspirations, Nina never became a writer. Like her husband, she painted instead and became a stage designer and landscape artist. In the 1980s, the couple held a number of local exhibitions and a book of Nina's art was published in France.

During the political thaw of the late 1950s and early 1960s, when many victims of Stalin's Terror were rehabilitated, including her mother, posthumously, Nina repeatedly applied for rehabilitation, but her appeals were declined because, at her trial, she had signed the indictment and confessed to the crimes she was accused of. In 1963, she wrote to Khrushchev saying that she had signed 'to end the torture', and her sentence was finally repealed – for lack of evidence.

Nina Lugovskaya-Templin died in 1993 at the age of seventy-four, having lived to see the collapse of the Communist regime and the end of the Soviet Union two years previously.

EXCERPTS FROM THE LETTERS OF NINA'S FATHER

These extracts from the letters of Sergei Fyodorovich Rybin in the NKVD investigation files are given without dates. Sergei wrote frequently to his daughters from exile and prison. His letters show a difficult, demanding father who was focused on inculcating his own moral standards and political beliefs in his daughters, even during his long absences. Even though most of the letters are addressed to her elder sisters, it is possible to see the influence of his ideas and attitudes on his youngest daughter.

To his elder daughter Eugenia

It's crowded back there in Moscow. It would be interesting to see how it's changed during these two years. I know that the population has increased by 200,000 to 250,000, but I can't imagine how this has affected the traffic. I suppose more unnecessary moving around and jostling for ration cards and other things. I'm fed up of these queues here, too. At least once or twice a month, I also queue up behind someone to get my pound of sugar, tobacco and flour, but I just can't appreciate this proletarian privilege in my life. No doubt, I haven't yet been properly boiled down in the proletarian cauldron. It would be interesting, of course, to read what you saw in the country on your outing, and on such a responsible errand, but I didn't get the letter from Lyalya anyway – it never reached me.

How did you manage to get so tired in the first term? Probably it's the new surroundings that affected you; that's what's making you concerned. It's good that you've parted company with the title of 'the shock-brigade class'. You, especially, little friend, don't get outraged, try to take a calmer attitude to your studies and consciously conserve your strength; restrain yourself from getting excited and nervous. This year will be difficult as far as food goes, you have to be serious about the need to be economical in expending your reserves of physical energy – yours and everybody else's are limited this year. This is a hungry place, too: I keep myself going with grain boiled in milk.

Sport is better, of course, it offers healthier and more varied movement and mobility, it develops and reinforces your strength. Skiing and ice-skating are interesting activities, but the way they give you drill every day doesn't sound very elegant, not musical. It's a drill when you load a cannon or a gun but, applied to people, this is strange and crude. In general, concerning your educators, they're not to blame for this, it's the system: everything is far too crude. Take a close look. It's as if they want to make people into a mechanical part of some machine or other, charging them and setting them going, and you have to spin round and round, like a lifeless, inanimate object. A long time ago, I happened to see the pieces performed by people doing PE in your school, and I was struck very clearly by this coarseness, the absence of beauty and grace. They do the same in the circus, only better, and the inner content of the life of circus artistes is perfectly repulsive. But the way you do it, it's like the army – no doubt they teach you how to stand and march in ranks, too, and how to hold a rifle.

In different conditions, everything would be different, but now we have to act as circumstances dictate. My dear, in beginning the struggle for your right to a human existence, you will have to invest a lot of energy in order to win that right, to occupy and hold a worthy position and not get lost in the crowd, like a grain of sand in the steppe. Remember, my little friend, from the age of fifteen, I began a life of total independence; I was a teacher in the village and I never pine over that. To this day, I have still not lost the energy for struggle and I feel I have enough strength not to get stuck in any one place.

You see, living in the capital, you have the opportunity to receive an education. You should see what the young people are like round here: the squalor's simply pitiful. Someone who has been through the seven-year school or junior technical college still doesn't know how to address someone politely, absolutely cannot read or write in Russian at all and is no good for any kind of work anywhere, with the possible exception of the Komi region. Probably it's the same everywhere in the autonomous republics. The young boys and girls are not taught, more 'entertained' with the awareness of their autonomy and independence.

* * *

And life is so empty and lacking in purpose. The summer's over, there's no more warmth, the time is taken up by working. Living just to live out one's time. You understand the tragedy of huge numbers of thousands of people just idling away their time. Right now, there are tens of millions of workers starving all round the world and, even in Russia, people are not well fed, especially office workers and their families. It's some kind of period of 'universal grief', despair and horror, while there are absolutely colossal reserves of food – as they say, there's nowhere to put it all. They often write off the surpluses in order to hold on to the money.

Write and say if you agree with my view of Tolstoy as a philosopher and politician. Check my opinion against his book. Only then will you be able to consider that you know Tolstoy, when everything becomes clear.

You know, you write the same things as Olga does, as if you had conspired. And so factory life is the same there and here. When you've lived in the world a little bit longer and observed life a bit more, you will see how low its level is in the thick of the people. Even in the village, I think it is probably higher than in a factory, but I might be mistaken now. And there's no point in even talking about this place. The moment it gets dark, everyone closes themselves in with shutters and sits in their closed rooms, and if there's a cow in the yard, they drag it into the hallway or the room for the night, otherwise it will get stolen. Thievery and banditry. The mixture of the thieves' element of Russia and the nomadic Cossacks has produced remarkable shoots. In all the shops – beggars, dozens of them. The drunks fight, and beside them lives a communist who has beaten his wife more than once during the night, and his brothers, and his mother. A depressing picture. In the army units, in the institutions, in the trading establishments, there is theft and embezzlement. The isolated individuals of culture are few in number and they flee from here at the first opportunity.

I know that you are going to study and devote yourself completely to pure art, but you should know in advance that for a long time your path will be a thorny one and that great willpower is required to overcome all the obstacles. And then, time and again, your practical painting skills will come to your aid. Only take post-graduate studies if they will not distract you from your direct studies or exhaust you with petty details. Of course, there is still enough time ahead to think all this through carefully more than once. You know, be as active as you can in the college. I believe that 'practical' people win advantageous positions at the right time – for themselves and their work – and, in any case, they do not just go where they are told to go.

I recommended Lyalya and I recommend you to read Kropotkin's *Mutual Help as a Factor of Evolution among Animals*. An interesting book. Probably that's enough; after all, now you will be very busy with your studying.

Mutual Help, by the famous anarchist and outstanding sociologist

Pyotr Alexeevich Kropotkin (1842–1921), was published in London in 1902. He sums up his central idea as follows: 'Mutual help, justice, morality – such are the successive stages that we observe in studying the world of animals and man. They constitute an organic necessity which carries its own justification within itself and is confirmed by everything that we see in the animal world ... The feelings of mutual help, justice and morality are deeply rooted in man by all the power of instincts. The very first of these instincts, the instinct of Mutual Help, is the most powerful.'

To his elder daughter Olga

I find the school of our time incomprehensible. You have every possible freedom and liberty, all you have to do is study, but your boys and girls play the fool and the hooligan, as you say. Why is that? What issues could there be now, especially in a group where 90 per cent are members of the Komsomol? In former times, we were driven to that by special issues, issues of principle, for which we suffered, but still did not regret it, since we considered the sacrifice necessary. But now you play the hooligan because there are no serious issues in your circle.

But the purge here is continuing; the way the Komis [*the local native tribe*] here relish everything is comical. The people are undeveloped and take every petty detail seriously, they spend weeks rummaging through each other's books, identifying deficits, writing reports about their work. If Soviet power is to be regarded as the ideal of modernity in all its manifestations, then you have to come here and look at the way these non-Russians, who are now national minorities effectively possessing all the rights of the majority, even, in fact, the most important right – the right of the majority: you have to come and admire just how conscientiously and willingly they put all of Moscow's designs into practice and, yet, even with that kind of attitude to work, things do not go well. And they have no doubts about anything.

Absolutely everybody is hostile to everybody except himself. Appreciate that fact and do not forget it. Do not try to do anything with them or help them, keep as far away as possible from any dunghill that stinks and poisons the air. For instance, you wrote that you were thinking of entering the *fabzauch* [*factory and plant college*], but think whether the situation there is the best. The system of education practised by them is the same everywhere, but I think it is probably even worse there, since the situation is further worsened by coarseness and vulgarity, with the compulsory addition of informing on each other. When you think things over a bit, then, with age and time, you will come to understand and realize what kind of situation they have in other places, where people die like flies, when they know how to die in protest against such a life. You have to get good books from somewhere, enrol in a library and, if necessary, it's better to pay a little for using books.

You shouldn't read any more rubbish like Verbitskaya. People were enthusiastic about her after the first revolution of 1905, as soon as reactionary viewpoints and decadence started to spread. Also, in the theatre, it is ten times more interesting and useful to watch a classical piece than Gorky. Alexei Gorky is no classic, after all, no matter how much they may shout about him. Let's talk about what you're going to do next year, that is, when you go to college. I think that you and I will not waste our life cheaply.

That means you'll have to work harder at physics. I thoroughly approve of your choice. In general, building and producing something new, and especially a machine that makes man's work and life easier, is enjoyable, interesting and attractive work. I think the future belongs to machines in all areas of life, and especially in Russia, where we have fallen far behind other countries. Meanwhile, you get on with your studies, and we'll see what happens. After all, this is an extremely complex and wide-ranging cycle of sciences, and you will have to choose among them. I shall be glad if you are not shock-workers.

Among my books there you will find Kropotkin's *Mutual Help as a Factor of Evolution among Animals*. I don't remember the precise title right now, but you'll be able to figure it out yourself. Kropotkin is a really major scholar in Russia and abroad, the founder of anarchism; he is also as famous in his own area as Tolstoy is in literature. I advise you to read this book and get a fresh impression; it will explain many things, it is easy to read and will be useful in biology at school. So you are beginning to read – well, that's good. Take a critical attitude to everything, check everything, take nothing on trust, clarify things in other books, write to me about your doubts, and I shall always be glad to answer you, although, of course, you can't say everything in a letter. The main thing is, do not be in a hurry to construct your own 'convictions' out of two or three books that you have read, do not hurry. For that is not everything. You need to know all the objections and the opinions for and against. You know, sometimes you can't find the reading matter you need on one question or another, but you need to know and therefore you'll have to ask.

A. A. Verbitskaya (1861–1928) was the author of numerous women's novels that were topical but extremely superficial. Alexei Gorky is Maxim Gorky. The writer combines the author's name, Alexei Peshkov, with his pseudonym, Maxim Gorky.

To his elder daughters, Eugenia and Olga

I thought from the very beginning that you were too over-burdened with serious studies, but it seems that you have a lot of free time and have taken up singing and gymnastics, not as part of your school studies, but in special clubs. Lyalya is evidently planning to be a wrestler, and Zhenya a boxer. I imagined that in the seventh group, the so-called 'shock-brigade class', you would really get down to serious work, but you still continue to immerse yourselves in uninteresting or, rather, absolutely useless pastimes. I used to write you more serious letters; you did not answer them, you were not capable of it. Have you not concluded from this that you are very backward?

At the present time, the person who will survive is the one who is most intelligent and developed, the one who knows the most. You yourselves do not notice how the superfluous burden of these useless clubs overtires you. In this way, these clubs are simply harmful to you, and I advise you to give them up and in general devote more attention to studying at home, since these clubs of yours are simply time for idle chatter. Your schools are second-level, with a more demanding programme than the old grammar schools and, in addition, with a bias to 'social studies' and empty time-wasting. The most important thing, my dears, is for you to be truthful with me and your mum. We have a lot of experience of life, we will understand everything you have to say.

How is your reading? Has no desire appeared to read scholarly books and, if it has, in what disciplines? In a year or so, you will be reading my library, too, it has a lot of interesting and valuable books in it. Soon, your social-studies teacher will appear again and start wearing you out. Now, he's probably giving your class the resolutions of the latest party congress to study but, by that time, life will have moved on far ahead and the mistakes of this congress will be evident. But, then, only the blind never notice their mistakes.

You know, your school, and any school, no matter how good it might be, constantly provides that monotonous education, which is advantageous at a particular time and, generally speaking, to the owner of the school, and the owner of the school is the state. Consequently, you will not learn very many good things or complete sciences in school, but only on the side, by means of self-education.

You will remember these youthful sufferings for a long time, these injustices and outrages, the disgusting way I have been treated after devoting my entire life to the social cause of the oppressed and offended. You are only just beginning to read the newspapers, but when you learn to understand and make sense of political matters, then, naturally, you will learn about politics from the judgements of not just the ruling groups but of many movements and tendencies. Every question is illuminated from every side and by every party from its own point of view. Only then will you gain a thorough understanding of the significance of the social sciences in the development of modern society and learn to assess every question independently of orders from school or anybody else. But, right now, the most important thing for you is not to study politics but mostly your subjects, and do a little bit of politics, so as not to fall behind the others. Remain independent at school, don't get involved in any underground societies if they are set up, especially from any kind of tendencies of the ruling party. Because they won't show you the real truth. It is hidden away beyond the reach of all of your clubs. Many of the bearers of this truth cannot speak out either openly or underground, and through no fault of their own. But all your various tendencies jostle about as if they are blindfolded in a big room, imagining that they can see everything but, in reality, they forget to take off the blindfold.

Don't go to the demonstration for the October holidays: it's a long way away from you, it's hard, exhausting and absolutely uninteresting. Better use the money for some healthy relaxation. Don't stay in school until nine or ten o'clock, try to finish earlier and go home. It's bad for your health and it's not 'the communist way'. They talk about a seven-hour working day, but they've loaded down the boys and girls for a full fifteen.

You have to remember that your position is worse than the others' and therefore you can avoid taking part in any social clubs with a clear conscience. Let the ones who enjoy this society, who feel the benefits of this society, engage in charity work. One thing you must do is study as hard as possible, build up a store of knowledge, read more, so that you are ready at any moment to struggle for your own life, and you can have fun at home with Mum. Your position sets you a head above the whole of your class. Accept this as an inevitable, bold necessity, and regard everything around with an awareness of your own sense of dignity.

Most often, a man has average abilities and intelligence, and the extremes are great minds, geniuses and talents on the one hand and idiots on the other. Society and the state live by average minds, advancing them to positions of authority in accordance with their known gifts, abilities, etc. All of this is created by the man or his circle, those close to him. You will be able and you must prepare in the most serious manner to develop yourself into an exceptional person, truly, a person who does not simply swim with the current or drag along in the rear, but leads others from the front. This is not always easy – most often it brings a man great pain, deprivation and misfortune, but it also brings him a delight, pleasure and self-satisfaction that neither wealth nor high rank can bring.

Be persistent in your efforts, develop your will – that is the main quality of a human being. And then be courageous and never be cowards. An entire nation has the nickname of cowards – the Jews: they lost their homeland and state-hood through cowardice, out of cowardice they do not serve in the army or, if they do, then they try to stay at the rear, managing the stores, but still everything to do with cowardice is labelled with the nickname of coward and so on. Of course, perhaps, not all of them, but the majority are undoubtedly like that.

The Russians have a bad trait – to give way to 'cheek', to cave in, as they say. You should not do this – quite the opposite. You must have civic courage, be actively out-raged by this and put the insolent villain in his place. The Russians have another trait too, a bad one, which I would not like you to have – it is excessive affability. We like to smile senselessly and, while we are smiling, forget to use our minds.

If it does not seem too boring, read political economy; I have some there. You should read a little bit at a time, like your lessons. On economics, my student lectures are particularly interesting, *The History of Economic Doctrines* by Bulgakov. But, first, you need to read political economy, in order to know what he is talking about. If it seems difficult, then perhaps it is still too early for you to strain your brains. There are several books by Kropotkin there. Only remember – don't repeat what you are thinking aloud in school. You have to know how to tell things apart and know how to keep quiet when it's the right thing to do.

You see, I've already mentioned earning money. You are still children, generally speaking, I ought to see more of you, but I keep preaching to you, either about taking your studies seriously or, now, about earning money. This, my young ones, is because life has changed your path through the world abruptly. It's not enough that your life is half-hungry, but all of us are also in poor health; in conditions like this, we shall quickly grow old, if nothing worse happens to us. Therefore, you will have to live independently significantly earlier than if these circumstances were different.

You know that I don't know how to dance at all, I can't play a single instrument, I can't skate, I don't even know how to laugh properly. Why? Well, it's obvious, the way my life has gone has meant there was no time to learn these things. But I don't complain to life about that; I have replaced these pleasures by always living in close union with an idea. I have never understood philistine whining and never dreamt of philistine contentment; it has always been completely alien to me. And, if I were offered a sackful of gold and a life of bourgeois 'bliss' on condition that I could not be any more than a philistine, that is, not take any interest in social, political and scientific matters, I would refuse. I simply would not survive in such philistine comfort, it is all so alien and incomprehensible to me.

You can speak at your social-studies lessons on several questions on which there is no sharp difference between various views and parties: for instance, social insurance, questions of the organization of public healthcare, etc. You can read about this matter and express your own opinion, that is, of course, if you have one. But if you are afraid, then keep quiet.

So many scientists are needed now that they will take people who know something into the institutions of higher education – just present yourselves properly. The fact that you are not a shock-brigade group is only a good thing. As a speciality, music does not promise anything interesting: either being a teacher or a sidekick in the sense of an accompanist for a performer. That's not interesting. It is good to know music for yourself, for the satisfaction of playing and distracting yourself from the misfortunes of daily life, and so don't forget it but keep on playing.

I think, my dears, that you will understand political economy; you have many advantages in your studies as compared with our time. Social studies also give you something. If you decide you want to read something, then try Chuprov. He is simple, easy to understand and not too grand. Write your impressions of this book (I studied it for an examination in the Commercial Institute). But you have to remember and be able to distinguish the concepts and formulations of political economy. If this subject turns out to be enjoyable, afterwards, you will read the history of economic doctrines. I have Bulgakov there: it's all expounded very well, interestingly. Of course, your social-studies teacher will recommend different authors.

When humanity moves forward, studying, educating itself, inventing, then this movement of humanity is called progress. These are individual personalities: scientists with profound intellects, artists and writers gifted with talent by nature (Tolstoy, Gogol, Esenin), composers, painters, sculptors, architects. They are few, very few; apart from them, a large number of all sorts of others do the same – in the way that a sterile flower blossoms, they think that they are the individuals who carry forward the progress of humanity, but, in actual fact, they are pitiful imitators without talent who often harm the cause. All the rest merely imitate the capitalists, acting for profit, for gain: the young ladies in order to be liked, your teachers in order to get ahead at work; and your social-studies teacher is especially stupid, with his collective farms and all sorts of hocus-pocus, and all his threats about excluding you from the shock-brigade group.

In your place, during a week's holiday, I used to read a dozen books that are worth more than your empty pastimes. The works of V. G. Korolenko are being published in a magazine now. He didn't write big things, but his stories have substance. Get them and read them.

Now, about my advice to you. I particularly want you to turn out to be real human beings, cultured, serious and intelligent. Therefore, I take great care to watch your every step. You must be quite serious in your behaviour, and I have no doubt that you are. But I have spent a lot of time observing our modern Komsomol youth, and I do not like it. Their morals are too lax. There is a lot that is bad among them; there is often a series of all sorts of reports about it in the newspapers. Your educators (if that's what they really are) have an unhealthy bias. Unfortunately, they don't wish to notice that in giving too much weight to the social and political training (processing) of young people, they have forgotten the main thing – the human personality, its integrity, and their public spirit is substantially below average.

Once again, these comic Komis don't wish to do anything for themselves. Their savagery is still evident at every step. Semi-barbarians, as the Germans say about us. But then we shall soon all of a sudden become super-civilized. If only history does not turn this experiment into a joke.

I remember that two years ago you had girlfriends round for your birthdays and you enjoyed yourselves, but now things are different. How things have changed for our family. Well, you must understand that as well, and not feel any resentment for your fate. After all, this is no accident, no exclusive phenomenon, but rather an 'every-day' occurrence. You should not forget that we are living through a time which only comes once in several centuries in the life of a nation. And it is very interesting that you are living at precisely this time; in your future life this period will provide you with extremely interesting memories.

To his youngest daughter, Nina

It's not that I'm growing old in spirit but, somehow, I feel superfluous or, rather, an outsider in this life, although I do find this painful, since my whole life has been tightly bound up with this life and the people. Having bound my fate completely to the people, I must also bear full responsibility for their successes and failures.

You have read *Spartacus*, and it's an interesting book, and I find it especially interesting from the historical point of view, like Sienkiewicz's *Quo Vadis*. I strongly advise you to read that as well. You can't really reproach the Romans with great crudeness: times were different then, after all. If you compare modern fighting (boxing) and other things, as well as customs, and the whole of reality in general, then it would seem quite incredible, if it weren't a fact. In these days of famine, our modern version of cannibalism is a sort of atheism, accompanied by 'society's' total indifference to the terrible events of today. When I look back at you over the past years, and also as you are right now, I see so many similarities with my own youth.

The novel Spartacus (1874, translated into Russian in the

372

1880s) was about a rebellion by slaves and gladiators during the Roman Empire, written by Raffaello Giovagnoli (1838–1915), who participated in the Risorgimento as an associate of Garibaldi. The epic novel Quo Vadis *was also popular in Russia. Written by the Polish author Henryk Sienkiewicz (1846–1916), it depicted the struggle of the early Christians against the despotic Roman Emperor Nero.*

It is curious why the NKVD picked this particular letter to Nina as part of their investigation, given its brevity. It could be that it was considered important because of the reference to Spartacus *and* Quo Vadis, *which might have been interpreted, in the general atmosphere of suspicion, as a coded call to rebellion against a despotic regime. The first paragraph, where Sergei describes feeling old and a failure, is touching, and it shows him revealing a more vulnerable side to his youngest daughter, compared to the hectoring tone in the rest of the letters.*

Sergei was released from prison in 1947 after ten years' hard labour, and he died in the late 1950s.

BIBLIOGRAPHY AND FURTHER READING

Amis, Martin, *Koba the Dread*, Jonathan Cape, London, 2002

Applebaum, Anne, *Gulag: A History of the Soviet Camps*, Penguin, London, 2004

Bardach, Janusz, *Man is Wolf to Man: Surviving Stalin's Gulag*, Scribner, London, 2003

Conquest, Robert, *Stalin, Breaker of Nations*, Weidenfeld & Nicolson, London, 2000

Fitzpatrick, Sheila, *Everyday Stalinism: Ordinary Life in Extraordinary Times*, OUP, New York, 1999

— *Education and Social Mobility in the Soviet Union, 1921–34*, Cambridge University Press, Cambridge, 1979

Garros, Korenevskaya and Lahusen (eds.), *Intimacy and Terror: Soviet Diaries of the 1930s*, The New Press, New York, 1995

Ginzburg, Evgenia, *Journey into the Whirlwind*, Harcourt, New York, 1975.

Gorky, Maxim, *My Universities*, Penguin, Harmondsworth, 1992

— *My Childhood*, Penguin, Harmondsworth, 1990

Grossman, Vassily, *Life and Fate*, Harvill, London, 1995

Pushkareva, Natalia, *Women in Russian History from the Tenth to the Twentieth Century* (ed. and trans. by Eve Levin), Sutton Publishing Ltd, Stroud, 1999

Sebag Montefiore, Simon, *Stalin: At the Court of the Red*

Tsar, Weidenfeld & Nicolson, London, 2003

Thurston, Robert W., *Life and Terror in Stalin's Russia, 1934–1941*, Yale University Press, New Haven and London, 1996

Tucker, Robert C., *Stalin in Power: The Revolution from Above 1929–41*, W. W. Norton, New York, 1992

Westerman, Frank, *Engineers of the Soul*, Harvill, London, 2006

Fiction

Fine, Anne, *The Road of Bones*, Doubleday, 2006

Orwell, George, *Animal Farm*, Penguin, Harmondsworth, 1999

Shlamov, Varlam, *Kolyma Tales*, Penguin, Harmondsworth, 1994

Solzhenitsyn, Alexandr, *The Gulag Archipelago, 1918–1956*, HarperCollins, London, 2002

— *One Day in the Life of Ivan Denisovich*, Penguin, London, 2000

Nina's reading list

Chekhov, Ivan, *Ivanov* (Five Plays, Oxford Classics)

— *The Seagull* (Five Plays, Oxford Classics)

Goncharov, I. A., *Oblomov* (Penguin Classics)

Kuprin, Alexander, 'Temptation', in *Selected Russian Short Stories* (ed. and trans. by A. E. Chamot) (World's Classics, out of print). *The Garnet Bracelet and Other*

Stories (Fredonia Books) and *River of Life and Other Stories* (Lightning Source) are both available but do not contain 'Temptation'.

Lermontov, Mikhail Yurevich, *A Hero in Our Time* (Random House, New York)

Pokrovsky, Mikhail Nikolayevich, *Russian History from Ancient Times* and *Brief History of Russia* (International Publishers, New York)

Pushkin, Aleksandr Sergeevich, *Eugene Onegin* (Oxford World's Classics)

Shakespeare, William, *Hamlet* (Penguin or Arden)

Tolstoy, Leo, 'After the Ball' in *The Death of Ivan Ilyich and Other Stories* (Penguin Classics)

— *Anna Karenina* (Wordsworth or Penguin Classics)

— *Childhood, Boyhood and Youth* (Penguin Classics)

— 'The Devil' in *The Death of Ivan Ilyich and Other Stories* (Penguin Classics)

— *Hadji Murat* (Hesperus)

— *War and Peace* (Wordsworth or Penguin Classics)

Turgenev, Ivan, *Smoke* (Wildside Press). He also wrote *Fathers and Sons* (Penguin Classics), which she would presumably have read.

Nina also mentions Tolstoy's poetry; Behind the Closed Door by Lev Friedland (not translated); V. P. Avenarius's biography, Gogol the Schoolboy (not translated); a biography of Lermontov (untraceable and most likely untranslated), and a novel about Russian terrorists (also untraceable).

PICTURE ACKNOWLEDGEMENTS

All the images in the photo section are sourced and supplied by Irina Osipova except for the following:

May Day parade: Mary Evans Picture Library/Meledin Collection

Ukraine famine: Mary Evans Picture Library; Nadia lying in state; Young Pioneers; Stalin at Kirov's funeral; pilots who rescued the *Cheliuskin*: David King Collection; the *Maxim Gorky*: RIA Novosti

Prison camp Siberia: David King Collection

NKVD headquarters: David King Collection

THE LEMON TREE
by Sandy Tolan

'MOVING AND PAINSTAKINGLY RESEARCHED'
Marina Lewycka, author of *A Short History of Tractors in Ukrainian*

In the summer of 1967, Bashir – a young Palestinian man – knocks on the door of his childhood home in the town of Ramla in Israel, a home from which his family was driven some twenty years earlier. The door is opened by a young Jewish woman, Dalia, whose family were settled in the house after fleeing persecution in Bulgaria at the end of the Second World War.

Thus begins an unlikely and difficult friendship, which bridges religious divides and last more than four decades. *The Lemon Tree* tells the story of this extraordinary friendship and offers a much needed human perspective on the Israeli–Palestinian conflict.

'READS LIKE A NOVEL . . . AN INFORMED TAKE FOR ANYONE INTERESTED IN THE HUMAN STORIES BEHIND CONFLICT'
New Statesman

'A FASCINATING AND HIGHLY ABSORBING ACCOUNT FULL OF WARMTH, COMPASSION AND HOPE'
Belfast Telegraph

'EXTRAORDINARY . . . A HIGHLY READABLE AND EVOCATIVE HISTORY'
Washington Post

'AFFECTING . . . SENSITIVELY TOLD. HUMANE AND LITERATE – AND RATHER DARING IN SUGGESTING THAT THE FUTURE OF THE MIDDLE EAST NEEDS NOT BE VIOLENT'
Kirkus Reviews

9780552155144

BLACK SWAN

THE PAST IS MYSELF
by Christabel Bielenberg

'IT WOULD BE DIFFICULT TO OVERPRAISE
THIS BOOK. MRS BIELENBERG'S EXPERIENCE
WAS UNIQUE AND HER HONESTY, INTELLIGENCE
AND COMPASSION MAKES HER ACCOUNT
OF IT MOVING BEYOND WORDS'
The Economist

Christabel Bielenberg, a niece of Lord Northcliffe,
married a German lawyer in 1934. She lived through
the war in Germany, as a German citizen, under the
horrors of Nazi rule and Allied bombings. *The Past is
Myself* is her story of that experience, an
unforgettable portrait of an evil time.

'THIS AUTOBIOGRAPHY IS OF EXCEPTIONAL
DISTINCTION AND IMPORTANCE. IT DESERVES
RECOGNITION AS A MAGNIFICENT CONTRIBUTION
TO INTERNATIONAL UNDERSTANDING AND AS A
DOCUMENT OF HOW THE HUMAN SPIRIT CAN
TRIUMPH IN THE MIDST OF EVIL AND PERSECUTION'
The Economist

'MARVELLOUSLY WRITTEN'
Observer

'NOTHING BUT SUPERLATIVES WILL DO FOR
THIS BOOK. IT TELLS ITS STORY MAGNIFICENTLY
AND EVERY PAGE OF ITS STORY IS
WORTH TELLING'
Irish Press

'INTENSELY MOVING'
Yorkshire Evening News

9780552990653

CORGI BOOKS

THE HOUSE BY THE DVINA
A RUSSIAN CHILDHOOD
by Eugenie Fraser

A unique and moving account of life in Russia before, during and immediately after the Revolution, *The House by the Dvina* is the fascinating story of two families, separated in culture and geography, but bound together by a Russian–Scottish marriage. It includes episodes as romantic and dramatic as any in fiction: the purchase by the author's great-grandfather of a peasant girl with whom he had fallen in love; the desperate journey by sledge in the depths of winter made by her grandmother to intercede with Tsar Aleksandr II for her husband; the extraordinary courtship of her parents; and her Scottish granny being caught up in the abortive revolution of 1905.

Eugenie Fraser herself was brought up in Russia but was taken on visits to Scotland. She marvellously evokes the reactions of a child to two totally different environments, sets of customs and family backgrounds. The characters on both sides are beautifully drawn and splendidly memorable.

With the events of 1914 to 1920 – the war with Germany, the Revolution, the murder of the Tsar, the withdrawal of the Allied Intervention in the north – came the disintegration of the country and family life. The stark realities of hunger, deprivation and fear are sharply contrasted with the day-to-day experiences, joys, frustrations and adventures of childhood. The reader shares the family's suspense and concern about the fates of its members and relives with Eugenie her final escape to Scotland.

'EUGENIE FRASER HAS A WONDROUS TALE TO
TELL AND SHE TELLS IT VERY WELL. THERE IS NO OTHER
AUTOBIOGRAPHY QUITE LIKE IT'
Molly Tibbs, *Contemporary Review*

'A WHOLLY DELIGHTFUL ACCOUNT'
Elizabeth Sutherland, *Scots Magazine*

9780552128339

CORGI BOOKS

THE GOD SQUAD
by Paddy Doyle

Paddy Doyle's mother died from cancer in 1955. His father committed suicide shortly afterwards. Paddy was sentenced in an Irish district court to be detained in an industrial school for eleven years. He was four years old.

This award-winning bestseller is a moving and terrifying testament of the institutionalised Ireland of only thirty-five years ago, seen through the bewildered eyes of a child. During his detention, Paddy was viciously assaulted and sexually abused by the nuns charged to care for him, and within three years his experiences began to result in physical manifestations of trauma. He was taken one night to hospital and left there, never to see his custodians again. This period of his life, during which he was a constant witness to death, culminated in brain surgery at the age of ten – by which time he had become permanently disabled.

This is the remarkable true story of a survivor, told with an extraordinary lack of bitterness. In Paddy Doyle's own words: 'It is about a society's abdication of responsibility to a child. The fact that I was that child, and that the book is about my life, is largely irrelevant. The probability is that there were, and still are, thousands of "me"s.'

'DOYLE NARRATES WITH GREAT CONTROL AND DIGNITY
Guardian

'UNBEARABLY SAD . . . IT IS IMMENSELY CHEERING THAT DOYLE SHOULD NOW BE MARRIED, HAVE THREE CHILDREN AND HAVE WON THE FIRST CHRISTY BROWN MEMORIAL PRIZE FOR LITERATURE'
Irish Independent

'THE STORY OF A HIDDEN IRELAND; OF THE HELL OF INSTITUTIONS AND HOSPITALS THROUGH WHICH ITS AUTHOR PASSED BEFORE FINDING THE HAPPINESS HE HAS TODAY'
Irish Times

9780552150279

CORGI BOOKS

FINDING PEGGY:
A Glasgow Childhood
by Meg Henderson

Scottish journalist Meg Henderson grew up in Glasgow
during the fifties and sixties as part of a large and often
troubled family. The tenement block in which they lived
collapsed and they were moved to the notorious Blackhill
district, where religious sectarianism, gang warfare and
struggles with hostile bureaucrats were part of daily life
for the people. Meg was born into a mixed-religion family,
where there was warmth and laughter as well as conflict.
She had a close relationship with her mother, Nan, and
her mother's sister, Meg's Aunt Peggy, two idealistic,
emotional women who took on the troubles of the
world. Together they shaped Meg's life, shielded her
from the effects of her father's heavy drinking and
helped her to move on, eventually, from
the slums of Glasgow.

A hopeless romantic, Peggy searched for a husband
until late in her life then endured a harsh, unhappy
marriage until she died tragically in childbirth. Her
death devastated the family and destroyed Meg's
childhood, but it was only as an adult, after the death
of her own mother, that Meg was able to discover the
shocking facts behind Peggy's untimely demise.

'BEAUTIFULLY WRITTEN AND
IMMENSELY ENJOYABLE. CAPTURES GLASGOW
PERFECTLY WITH NO ROSE-TINTED GLASS'
Alan Taylor

9780552141857

CORGI BOOKS